In recent years an increasing nu and
verbal ironies widely distribute. in Mark's gospel. This head study makes
an important contribution to our understanding of Marcan irony, and combines a literary–critical approach with insights gained from the sociology
of knowledge. Professor Camery-Hoggatt argues that the Marcan ironies
are intentional, and that irony comprises an integral factor in Mark's overall
strategy of composition: irony is a subtle means to achieve apologetic and
paradigmatic ends.

SOCIETY FOR NEW TESTAMENT STUDIES

MONOGRAPH SERIES

General Editor: G. N. Stanton

72

IRONY IN MARK'S GOSPEL

Irony in Mark's Gospel

Text and subtext

JERRY CAMERY-HOGGATT

Associate Professor of New Testament,
Southern California College,
Costa Mesa, California

CAMBRIDGE
UNIVERSITY PRESS

CAMBRIDGE UNIVERSITY PRESS
Cambridge, New York, Melbourne, Madrid, Cape Town, Singapore, São Paulo

Cambridge University Press
The Edinburgh Building, Cambridge CB2 2RU, UK

Published in the United States of America by Cambridge University Press, New York

www.cambridge.org
Information on this title: www.cambridge.org/9780521414906

© Cambridge University Press 1992

First published 1992
This digitally printed first paperback version 2005

A catalogue record for this publication is available from the British Library

ISBN-13 978-0-521-41490-6 hardback
ISBN-10 0-521-41490-3 hardback

ISBN-13 978-0-521-02061-9 paperback
ISBN-10 0-521-02061-1 paperback

CONTENTS

PREFACE

Anyone familiar with the study of irony in the biblical narrative will be struck by two outstanding developments. First, before 1970 discussions of irony were widely scattered. When it was discussed, it was primarily as a matter incidental to some other concern. Studies which focused on irony *as such* were exceptional, and were often dismissed as speculative. Since 1970 however, something remarkable has happened. There has been a growing interest in irony, not only in the Gospel of Mark, but throughout the biblical narrative. Studies of irony have appeared more frequently, have treated irony as a literary phenomenon worthy of exploration in its own right, and have discovered irony in places where it would been virtually invisible before. In this essay, I have argued that the wide distribution of irony suggests that it was born of the author's conscious intent. Irony lies close to the narrative's core.

We are brought in this way to my second point: I would go so far as to say that the interest in irony is evidence that the interpretative paradigms employed in the study of the Bible are undergoing a fundamental shift. The shift raises basic questions which bring into focus important dimensions of the current hermeneutical climate. If irony lies close to narrative's core, why has it been noticed with regularity only within the last two decades? Why was it for so long overlooked? What configuration of intellectual resources converged in the 1970s to make the shift possible? These are large questions, and they raise large implications. Some of those implications will occupy our attention in the pages which follow. For now, however, three want special attention.

First, the hermeneutical shift is an indication of increasing crossover scholarship from other academic disciplines, in particular, literary scholarship and folklore study. Folklore study finds ready hearing here because of biblical criticism's ongoing concern for the laws which govern the transmission of oral literature. Among the concerns which were operative for the folklorists were the reiteration of formal elements and plot functions, and the distinctiveness of the story-telling event as performance, rather than as a receptacle for historical or traditional information. Understood in this way, a story could be discussed in a manner which stressed its disconnectedness from its sources, from other forms of narrative, and from all previous performances.

Second, with the conception of the story as performance has come also a growing respect for the integrity of the narrative *as such*, and a resistance against the habit of historical scholarship to dismantle the narrative in search of earlier strata of the tradition. Respect for the integrity of narrative requires sensitivities which are more clearly attentive to the dynamic movements of the narrative transaction. For literary scholarship, what this means is a refinement of our understanding of what constitutes narrative meaning. Rather than identifying the meaning of the narrative with its historical antecedents, or with specifically theological or devotional nuggets which can be mined beneath its surface, the literary scholars have understood "meaning" more broadly to include the range of reactions evoked within the reader.

Third, there is a growing recognition that, though that range of reactions is informed and shaped by the narrative itself, as a kind of coinage of exchange, there is more involved. The narrative is not all that matters in the narrative exchange. The "reader" is someone who possesses specific competencies – skills and bodies of knowledge – against which the details of the narrative work out their rhetorical play. Those competences can only be understood within the social and linguistic matrix which the author or redactor assumes. Thus sociology of knowledge is receiving increasing attention in literary scholarship. In the study of irony, this has entailed a subtle shift even in the way that irony is recognized and understood. Rather than viewing irony as a property resident within the *text*, scholars now recognize irony as somehow resident within the reaction of the reader. This is a shift which reflects increasing interest in the narrative exchange as a genuine human transaction, worthy of exploration in its own right.

Part of that interest has been nourished and informed by the influence of cross-over interdisciplinary scholarship by those trained elsewhere in the classical humanities. The literary scholars brought with them the insistence that the complexities of language are seldom explicit. Systematic and logical discourse is exceptional in its effort to prune its vocabulary of extraneous and ambiguous nuances. Narrative, in contrast, heightens and exploits suggestive ambiguities and connotative subtleties. Narrators strategize the presentation of information by timing the story elements against the literary repertoire they know they can assume on the part of their readers. They also overload language with allusions and connotations. Narrative tries to surprise. This conviction on the part of the literary scholars stands as a needed corrective to the historian's habit of dismantling the narrative in search of information about history. It also counterbalances the theologian's habit of stitching the narrative together with other biblical narratives in the hope that the combination will tell us something more about God than the Bible itself tells us about God. Either approach treats the account itself as something of secondary worth. When we ignore the non-logical aspects of language we necessarily miss important dimensions of the Bible's depth and power.

None of these ideas is entirely new in the study of scripture. What is new is the clarity and force with which they are converging. I would go so far as to say that the study of irony provides a unique access to that convergence. We do not uncover irony by looking for it, exactly. Irony requires no skills which are different in kind from those we use when we read anything naturally. Irony is simply uncovered in the course of normal reading. Yet if it is to be recognized, it calls for refined levels of sensitivity, which are different not in kind, but in degree.

I am privileged to have been taught by members of the scholarly guild in whom those ensitivities appear with special grace: Howard Clark Kee and Carolyn Williams of Boston University read my manuscript with care. Dr. Kee was the adviser of the dissertation upon which it is based. Both he and Dr. Williams have made thoughtful suggestions which make this at once more readable and more true. Amos Wilder provided special insight in a semester of conversations which took place in his office in the depths of the Harvard Divinity School. If you find something here not to your liking, do not blame them. They did the best they could with me.

I am grateful also to my readers and copy-editors at Cambridge University Press, particularly Graham Stanton and Gail Turner, whose comments have made the manuscript both more accurate and more readable.

This book is dedicated to my wife, Shaleen.

ABBREVIATIONS

BibRes   *Biblical Research*
BTB   *Biblical Theology Bulletin*
BibZeit   *Biblische Zeitschrift*
CBQ   *Catholic Biblical Quarterly*
EpTheolLov   *Ephemerides theologicae lovanienses*
EvT   *Evangelische Theologie*
ExpT   *Expository Times*
HTR   *Harvard Theological Review*
Interp   *Interpretation*
JAAR   *Journal of the American Academy of Religion*
JBL   *Journal of Biblical Literature*
JRel   *Journal of Religion*
JSNT   *Journal for the Study of the New Testament*
JTS   *Journal of Theological Studies*
NovT   *Novum Testamentum*
NTS   *New Testament Studies*
RevBib   *Revue biblique*
SBK   Kommentar zum Neuen Testament aus Talmud and Midrasch, by H. L. Strack and P. Billerbeck, 5 vols. (1922–55)
SBLDS   Society for Biblical Literature Dissertation Series
SJTh   *Southwestern Journal of Theology*
StEv   *Studia Evangelica*
StTh   *Studia Theologica*
TDNT   Theological Dictionary of the New Testament, ed. G. Kittle and G. Friedrich, 10 vols. (1964–76)
TheolZeit   *Theologische Zeitschrift*
VT   *Vetus Testamentum*
ZAW   *Zeitschrift für die alttestamentliche Wissenschaft*
ZNW   *Zeitschrift für die neutestamentliche Wissenschaft*

1

INTRODUCTION: THE PROBLEM OF IRONY IN MARK

The subtitle of this book − "Text and subtext" − is taken from a discussion of the relationship of language and thought in James Miller's "rhetoric of imagination," *Word, Self, Reality*. In that essay, Miller puts his finger on the pulse of the linguistic reality which makes irony possible. The passage in view discusses the view held in theatrical circles that there are often differences of nuance between the surface meaning of the dialogue − the "text" − and the underlying connotative meanings − the "subtext." Often, the "play" itself resides in the interplay between these two: "When actors come to understand the subtext of the play, they can then give the interpretation that makes for great performances."[1] Miller's distinction between text and subtext lies at the core of this rhetoric of irony. Irony occurs when the elements of the story-line provoke the reader to see beneath the surface of the text to deeper significances.

Sometimes the two dimensions of stress are extensions of each other, but sometimes they stand at odds. When the former takes place, the basic thrust of the message can be heightened by the congruity with its form; when the latter takes place, the incongruity can evoke reactions which are downright visceral. For this reason, the relationships between text and subtext can be extraordinarily complex or subtle. We are prone to overlook them whenever we insist that the "meaning" of the language can be reduced to a single, unified field of reference. Because irony is complex, our natural tendency is to treat the ironic as something exceptional, something created by conscious literary artifice, and therefore as somewhat removed from the ordinary operations of language. But this is misleading. Miller has pointed out that ordinary language is replete with subtexts. If this is so in English, then perhaps also in the "ordinary" language of the Bible. Thus we are brought to the subject of irony in the Gospel of Mark.

The state of the question

The observation that there is dramatic irony at work in the Gospel of Mark is not a new one. As early as the seventeenth century, Sir Thomas Hobbes noted in his "York Tile Maker's Play" the presence of irony in the mockery of the soldiers in Mark 15.18: "Hail, King of the Jews."[2] This first example provides an opportunity to refine more closely a methodological distinction which will later prove critical in our discussion of the social implications of Markan irony: sometimes the irony of an event or a saying is available to the characters "inside" the story. That is the case with the clear verbal sarcasm of the soldiers' mockery. It is clear that their mockery is precisely that. By hailing Jesus "King of the Jews" they intend exactly the opposite of homage. The gallows humour by which they have dressed him up to die is intended as an affront, not to Jesus only, but to the Jewish nation itself. What they *mean* is in balanced dissonance with what they *say*. The text and the subtext are in diametrical opposition. The soldiers are quite aware of that opposition, as is everyone else inside the story. But the soldiers have no way of knowing that for Mark's readers the designation of Jesus as "King of the Jews" is exactly right. In their impudence, the soldiers have made an unknowing acclamation. The soldiers have no way of knowing that, for Mark's readers, the spindles of the crown of thorns would have appeared a peculiarly appropriate corona. There is, therefore, a second sense in which the dramatic ironies of the soldiers' sarcasm are available only to the reader, who stands outside the narrative action and views it from a different vantage-point. It is this latter level of irony – dramatic irony – which interests us here. Simply put, dramatic irony occurs when the story-line itself plays upon the reader's own repertoire of knowledge and convictions to produce a distinctive subtext. Though the reactions of the *reader* are orchestrated against that repertoire, the reactions of the story's characters cannot be. The characters are participants in the event, but they cannot know that the story about the event will be told in precisely this way.

I mention this now because, in the earliest discussions, the distinction between irony which is *within* the narrative and that which is *carried* by the narrative is often obscured or ignored. The result is that such studies were sometimes truncated or distorted by an interpretative point of view which was blinded to the literary dimensions of the story-line *as such*. A primary example is Jakob Jónsson's

Humour and Irony in the New Testament, which appeared in 1965.[3]
A good deal of Jónsson's discussion is concentrated on the gospels,
but for all its attention to the humour of the Jesus sayings, this book
misses entirely the obvious ironies the Jesus story would have held
for the gospels' reader.

Sometimes the two levels are congruent, and differ primarily in
degree. In 1950 Albert Descamps briefly called attention to the irony
of the saying in Mark 2.17, "I came not to call the righteous, but
sinners."[4] The ambiguity here is quite subtle. On the surface of it,
Jesus could simply have meant that the zeal of the "righteous" stood
them in good stead already, and that the call of God was now extended
beyond them to include sinners. But the context here militates against
that view. The open hostility of the "righteous" sets them against
the sinners who are called, and thus over against the one who calls
them.[5] Put another way, because Jesus has come to call sinners, his
call positively excludes the "righteous". All of that would have been
accessible to Jesus' listeners, but we can suppose that, in Mark's context, in which questions of ritual purity and the extension of salvation
to the Gentiles had raised the antagonism of Jewish detractors to a
higher pitch (see Mark 7.1–23), the saying "I came not to call the
righteous, but sinners" would have become a good deal more potent.

At other times the second level of irony is so thoroughly embedded
in the narrative *as such* that it is available to the reader in a sense
which completely excludes the story's characters. A good case in
point is the irony of the trial of Jesus in 14.55–65, which has been
interpolated into the story of Peter's denial in 14.54, 66–72. Here,
because the reader has been guided into the story-world by the
narrator, he is able to follow events which are happening simultaneously for two sets of characters. He has also been privy to Jesus'
prophecy of Peter's denial which had appeared earlier in the chapter
(14.30). With these resources in hand, he is able – as a reader –
to perceive a critical irony in the unanswered demand that Jesus
prophesy in v. 55. William Lane's analysis comes closest to recognizing Mark's narrative strategy here:

> The irony inherent in the situation is evident when the force
> of juxtaposing verse 65 and verses 66–72 is appreciated.
> At the precise time when the court attendants were heaping
> scorn and derision upon Jesus' claim to be the Messiah, the
> prophecy that Peter would deliberately deny him was being
> fulfilled.[6]

But there is something subtler here, which Lane overlooks. The scorn heaped upon Jesus centered upon his failure to prophesy, while Peter's denial in the courtyard was a precise vindication of Jesus' prophetic ability. If the prophecy in 10.33 is drawn into the picture, the very fact that Jesus is standing trial further vindicates his prophetic identity. The reader is called upon to pass judgment against the authorities at the very moment they pass judgment against Jesus. So this is a trial with two verdicts, one leveled by the authorities, and one leveled against them.

From here it is but a short step to the realization that the ironies in the narrative force the reader to a decision. This is one means of leveraging the opinion of the reader for or against the actions of the story's characters. In that way, a clever ironist can ask the reader to consolidate his or her commitments to the values of the group which considers the story sacred. That remark has been made already by Wayne Booth, in a comment on the irony of the soldiers' mockery which Thomas Hobbes had pointed out:

> It is true that Mark may in part intend an irony against the original ironists, but surely his chief point is to build, through ironic pathos, a sense of brotherly cohesion among those who see the essential truth in his account of this man–God who, though *really* King of the Jews, was reduced to this miserable mockery. The wicked and foolish insolence of those who mocked the Lord with the original "hail" is no doubt part of Mark's picture, but it is surely all in the service of the communion of Saints.[7]

This note is significant for its clear observation that irony creates a sense of community which – as Booth goes on to insist – is "larger . . . with fewer outsiders, than would have been built by non-ironic statement" (p. 29). The idea that irony contributes to community will occupy a significant portion of our attention in the pages which follow. As we shall see, there are three areas in particular in which irony contributes to the survival of the group. First, because it forces the reader to decision, and because the direction of that decision is clearly indicated, irony can serve legitimating functions, by which the group's institutions and practices are secured against threats and challenges. Second, because it divides its listeners or readers into "insiders" and "outsiders," irony aids in group-boundary definition. Third, because it can "overcode" language with new dimensions of significance, irony helps to keep the group's "language-world" open-ended and pliable. Traditional stories can be made to yield new, ironic meanings, and in that way can be appropriated for new and different circumstances. These are dimensions of the biblical tradition which have thus far hardly been noticed, much less explored.

One implication of what we have just suggested is that irony, which is carried through the medium of the narrative, itself can serve the sociological needs of the group. Sometimes those functions are also served by irony which lies within the narrative, as Madeleine Boucher pointed out in her discussion of Jesus' parables, *The Mysterious Parable: A Literary Study*. In this discussion, which appeared in 1977, Boucher ranges irony under the wider category of "trope," along with metaphor, synecdoche, metonymy, and − as a special instance of metaphor − allegory:

> A trope, as its name implies, is a turn or change which occurs when an unexpected word is placed in a syntactic structure and is thereby given another meaning in addition to its literal one ... In every trope, then, the word has two levels of meaning, the direct and literal, and the indirect and tropical. Between the two levels of meaning there is both similarity and dissimilarity, with sometimes the one predominating, sometimes the other.[8]

In irony, though, the dissimilarity dominates (pp. 19f), and it often sharpens the dissonance between the two levels of meaning. In this way, the tropical qualities of irony and the tropical qualities of parables can be connected and compared. That a duality of meaning is constitutive of Jesus' parables Boucher understands to be patent (p. 22). It is for this reason that the parables can be understood as riddles or mysteries (Mark 4. 11f): they imply a comparison between two dimensions of reality which − since one is only implied in the other − "require insight on the part of the hearer if it is to be grasped" (p. 25). Yet that insight is not freely formed. It is, instead, patterned in response to the elements of the trope as they unfold against the backdrop of the reader's own knowledge and convictions. In the terms which we have used thus far, the tropical dimensions of a text are intended to be grasped against a particular subtext. "Insight" is as much a product of the parabolic event as it is a native skill possessed by the reader.

What is intriguing in our discussion of Markan irony is the possibility that Mark's narrative itself may have "tropical" nuances, may be parabolic, may shift in significance as it is appropriated for new and different circumstances. If that is so, the literary insights employed in parable research may prove helpful if applied to the narrative as a whole. That observation, which will later prove to be critical in our evaluation of Mark's rhetoric, has been made most recently in Werner Kelber's discussion of Mark's genre.[9] For Kelber, the programmatic key lies in the famous crux at 4.11f:

> To you has been given the secret of the Kingdom of God,
> But for those who are outside everything is in riddles;
> so that they might indeed see
> but   not perceive,
> and   may indeed hear
> but   not understand;
> lest they should turn again and be forgiven.

The following comments come just after Kelber's discussion of the parabolic quality of the book as a whole:

> The intriguingly difficult verses 4:10–12 contain the germ of Mark's so-called parabolic theory. In response to a question concerning parables Jesus states that "to those about him with the twelve" (4:10; au. trans.) the mystery has been given that pertains to the kingdom of God, whereas "to those on the outside" (*ekeinois de tois exo*) everything is "in parables" (4:11). One immediately observes an insider–outsider dichotomy. Insiders are admitted to the mystery of the kingdom, while outsiders are barred from it ... This, then, is the heart of the so-called theory on parables: parabolic discourse is the carrier of a cryptic message that casts to the outside those who cannot fathom it, while confirming as insiders those to whom it is revealed.   (p. 121)

Here, Kelber concurs with – and quotes – Boucher: "Mark has not taken clear, straightforward speech, the parable, and transformed it into obscure, esoteric speech, the allegory. He has rather taken what is essential to the parable, the double-meaning effect, and made it the starting point of a theological theme concerning the audience's resistance to hearing the word."[10] But Kelber runs beyond Boucher in discovering the "double-meaning effect" in the book as a whole.

If Kelber is right, we should not be surprised to discover that dramatic ironies are widely distributed throughout Mark's narrative. That suggestion has already been made by Gilbert Bilezekian, whose study of tragic action in Mark appeared in 1977.[11] Bilezekian based his understanding of irony on the definition set forth by Joseph T. Shipley: irony is "a device whereby ... incongruity is introduced in the very structure of the plot, by having the spectators [in our case, the readers] aware of elements in the situation of which one or more of the characters involved are ignorant."[12] With that definition in hand, he simply listed a wide variety of places in which irony or *double entendre* may play a role in the unfolding rhetoric of Mark's story. His list is organized under three headings:

1. Irony expressed as sarcasm or humour;
2. Irony emerging from the use of esoteric language which would have been clear to the audience; and
3. Irony which occurs "when the reverse of an expected course of action takes place, or when an effect or paradox or contrast is introduced". (p. 123)

Of these, we are interested primarily in the second and third. Of the examples given, perhaps half are open to question, and it remains regrettable that Bilezekian did not explore the literary and verbal dynamics by which the ironies he lists have been brought about.

In 1977 there also appeared in print Donald Juel's 1973 doctoral dissertation, *Messiah and Temple: The Trial of Jesus in the Gospel of Mark.*[13] In this study, Juel carried forward the observation of his mentor, Nils Dahl, that the Messianic Secret[14] is hidden only from the characters in the story. The reader has already been informed in Mark 1.1 that Jesus is the "Christ the Son of God." With that knowledge in hand, the reader's reaction to the elements of the narrative is leveraged over against the reactions of the story's characters. This basic assumption, that the narrative operates on two levels, forms the basis for Juel's analysis of the "temple charge" brought against Jesus in his trial before the sanhedrin in 14.58. He begins by noting the clear-cut ironies in the mockery of the soldiers (15.16–20; Juel, p.47), and in the taunts leveled at Jesus on the cross (15.29, 31f; Juel, p.48). In both instances, the taunts carry secondary levels of meaning for the reader. Since the charge brought against Jesus in 14.58 parallels these in content, it must also carry secondary levels of meaning (p.57). The movement between the superficial facts of the story and their theological implications Juel then notes in a series of Markan complexes, all related in one way or another to the trial and crucifixion.

That central thesis he developed more broadly in 1978 in the treatment of Mark in his introductory level survey of the NT as literature.[15] Although brief, and written for laymen, Juel's discussion here is in many ways the most exegetically responsible treatment of Markan irony yet to appear. He begins with the observation that the passion in Mark operates on two levels, and that therefore "dramatic irony runs through Mark's passion story" (p. 179). Those two levels – "revelation" to the reader and "mystery" for the characters – form the basic structures of his discussion. The narrative strategies by which the content of the revelation has been disclosed to the reader are surveyed, but only briefly, as follows:

1. The disclosure in the prologue,
2. Aspects of the trial and crucifixion,
3. Peter's confession,
4. The affirmations of Jesus as God's son, and
5. Notes about the special demands of discipleship.

In effect, what Juel has suggested is that irony in the narrative results from the skillful use of rhetorical devices which structure the reader's reactions in various ways. But Juel was not the first to point this out. Robert Fowler's 1973 doctoral dissertation included a systematic tabulation of the "reliable commentary" against which the Markan ironies could be articulated.[16] Note that the term "reliable" here implies a literary judgment, not an historical one. What Fowler had in view was the voice of the narrator as a reliable guide into and around the story-world. The reader or listener is expected to trust the narrator, and that expectation is rewarded appropriately.[17] We may, with Fowler, review briefly some of the rhetorical devices by which Mark's narrator builds up the reader's distinctive perceptions of the story and its elements:

I.   Direct comments to the reader
     A. The title and epigraph
II. Linking statements
III. Parenthetical constructions
     A. Explanations of foreign customs and concepts
     B. Translations of foreign words
     C. Winks at the reader
     D. Explanatory clauses
     E. Markan insertions
     F. Intercalations
     G. Doublets
IV. Inside views
V.   Unanswered questions

VI. Reliable characters
  A. Jesus
  B. The voice from heaven/the cloud
  C. The demons
  D. The centurion at the cross
  E. The young man at the tomb
VII. Prospective passages: build-ups and introductions

The idea that an author must provide guidance for the reader has a variety of collateral implications which will command our attention in the pages which follow. Fowler devotes an entire chapter to this question.[18] What he has left unexplored, however, is the implication that the very fact that such guidance is necessary implies a tension between the points of view of the characters inside the story, and those of its readers.

That dimension of the literature was explored in 1980 by Robert Tannehill, in an article, "Tension in Synoptic Sayings and Stories."[19] According to Tannehill, when the points of view of the story's characters are understood to be reliable or normative, their elucidation may be a call for conversion. On the surface of it, this point is obvious. But what about the points of view of the characters who are unreliable, or who are condemned in the narrative? When the characters or their actions are condemned – whether implicitly or explicitly is irrelevant – the reader is called upon to share the point of view from which the condemnation proceeds. Thus the challenges in the text may be sociologically or theologically potent. For Tannehill, that potency is heightened by Mark's ironic paradoxes, all of which reach a kind of acme in the passion.

> In the passion story the paradox is turned into drama in the mocking scenes which follow each of the main events in Jesus' way to the cross (the two trials and the crucifixion), for the same words that reject the dying Jesus are ironic confessions of him. The dramatic tension of these events is heightened by a series of suggestions of ways in which Jesus might escape. Those inclined to seek such escape from death are enticed to false hope: then hope is crushed as the ways of escape are closed one by one. Mark's readers must face the conflict between the way of Jesus and their own desire for security, a desire which will make them like the faithless disciples. And the tension is heightened by presenting Jesus' way as paradox and as triumph by irony.   (p. 150)

If this implies a dimension of narrative meaning which runs beyond the communication of mere information, it does so intentionally. Irony implies that more is going on than mere information can grasp, and that discipleship must be an activity of personal response as well as an activity of intellectual assent; that is, the ironic dimensions of the passion may *effect* the kind of commitment which for Mark lies at the core of discipleship.

There are other passages in which irony may be used in the service of deepening discipleship. One such pericope has been noted already by the director of this dissertation, Howard Clark Kee. In 1983, Kee published the fourth edition of his survey, *Understanding the New Testament*.[20] In this new discussion, he paused to focus briefly on the irony of the blind Bartimaeus story in Mark 10.46–52. It is, after all, an unexpected turn of events that a *blind* man should be the only one who sees clearly who Jesus is. When Bartimaeus hails Jesus as "Son of David" (in vv.47f), it is not the political but the eschatological implications of that name which inform his pleading (v.51; cf. Isa.35.5). This is only a passing note, but it is not without its broader significances. The story of blind Bartimaeus parallels the report of the healing of the blind man Bethsaida in 8.22–6. Together these two pericopae form an *inclusio* which frames the third major section of the narrative.[21] That major section has to do with the demands and disillusionments of discipleship, and is riddled with indications of the disciples' persistent blindness. It is not insignificant, then, that blind Bartimaeus, after he receives his sight, "follows Jesus on the way" (v.52).

So there is tension here, tension which forces upon the reader the necessity of deciding who will command his loyalties and on what terms. We may return briefly to Tannehill, whose larger study of tensive language in the Jesus sayings traditions – *The Sword of His Mouth* – is the source of the following quotation:

> Thus the tension in the text is necessary to its purpose. This tension enables the text to resist being digested by the prevailing patterns of interpretation and instead to challenge those patterns. The tension enables the text to speak with the necessary depth, to address the self on the level of the basic structures of his personal world rather than on the level of technical decisions, thereby awakening an answering tension within the self, which can lead to change.[22]

But what if the internal tensions generated by the story are not entirely resolved by the story's end? In that case we would have an indeterminate ending. Laurence Perrine has discussed the significance of both the indeterminate ending and the "unhappy ending."[23] Mark's ending is indeterminate, but Perrine's comments about the rhetorical functions of unhappy endings seem exactly right for our discussion of the ironic impact it holds:

> The unhappy ending has a peculiar value for the writer who wishes us to ponder life. The story with the happy ending has been "wrapped up" for us: the reader is sent away feeling pleasantly if vaguely satisfied with the world, and ceases to think about the story searchingly. The unhappy ending, on the other hand, may cause him to brood over the results, to go over the story in his mind, and thus by searching out its implications get more from it. (p. 66)

Such is the case with Mark's ending as it stands.[24] The reader is forced to a re-evaluation and reconsideration of everything which has preceded it. In literary terms, the narrative fails to bring to resolution a good deal of its major anticipations: a promised appearance of the resurrected Jesus (16.7); his promised return (9.1; cf. 13.14–37, esp. v.30); the anticipated sufferings of the disciple band, as a whole (13.9–13), and of James and John in particular (10.39). Mark's failure to bring his narrative to complete closure is especially evident when his Gospel is read or recited aloud before a live audience, I suspect because the ongoing movement of the plot forces the listener to continue rather than permitting him to dawdle on this or that intriguing detail. The result is that the narrative is taken in as a whole, and a larger number of its details remain close to the surface of the listener's consciousness. Thus the elements which have not been brought to resolution are more immediately apparent. This observation is perhaps more significant when we recall with Thomas Boomershine that, in the ancient world, narrative was read aloud as a matter of course.[25]

It is in this final sifting, this final "readerly work," that the inherent ironies in the text can be brought to their full fruition. Donald Juel has made this point in a discussion which depends for its cogency upon the essentially ironic character of the narrative itself: the ironies of the final verse leave the reader with an enormous residue of unfinished readerly work. Here the whole of the gospel is turned over and stood on its head. "What sort of good news concludes with 'and they said nothing to anyone for they were afraid?' " Juel asks.[26]

It may be that the ironies in the final verse should be somewhat more narrowly defined. Norman Petersen has argued against what he calls the *massive* approach to irony here.[27] Instead, the immediately preceding verses provide the basis for a kind of irony which is smaller in its scope but more potent in its impact: "A lesser irony costs less and purchases more" (p. 162). But what is that lesser irony? The reversal in v. 8 focuses attention on the words of the young man in v. 7: "To Galilee!!" The closing irony of Mark is a reminder that the risen Christ is yet at work, and that he has summoned his followers back to their original discipleship. The women are to tell the disciples to get themselves together and respond once again to the call of Christ!

What might all of this imply, and in what sense does it call for further elaboration? Even at this early stage, a number of general observations may be drawn which can help clarify our further inquiries. First, it is significant that irony has been found distributed throughout the book. We may review rapidly: Chapter 1 (Juel, following Dahl); Chapter 2 (Descamps); Chapters 6 and 8 (Fowler); Chapter 10 (Kee); Chapter 14 (Juel); Chapter 15 (Thompson, Juel, Tannehill); and Chapter 16 (Petersen, Juel). We can hardly avoid the conclusion that it is there by design. If that is so, any interpretative procedure which discounts its presence will offer truncated or distorted results. We would go so far as to suggest that the ironies noticed already in the scholarly literature signal the presence of a rhetorical strategy which is central to the narrative itself. Thus far, that possibility has remained unexplored. Even the studies just mentioned – with the exception of Donald Juel's suggestive comments in *An Introduction to New Testament Literature* and Robert Fowler's dissertation *Loaves and Fishes* – note only the presence of irony in passing or in isolated instances. What is called for now is a systematic re-examination of the book as a whole, with the possibilities of ironic nuances constantly in hand.

Second, the discussion as it stands lacks anything like a systematic theoretical basis. Reference is frequently made to the standard "rhetorics of irony" by Wayne Booth[28] and D. C. Muecke,[29] and occasional reference is made to Edwin Good's study, *Irony in the Old Testament*.[30] But Booth and Muecke draw their observations from English literature, and are removed by considerable distance from the social and literary contexts in which Mark did his work. Good, while suggestive, and in many ways programmatic for the study of biblical irony, has nevertheless been criticized for his failure to provide an adequate theoretical basis for his own conclusions.[31]

Third, we should note that discussions of Markan irony have generally been carried on in isolation from scholarly investigations into other matters – historical, theological or sociological. Yet if Mark deliberately employed strategies which evoke ironic responses on the part of his readers, the implications of that fact should be widely ranging. I am not here suggesting that historians, theologians and sociologists might incidentally glean some fruit left behind after the literary critics have finished their reaping. I am suggesting instead that the exploration of irony is of a piece with the reading of the narrative for any purpose at all. This third point is perhaps the most important, and it forms the final justification for this volume. We do not suddenly shift into another mode when we read irony. Rather, we encounter and recognize irony in the course of reading naturally. There is a sense, then, in which the subject of this study may hold critical implications for all of the reading we do in scripture. I hope to have organized its parts so that they can serve as a basis for wider reflections about reading.

There are related questions. Generally speaking, studies which appeared before 1970 tended to ignore any clear distinction between ironic functions operative within the narrative world and ironic functions of which the narrative is itself the carrier. After 1970, that distinction has been made with increasing forcefulness and clarity. Furthermore, irony seems to be turning up elsewhere in the biblical literature with increasing frequency.[32] But this poses a problem. If irony is everywhere, why was it for so long overlooked? Were there methodological blinders built into the interpretative canons we had been using before? And what configuration of intellectual resources converged in the 1970s to make this sort of awareness possible? What has happened in hermeneutics, anyway?

Irony and the "Academy"

Here we may attempt an answer to that question, albeit briefly. Irony is a function of interfacing and conflicting points of view: the points of view of the story's readers set against those of the story's characters. Its explication requires systematic attention to both the point of view of the characters and the point of view of the reader. But these two points of view are differently informed, and differently framed. The point of view of the characters is rightly contained within the narrative – a literary concern. The point of view of the reader is informed by the "language-world" of the community for which the text was intended – a sociological concern. As our store of that sort of information has improved, so also has our understanding of the interplay between the points of view which would have been operative for the reader. At the same time, we have needed vocabulary by which to describe that interplay. This has been provided by the literary critics, with their conscious attention to the narrative *as such.*

We have also pointed out that the ironies have a particularly potent effect on the reader. They summon the reader to make answering responses from within his own soul. Those "answering responses" are patterned, and not chaotic. A writer can strategize his presentation of the material to bring them about. For that reason, they are sociologically significant. It seems we have been brought round once again to matters of sociology.

In sum, the increasing clarity about ironies in the biblical tradition can be traced to methodological advances in our understanding of the social background against which the elements of the text must be read – sociology of knowledge – and about the literary strategies by which the text interacts with that background to achieve its particular patterns of tension and transformation – literary criticism.

In Chapters 2 and 3 we shall address those two concerns in greater depth, and in Chapter 4 seek a working rapprochement between them. The necessity of congruence should not be so difficult to establish as the present state of NT scholarship would suggest. The very fact that our sensitivities to irony have reached the levels I have described in this chapter suggests that the older antagonisms between practitioners of the various methodologies may be giving way to common interests and concerns. Indeed, it would appear that with the emergence of sociological analysis and literary criticism, the horizons of biblical interpretation are being brought into a new kind of balance.

2

THE SOCIAL FUNCTIONS OF IRONY

Chapter 1 closed with the remark that, with the emergence of sociological analysis and literary criticism as viable options within biblical scholarship, the horizons of biblical interpretation have been brought into a kind of balance. This point has been made before with specific reference to the Gospel of Mark. When William Lane offered his review of "The Gospel of Mark in Current Study" in 1978,[1] he noted as promising both the sociological and the literary approaches to gospel narrative. Indeed, one would expect that there would already be fruitful dialogue between them. If that dialogue has not yet come, I suspect it is because these two disciplines are based on differing theoretical foundations, and because they have thus far offered competing interpretations of the text and its significance. Their vocabularies differ significantly, and the uses to which they put the text appear to be almost mutually exclusive. Sociological analysis has used the text as a kind of lens through which to focus its descriptions of the dynamic social factors which shaped primitive Christianity. Literary criticism in gospel study — and by this we mean primarily the New Criticism — has tended to reject that inquiry out of hand, and has instead focused its attention on the text itself, as an independent literary or aesthetic object.

It is my contention that the obvious differences between these two approaches may disguise their underlying similarities and their common interests. The merging of their vocabularies may ultimately serve to broaden both approaches, while the frank recognition of their differing agendas may provide conclusions which, precisely because they are differently based, may be mutually illuminating. We shall begin with an exploration of the social functions of narrative, and of ironic narrative in particular. Then, in Chapter 3, we shall turn to the literary functions of the narrative's internal elements. Chapter 4 will draw these two discussions together into a single framework. Chapter 5 will employ that framework as a kind of lens through which to read the Gospel of Mark.

The notion that those vocabularies may be merged depends in part upon the creation of clear connections between sociological and literary concerns. Literature may be understood in *dialogue* with the "world" which is taken for granted in the environment in which it was created. Within NT scholarship, that matter is being addressed with increasing clarity by a group of scholars trained in the sociology of knowledge. Thus far, sociological explorations of the NT documents have tended to focus on the biblical texts as *expressions* of potent sociological factors, as Howard Kee notes in his study, *Christian Origins in Sociological Perspective*:

> Important clues about a work are the linguistic and literary features which it embodies, as indicators of the general cultural climate in which it was produced. (The literary critics) Wellek and Warren note that a literary work can be used as a social document and thereby "yield the outlines of social history."[2]

There is, of course, a sense in which the issues here are more subtle than discursive thought can penetrate. A community does not form a rationally coherent view of reality. Rather it formulates a "sacred cosmos" alongside, and more importantly, over against, other, competing sacred cosmoi. The content, values, and structures of the sacred cosmos are thus matters of issue – critical loci of loyalty – and are potent factors in the delineation of group boundaries. By recognizing the subtle and complex dimensions of world-constructing that take place within living communities, the sociologist can produce an evaluation of the evidence which is at once more broadly based and more sensitively nuanced.

It is clear that studies of this sort will run counter to the naïveté of the literalist or the bare mimetist. The literary critics René Wellek and Austin Warren have already pointed that out: an author is under no obligation to describe his social world in "official terms."[3] Rather, he interacts with that world in a dialogic fashion, both playing upon and transforming its basic traits. What Wellek and Warren have said about literature in general may be heightened somewhat in the case of literature which serves the needs of a religious community. At its most profound, religion is more than a series of truths to be endorsed. Rather it is a way of seeing and responding to all truth. Religious literature can be a summons to conversion, can ask the reader to leave one "world" and enter another, to change not only *what* he sees, but also the *ways in which he sees*. In its inner reality, that transformation is a matter of the spirit; who can know it but God alone? But transformation also has an outer face which it presents to the world. The outer reality of conversion is certainly subject to investigation. But how? One way is through the lens of sociological analysis, especially as it deals with the shifting perception made possible by shifting uses of language. It is accordingly to language that we shall now turn.

We shall begin with a summary: the conclusion of the sociologists Peter Berger and Thomas Luckmann – "reality is socially con-structed"[4] – has its implied correlative: the functioning boundaries of any social group are in significant measure determined by the extent to which its members construct reality in similar ways. That is, a common "life–world" – as Howard Kee has said, a common "cosmos" – represents a critical precondition of social solidarity, and is the functional matrix within which the group can build its common life. It is by means of language that that "cosmos" is created and sustained in the first place.

The social functions of language

It may not be insignificant that a great deal of contemporary theo-logical[5] and philosophical thinking has been informed by the con-viction that man is constituted Man insofar as he uses language in the structuring[6] and the ordering of his experience of reality. The entire enterprise of the "New Hermeneutic" – epitomized in the work of Ernst Fuchs and Gerhard Ebeling – attempts to take seriously the nature of the Word as *word*.[7] Ernst Cassirer called Man the *"animal symbolicum,"*[8] and predicated his "Philosophy of Sym-bolic Forms" on the notion that the intersecting point at which the various anthropologies converge is Man's use of language. Kenneth Burke called Man the "symbol using animal,"[9] and Hans Georg Gadamer suggested that it is language which transforms *Umwelt* into *Welt*: it is language that humanizes experience.[10] H. Richard Niebuhr constructed his entire system of ethics on the foundation stone of Man as "homo dialogicus."[11] In another vein, Richard Bandler and John Grinder[12] have applied Noam Chomsky's theories of transformational grammar[13] to the methodological issues of depth psychology. We could go on, of course. The current insistence that the human person is constituted human in his use of language may hold the promise of a conceptual and methodological *lingua franca* which all the humanities can hold in common.

What interests us here is the prominent place given language in sociological inquiry. The functions of language in the establishment and maintenance of social group boundaries have been enumerated extensively by Joyce Hertzler[14] and also — in an essay which is both more compact and more insightful — by Edward Sapir.[15] Sapir's work was early (the essay to which we are referring first appeared in 1933), and much of contemporary linguistic theory takes its bearings from it. So also will the remarks which follow. It is my contention that what Sapir said about language in general may be said as well of its various manifestations, such as epithet, wisdom saying, poem, discourse, or even off-handed conversation. As we shall see, this much is certainly the case with regard to narrative.

Language and the structuring of consciousness

Sapir began by stating the obvious: language is learned in childhood (p. 12). That it therefore represents both the mode and the content of primary socialization is an insight carried forward by George Herbert Mead.[16] Sapir simply pointed out that, from the beginning of articulated consciousness, experience and language interpenetrate. The implications for identity formation are not difficult to draw: the processes of personal development, of the child's mastery over his "self" and over the world in which he finds himself, involve the structuring of experience in a manner which is disciplined and given shape by the patterns of the language into which he is brought up.

The notion that experience is therefore inevitably and irrevocably qualified by the language we use is Sapir's distinctive contribution to linguistic theory. Our languages "predetermine for us certain modes of observation and interpretation" (p. 10). Sapir's student, Benjamin Whorf, carried this observation further:

> We dissect nature along lines laid down by our native languages. The categories and types that we isolate from the world of phenomena we do not find there because they stare every observer in the face; on the contrary, the world is presented in a kaleidoscopic flux of impressions which has to be organized by our minds — and this means largely by the linguistic systems in our minds.[17]

What is significant here is Whorf's conviction that the patterns of language not only provide us with tools for describing experience: they predispose us to experience reality in one way and not another. The implications of that thought were anticipated already in another of Sapir's early essays on language:

> The fact of the matter is that the "real world" is to a large extent unconsciously built up on the language habits of the group. No two languages are ever sufficiently similar to be considered as representing the same social reality. The worlds in which differing societies live are distinct worlds, not merely the same world with different labels attached.[18]

Thus the commonsense notion that language is primarily a medium of communication is a step removed from the matter. If Sapir and Whorf are right, language functions primarily in the structuring of experience. But here we must pause to express a hesitation: *if* Sapir and Whorf are right. In point of fact, they may well have overstated their case. It is not entirely clear that the categories of language are prior to those of experience, and that they are arbitrarily imposed upon experience. Tangible reality appears to be intractable, and to force language into *its* patterns. As we stand together talking in the garden, my German grandfather may say *Baum* where I would say *tree*, and it makes little sense to say that we live in completely different realities. It is for this reason that the hypothesis of linguistic relativity posed by Sapir and Whorf has been so often and so seriously challenged.

But is this adequate? Is it not that communal life is created and sustained by fundamental agreements about concepts for which there is no specific, objective, tangible entity – love, justice, loyalty? Anyone who has studied more than one culture will recognize just how broadly ranging such concepts can be, how deeply they can differ from one another, and how important agreement must be if the group is to survive. On the larger, metaphysical issues, the hypothesis proposed by Sapir and Whorf possesses enormous heuristic value. The distinctive patterns of thought shared by speakers of the same language create the pre-conditions necessary for group cohesiveness by providing the basis and understructures of a common "life-world" or "language-world", and this even before anything specific is said.[19]

Structured experience and social solidarity

The implication that a common language represents a symbol of social solidarity is evident in the tendency of any given social group to evolve over time its peculiar dialect, from which − by psychological or social necessity−outsiders are barred (pp. 16, 28). In their own ways, by defining the limits of membership in the group, these dialects and "mini-dialects" help to create the conditions in which the group can exist.

The custom of imposing taboo restrictions reflects this reality on the inverse. The social effects of taboo may be differentiated according to their manifest and latent functions.[20] Thus the manifest effect of taboo may be to establish the standard boundaries of experience open to the members of the group by interdicting as impermissible the language by which forbidden − or holy − experiences are described. On the other hand, the latent effect of taboo may be the creation of special groups, provinces or circumstances in which such restrictions are temporarily suspended. The movement into such provinces or groups may represent migration to a different social location. Thus, in this culture, the adolescent's use of invective or of sexually explicit language may infuriate his parents not only because it violates their sense of taboo, but also − perhaps more so − because it represents his attempt to migrate to a social status in which he will no longer be under their control.

Sapir also pointed out the role of language in the accumulation and transmission of culture (p. 16). That communities collect and communicate information by means of language is "obvious and important" (p. 16). From Sapir's perspective, and later more clearly from Whorf's,[21] what is perhaps more significant is the role the inherent structures of language themselves play in patterning and shaping the information thus conveyed. What is more, the accumulated body of biases and information embedded in the language represents implicitly the preservation of the group's history, and its sense of "place" within the social structures of the wider culture in which it finds itself.

It may be best to clarify the role of language in identity formation with this realization firmly in mind. If language qualifies and shapes man's experience of the external world, it also creates and sustains the structures of his inner experience. Here we leave Sapir briefly for a comment from the Catholic scholar Luis Alonzo-Schökel:

In language man also interprets his inner experiences, articulating them in significant and communicable forms; even though a man has beforehand in his mind a vague idea of what he wants to communicate, this idea is complete only when it is formulated into words. Man makes an interpretation of his own internal experience as he transforms it into language, in a sort of creation in which he reveals himself to others and to himself.[22]

But there are subtler matters afoot here. The style and "texture" of a person's language – its patterns, its vocabulary, even its resonances – have always served as ready indicators of personality (Sapir, p. 17). Further, the language one uses both determines and reflects his social location. (The very fact that I have chosen to use the masculine pronoun will make this volume difficult for some readers to swallow, even though the matter of gender has absolutely nothing to do with the question at hand!) Joyce Hertzler points out that in many cultures different social classes actually use distinct languages: "People live in their social class intuitively, habitually, and *verbally.*"[23]

Since this is so, the movement between social locations involves a fundamental shift in habituated language patterns. That change is obvious in the movement from one country to another, but even though it is more subtle, it is no less significant in the movement from one social class or social group to another. Anyone who has returned home after extended schooling will recognize the basic irony that an expanded vocabulary can inhibit communication. What is revealed in that homecoming is more than, and different from, a simple change in communication skills. One learns to his horror that the world of his childhood has been called into radical question, and that – for him at least – it has ceased to exist. One also learns that the potencies of language are not exhausted by precise "lexical" definitions. They involve as well a widely ranging fabric of linguistic patterns, relations and assumptions against which individual sentences are articulated. Those relations and assumptions must be shared by both speaker and hearer, there must be a shared semantic field, in order for communication to take place effectively.

Because those patterns are latent within the "logic" of the language's grammar, and because language and experience appear to interpenetrate, to those who hold them the understructures of the "language-world" appear to be endemic to the structures of reality itself. But the facts that they differ from group to group, and that they shift for individuals over time, suggest instead that they derive from a kind of contract to which the speakers of a language subscribe as a precondition of its use. Whorf made this observation in perhaps its most explicit form (in the quotation which follows, the emphasis is Whorf's own):

> We cut nature up, organize it into concepts, and ascribe significances as we do, largely because we are parties to an agreement to organize it in this way – an agreement that holds throughout our speech community and is codified in the patterns of our language. The agreement is, of course, an implicit and unstated one, BUT ITS TERMS ARE ABSOLUTELY OBLIGATORY; we cannot talk at all except by subscribing to the organization and classification of data which the agreement decrees.[24]

We are brought in this way to the point at which our inquiry began: if Sapir and Whorf are right, language imposes coherence on experience, and each language or family of languages or dialect does so in a distinctive way. The implications for sociological analysis are extensive. A common language represents a usual minimum condition for social groups to exist, not because it facilitates communication, but because it creates the preconditions for a common experience. The phenomenon of taboo may represent this reality on the inverse. Language makes possible the accumulation and transmission of culture, embodying and shaping that culture in the very process of transmission. Similarly, the formation of identity is at once made possible and radically circumscribed by the structures of language as a primary vehicle of socialization. The language one uses both determines and reflects his social location. Migration to a new social group may reflect a fundamental shift in one's habituated language patterns, in effect the exchange of one "language-world" for another.

Linguistic dissonance

From what has been said thus far it would appear that language is always consolidative, or that its phonemic, semantic, and rhetorical structures are congruent and whole in the same way that our experiences of reality are congruent and whole. But herein lies a problem. If our experiences of reality were consistently and entirely integrated, and therefore fixed, growth would be unnecessary, and conversion impossible. The varying textures of experience could be flattened out and assimilated to a single, coherent, rationally defensible system.

The problem lies in the fact that our experience of reality all too often leads in exactly the opposite direction. In the realms of experience we take to be most significant, "reality" often proves to be slippery, it forces us into radical shifts in our modes of thought, it bedevils us into conversion. Language, too, can be full of mystery, can tease and then guide us in the movement from one reality-sense to another, can enrich experience by bursting open the customary and the superficial. Thus the impression of seamlessness in any given language-world ultimately proves illusory. We are not here discussing the limitations of language, but rather exactly the opposite. Its capacity to unmask the superficialities and inadequacies of our customary modes of perception is part of what gives language its characteristic depth and power.

The illusory quality of language-worlds is evident in a modest sense in those instances in which synonyms, homonyms, and oxymorons provide occasion for linguistic dissonance. In these minor disruptions of the language-world often lies the pleasure of the joke. If the bumper sticker on the automobile in front of us reads "librarians are novel lovers," we laugh at the incongruity. We remember with a certain sense of pleasure the cleverness of the sloganeer: "I believe in resurrection, and if I died tonight I would believe in resurrection tomorrow!" But linguistic dissonance can be deadly serious as well. US military officials reportedly dropped the atomic bombs on Nagasaki and Hiroshima because they misunderstood a communiqué from the Japanese government. The potencies of language become especially evident when misunderstanding leads to conflict, but they are not restricted to that. Language is often explosive in its own right. Sometimes what is detonated is the hearer's own reality-sense. Whole linguistic worlds can be created and then − when the weight of the speaker's wit reaches its critical mass − can be completely blown away.

The idea that language-worlds may be exploded has already shaped a great deal of the debate which is currently raging about the significance of Jesus' parables. One such study provides the basis of the general remarks about imaginative language which will occupy the next few pages. In his important and programmatic analysis, *The Sword of His Mouth*,[25] Robert Tannehill has explored the forceful and imaginative rhetoric of the synoptic Jesus sayings with an eye toward showing that the jolts they inflict on the hearer can challenge or illuminate, precisely because they disrupt the fixed structures of meaning which he supposes inhere in the nature of reality itself.

Tannehill is right. Even the most casual reader of the gospels may be struck from time to time by the almost quixotic depth and penetration of the sayings that are found there. On the other hand, even the practiced eye of the most thorough and systematic of exegetes may be blind to the dynamism, the potencies, even the humor of the text; that is, in the quest for clarity and precision, the reduction of language to informational content may represent a failure of vision.

I have mentioned the matter here because it is significant for our exploration of the functions of language generally, and of the functions of narratives specifically. Occasionally one reads even in the standard literary handbooks such well-meaning but misguided notions as this: "The student ... must translate his experience of literature into intellectual terms, assimilate it to a coherent scheme which must be rational if it is to be knowledge." Wellek and Warren, from whose book this quotation is taken (p. 15), are hardly naïve. Yet there is a sense in which they overlook the critical integrity of narrative, and the legitimacy of that integrity even when it juxtaposes dissonant elements. The dismantling of tension-ridden language, and its reassembly into a coherent framework in the interests of knowledge, represent the violent imposition of order. But here we have run beyond the topic at hand.

Tannehill opens his discussion proper by directing attention to the work of Philip Wheelwright. It may not be inappropriate, then, if we turn aside briefly to a discussion of Wheelright's essay, *The Burning Fountain*.[26] It seems clear that there are fundamental differences between scientific language and "literary" language. Wheelwright carries that distinction further. Scientific language, with its effort at logical coherence and definitional precision, he refers to as "steno-language," and he points out its refusal to recognize the rhetorical significance of allusions, contrasts, and "extraneous" linguistic nuances. The poet − and, we add, the prophet − may exploit precisely those possibilities in a movement which enriches experience by conjuring up metaphorical and allusive associations which would otherwise be systematically suppressed.[27] According to Wheelwright, the language of poetry and art may be plurisignificant: insofar as it "carries more than one legitimate reference, its full meaning involves a tension between two or more directions of semantic stress" (p. 81).

The plurisignificance of signs represents something of a problem for the interpreter who understands as his task the distillation of the content of the text into a single coherent system. If Wheelwright is correct, we must understand as constitutive of meaning not only the straightforward assertions of the text, but also the incongruities, the disruptions, associations, and allusions which so liberally season the linguistic potpourri which comprises the biblical literature. They give the text its distinctive flavors, and it is often exactly the aroma of those flavors that we stop to savor. The attempt to boil down metaphorical language to its bare bones informational content may preserve some small measure of its nutritional value, but it does so at the expense of its palatability and texture.

The possibility that tension-ridden language may be elusive or explosive should not prevent us from affirming the roles it may play in the establishment of social solidarity and in group-boundary definition. There are at least three ways in which such tensions may help maintain the vitality, and therefore the viability, of the language-world which lies at the core of the group's commonly structured sense of reality.

First, tensive language disrupts the superficialities of ordinary language, opening up new and richer possibilities of understanding. In Wheelwright's terms, by the disruption of the patterns of steno-language, "depth" language unmasks dimensions of human experience to which logic and precision are fundamentally inadequate. We return to Tannehill:

> The language of logic and clear definition has greater efficiency and precision, but it abstracts from the rich significance of man's encounters with reality. The reality encountered is not allowed to be fully present, and important dimensions of meaning for man are ignored. Depth language seeks to respond more appropriately to the richness of reality.
> (p. 13)

That is, because of its immediacy and its refusal to engage in reductionism, depth language actually contributes to the building of a more fully orbed picture of reality.

Second, tensive language provides a linguistic matrix in which the imagination can function, and therefore also a medium with which the living community can interact with its tradition, shaping and evaluating its contents and appropriating them for new and different circumstances. The importance of this interaction for living communities is well documented within the social sciences, and has been reasserted for religious studies in the pioneering work of Amos Wilder[28] and Will Beardslee.[29] Tannehill continues his discussion by exploring revelation in the light of Ray Hart's book, *Unfinished Man and the Imagination*:[30] Revelation is disabled when the imagination is crippled, and the imagination is crippled when the meaning of language has been strait-jacketed into old and ossified categories. To be set free, language must be shocked by confrontations with new and challenging dimensions of meaning. According to Tannehill, it is in that confrontation that revelation can occur.

Finally there is what might be called "the camaraderie of the shared joke." Even the most subtle disruptions of the language-world create moments of tension, and the appropriate resolution of the tension – the laughter at the punchline, the delight in the enlightenment – may represent a moment of harmony and balance, a pleasure shared by speaker and hearer. On the other hand, the disruption may baffle or horrify the listener, may even occur at his expense. The joke may create a minor crisis of loyalties, a subtle dividing between insiders, who share its pleasures, and outsiders, who do not. There is therefore a certain precariousness latent in the act of "languaging" a world, and it is a precariousness which holds out to us the possibility of antagonism, illusion, and possibly damnation. But it also holds the promise of camaraderie, development, movement, and growth.

The social functions of narrative

In his discussion of the social functions of language, Sapir contented himself with illustrations drawn from the smaller and more manageable linguistic constructions – phonemes, clauses, and individual sentences. I here recall my contention that what may be said of language in general may be said as well of its various manifestations, including such larger linguistic units as discourses and narratives. At this point in our discussion, what is of interest is not the internal structures or constitutive elements of narrative. We will come to those matters in Chapters 3 and 4. Here we are interested rather in the social impact of the story-telling event itself.

In Chapter 3 we shall deal with story-telling under the rubric of what Alfred Schutz has called "finite provinces of meaning."[31] Stories, as distinct from "normative" (Schutz used the term "paramount") reality, represent "sub-universes" which operate according to their own laws. Like other finite provinces of meaning, their reality lapses with attention. We migrate into them by crossing a threshold. They involve the suspension of doubt. If stories are examples of Schutz's finite provinces of meaning, it may be appropriate to ask what is their relationship to "normative" reality. By framing the question in this way we touch upon a discussion which has already been for some time a matter of debate among the literary critics, particularly those of a mimetic bent. The positions set forth in the literary debate run the gamut of an entire spectrum:

1. Paramount reality is inherently structured, and stories reflect that structure;
2. Stories derive their structures from the inherent patterns of thought or consciousness;
3. The dynamic patterns of story-telling are superimposed on thought: stories structure consciousness, rather than the other way around; and
4. Reality is inherently chaotic, fluid and paratactic;[32] and the "structured-ness" of stories imposed upon reality represents a kind of violence.

What is important here is that all four positions hold in common the notion that the structures of reality, the structures of consciousness, and the patterns of narrative *appear* to be interrelated. That impression — naïvely taken, without respect to its critical validity — forms what I take to be the basis for the social impact of story-telling. If we find stories engaging, if we interpret reality by means of stories, if we pattern our recollections of the past and our hopes for the future in story form, it is because — so we tell ourselves — "this is the way things really are."

Stories and the structuring of consciousness

Here, then, we can return to the point at which we left Sapir's analysis of language: just as language and experience interpenetrate, so also narrative consciousness and experience interpenetrate. It may be for this reason that stories provide such radically effective tools of primary socialization. On the one level, they provide paradigms which reveal to their listeners socially appropriate patterns of behavior. At the same time — and this may be much more important — they inculcate the values and perspectives which inform the actions of the group and its heroes, and which appear to its members to be given. I once asked Amos Wilder if stories were found in every civilization. His answer turned my question on its head. He will forgive me if I only approximate his response:

> Civilizations are not found where stories are wanting. That is because we learn from stories that there are consequences to our actions. Stories therefore provide the basis for moral thinking, and are a *prerequisite* for civilization.

The significance of stories for child development has been explored extensively by Bruno Bettelheim.[33] As a psychoanalyst, Bettelheim was "confronted with the problem of deducing what experiences in a child's life are most suited to promote his ability to find meaning in his life" (p.4). His conclusion:

> Regarding this task, nothing is more important than the impact of his parents and others who take care of the child; second in importance is our cultural heritage, when transmitted to the child in the right manner. When children are young, it is literature that carries such information best.
> (p.4).

In another place, Bettelheim relates this process to the complex interior structuring the child must master as part of his maturation processes:

> Just as his life is often bewildering to him, the child needs even more to be given the chance to understand himself in this complex world in which he must learn to cope. To be able to do so, the child must be helped to make some coherent sense out of the turmoil of his feelings. He needs ideas on how to bring his inner house into order ... The child finds this kind of meaning through fairy tales. (p.5)

Narrative consciousness and social solidarity

What for our purposes is equally significant is that the mastery of those patterns of moral behavior and interior structuring is a necessary prerequisite for participation in the life of the group. Insofar as different groups affirm differing moral values or practices, those patterns themselves represent "carriers" of the cultural heritage to which the child is heir. Sapir pointed out that language facilitates the accumulation and transmission of culture. In a similar vein, stories provide the primary mode of preserving and transmitting the group history. This is not simply a matter of providing information about the group's collective past. The very act of telling a story involves taking a point of view, a particular "slant," on the relative significances of, and the relationships between, its various elements. By telling the group history in one way and not another, the storyteller may create a version which reveals to the newcomer the legitimacy of the actions of the group and its heroes. If he does so, at the same time he discloses the values and perspectives which inform the group's decisions about what is legitimate and heroic.

One particular telling of the story may even attain recognition as the "official" version, the standard against which all other tellings are measured. In that case, the newcomer is faced with the difficulty of learning, not the "bald" historical facts surrounding the group's origins, but the official version of the facts. In some settings, the degree of loyalty an individual holds to that version of the group's history may be taken as an indication of his loyalty to the group itself. In this assertion it is not insignificant that the legitimacy of social institutions is functionally established on the basis of their origins and history.

Stories may thus provide aetiologies for present institutions, circumstances or practices, and in that way function as legitimating elements within the overarching social framework.[34] Perhaps the most telling examples of functioning aetiologies are the cosmogonic myths, which, in primitive cultures, locate the tribe in the center of the "sacred cosmos" and provide a comprehensive basis for ordering and structuring the sacred reality. Mircea Eliade has examined already the significance the "Sacred Space" in his widely read study, *The Sacred and the Profane*.[35] Less widely known is his earlier work, *Cosmos and History*, from which we take the following quotation:

> Obviously, the metaphysical concepts of the archaic world were not always formulated in theoretical language; but the symbol, the myth, the rite express, on different planes and through the means proper to them, a complex system of coherent affirmations about the ultimate reality of things, a system that can be regarded as constituting a metaphysics.[36]

Earlier we illustrated the role of language in social location by pointing out that a shift in habituated language patterns accompanies migration to a different social group. Something similar is afoot in the appropriation of the group's history. It is not enough that the newcomer learn or endorse the official version of the group's history; ultimately he must accept that history as the key to his own: that is, he must re-shape his telling of his own story in the light of the biases and perspectives which he has learned in his hearing of the group's story. Often enough, the degree to which the newcomer accommodates his own history to that of the group represents a telling register of his assimilation into the group.

Thus stories in their own ways reflect another of Sapir's generalities about language: like language, the stories he tells – their contents and their points of view – locate the individual within a specific social group. The converse of that statement is also true: the stories that its members tell one another help to create the conditions necessary for the group to exist at all. As we have already suggested, this is the case with respect to the group's perspectives on its own history; the inculcation of the group's characteristic beliefs, perspectives, and behaviors; and the legitimation of the group's practices and institutions. It applies, in short, to the clarification and transmission of the group's very identity. Stories, like language in general, create the preconditions of group cohesiveness by providing the basis and understructure of a common life-world.

It may be possible to discern differentiation in the life-world of a specific social group by investigating the selectiveness by which its stories are withheld from its various sub-groups. Stories, like language in general, can be subject to rules of taboo. Eliade, for example, has investigated the role of sacred myths in demarcating the limits of manhood in the initiation rites of primitive cultures. For the initiate, the hearing of such sacred stories represents a mark – and a means – of emigration to a different social status.[37]

Stories thus play a major role not only in primary identity formation, but also in secondary socialization. When we ask "who" a person "is," the most common response in our culture is that he will name his profession. If we press further, eventually the answer will emerge in the form of story.[38] By telling "my story" I am disclosing the arena of social relationships which I take to be my significant field of action. I disclose at the same time the unique perspective by which I view that field of action. As I move to a new social group, I may change my telling of my story significantly, and not only by extending its parameters to include a wider field. Instead, I may find that my past history has itself become "past history," that it wants to be re-told in the light of the new situation in which I now must orient myself.

We have seen that stories, like language, shape the world of their hearers on a variety of levels. As with language in general, the common-sense notion that the primary functions of stories lie in description or entertainment overlooks their role in pre-orienting their hearers to experience reality in one way and not another. As larger linguistic units, stories create the preconditions of social solidarity by establishing rapport between individuals, by articulating a group history and thereby a locus of loyalty, by legitimating the practices and institutions of the group, and by structuring the thinking of newcomers – children and initiates – in patterns appropriate to the group's assumed values and perspectives.

Narrative dissonance

From what has been said so far, it would appear that stories are inherently "constructive," that they are used primarily to "positive" purpose. But that impression belies the heterogeneous character of society in general. Social forces militate against one another. Subgroups square off against major groups in a never-ending ritual of challenge and reaction. The implication of that fact is critical for our understanding of the social functions of the gospel stories: what is legitimating for one institution at the same time implicitly challenges the legitimacy of its rival. Thus Jesus' response to the authorities in the temple ultimately calls into question the legitimacy of the assumptions on which their authority is based.

At this point it is helpful to recall Philip Wheelwright's discussion of plurisignificance in language, and the tensions which result when multiple levels of meaning confront and conflict with one another. I raise the matter here because the functions of tensive language on the semantic level may parallel the functions of ironic language on the narrative level. Ironic stories involve the creation of dissonant and competing points of view. As with language generally, the tensions thus created may help to maintain the vitality, and therefore the viability, of the storied language-world which lies at the core of the group's commonly structured sense of reality. I have suggested that there are three reasons why this is so: such language unmasks the superficialities of "customary" experience, it provides a matrix in which imagination at work in the living community may shape and appropriate the content of tradition, and it provides occasion for what I have called the "camaraderie of the shared joke." We might here point out that it is precisely this quality of tension which characterizes narrative irony, and that it is for that reason that such considerations are especially significant in our exploration of irony in the Gospel of Mark.

First, ironic narratives disrupt the superficialities of ordinary experience, opening up new and richer possibilities of understanding. In a sense, this is true of all narratives, since they are all in one sense or another interpretations of the experiences they convey. Irony, however, can carry that inherent tendency to an extreme, setting one interpretation of an event over against another. In that sense the deeper reading of the narrative unmasks dimensions of the event to which its participants would have been fundamentally blind. Here, then, is the suggestion that in human experience "more is going on than meets the eye."

What is significant about this quality of irony is that it suggests that the interpretative keys for experience may lie outside the parameters of the event itself, in its final outcome perhaps, or in the deeper implications it may later come to hold for the listener. With that affirmation, we come to a matter which has been the subject of continuing debate: must we base the significance of our experiences on factors which are removed from the experiences themselves? Is the significance of experience only to be discovered after the fact? And does that not in some way diminish the value of the moment, as Ted Estess has asked?[39]

But this matter could be approached differently. In the affirmation that the significance of events may lie outside their immediate parameters lies the implicit assumption that they are part of a wider scheme of things, that they can yield their significances only within wider contexts. At times, the end toward which the plot is leading may be understood as an absolute disconfirmation of its elements as they appear when they first unfold. In that way, the *telos* of the story may represent a kind of judgment on its parts. In theological terms, the eschatological judgment toward which history is leading significantly shapes what we make of events as they unfold; eschatology is not only the study of "end times," but is also the study of "the way all things relate to the end." If that assumption lies at the basis of the apocalyptic view of history, we should not be surprised to discover that much of the biblical narrative is ironic in its inner movements. There is, of course, a sense in which the details of the Jesus story are to be understood in the light of the resurrection which forms their *telos*. But more than that, the biblical writers insist that in that *telos* is configured the end of all things.

What is perhaps more interesting is the question of *why* the biblical narrators should have been so keenly attracted to the cognitive potentials of ironic narrative. The solution to that question lies in the second affirmation we had made about tensive language in general: irony in narrative creates a linguistic matrix in which the imagination can function, and therefore also a medium with which the living community can interact with its tradition, evaluating and shaping its contents, and appropriating them for new and different circumstances. Within the biblical literature, what this means is that the living communities, which preserved the oral and literary traditions underlying the gospels, did so because they understood those traditions to be significant in some way for the immediate circumstances in which they found themselves. They told the stories of their origins in such a way that new and different significances could be discovered there. We have direct evidence of this tendency at work on a variety of planes, perhaps most obviously in the early Christian appropriation of Jewish literary traditions wherever they could be made to serve apologetic ends.

Clearly in this action the Church stood in direct confrontation with its Jewish counterparts. It defended that activity by claiming that it had been given the "secret" of the Kingdom of God (Mark 4.11), or that the resurrected Jesus himself had "interpreted" for it "all the scriptures concerning himself" (Luke 22.27), or that it had been given the "Spirit of Truth" (John 14.17; 16.3). We should not overlook the basic element of irony which attends all of the Church's hermeneutical activity: from the standpoint of the Christ-event, the entire OT economy takes on a new and sometimes startlingly different aspect. If the Church approached the traditions about Jesus in the same way, it may be because central to its convictions was the belief that the living and incarnate Word will remain potent even when the circumstances in which it was originally spoken have been radically changed; or it may be because they held the conviction that the central truths of the gospel traditions could only be appropriated when they were consciously translated into real life expressions of piety. In either case, the possibilities of tensive language, of plurisignificance, and of narrative irony represent movements within living traditions which ultimately function to keep those traditions supple and healthy.

We had also said of the "camaraderie of the shared joke" that such tensive language may create a minor crisis of loyalties, a "subtle dividing between insiders, who share its pleasures, and outsiders, who do not." That this operation is constitutive of irony is clear. A story is told in which the perspective of the characters is faulty in some way. The narrator takes care to inform the audience of the facets or implications of the story to which the characters are blind. Frequently the possibility of a second – better informed – vantage-point is introduced with a literary device which hints that more is going on than meets the characters' eyes. In this way, a subtle tension is set up between the two perspectives, a tension mirrored by an internal dissonance within the consciousness of the audience itself. The natural reaction of the audience is to opt for the better informed perspective, and thereby to resolve its own internal tensions in a manner which is consistent with the story-teller's point of view.

Thus competing stories may set one reality against another, and ironic stories may provide competing perspectives on the same reality. In doing so, they create "crises of loyalty" between which their listeners are asked to choose. As the listeners do so – as they align themselves with this telling and not that, as they say to themselves, "This (and not that) is what life is like" – they confirm and consolidate their commitments for and against particular social groups.

We began this chapter by suggesting that what was needed in the investigation of primitive Christianity was a sociological paradigm which could be tailored to the peculiar nature of the evidence it has left us. In the cases of the evangelists' communities, the fact that the bulk of their theological traditions is preserved in narrative form may begin already to suggest some general observations. The gospel narratives root their communities within a specific history, and they thereby legitimate with reference to their origins the communities' characteristic institutions and practices. In the telling and the hearing, they inculcate the peculiar biases and perspectives which newcomers must endorse as the price of initiation into their churches. In this way, perhaps more than any other, community origins are appropriated as the basis of a common experience, a common "life-world." By telling their stories in one particular way, rather than any other, the evangelists begin to establish "loci of loyalty," with reference to which their readers identify and consolidate their similarities to one another, and their differences from those who tell different sacred stories, or who tell the same stories differently. Their churches are communities precisely because their members share common experiences of reality, and common vocabularies with which to understand them. The evangelists supply both. In the process, they also provide the initiate with the raw vocabulary and the interpretative agendas he needs for that retelling of his own story which represents the price of his admission to the group.

3

THE LITERARY FUNCTIONS OF NARRATIVE

In Chapter 2 I suggested that the telling of stories represents a kind of informal or pre-formal epistemology, a way of structuring and understanding the world which is critical to the establishment of group-boundaries. Here I wish to suggest that the interpretative power of story lies in the fact that it stands removed from the "real" world in significant ways. A relationship exists between brute reality and narrative, but that relationship is never straightforward or simple. It is always manifold and complex. In this chapter we shall concern ourselves with the functions of the narrative's internal elements which make that complex relationship with brute reality possible. The critical term here is "function," and we shall be using it in a sense which has somewhat different nuances from those in Chapter 2. In our discussion of the social functions of narratives we dealt with the significance of the narrative or its details for the community of the teller and listener. In our discussion of literary functions we shall deal with the relationship of the narrative elements to one another. We might express that difference in other terms: in the sociological study of literature we have explored the role of the narrative elements in orienting the reader within his own world; in literary study we shall explore the role of the narrative elements in orienting the reader within the world of the narrative itself.

Before we make that move, however, it may be helpful to note in passing the critical link between the two "worlds." We shall base the remarks of the next few pages on the vocabulary of one of sociology's prophetic figures, Alfred Schutz. In his essay, "On Multiple Realities,"[1] Schutz argued that the world of unmediated, tangible experience was in some sense "paramount" (p. 342), and that, standing in tension with paramount reality – alongside, and often over against it – are alternative arenas of perception, which Schutz called "finite provinces of meaning." Such "provinces" may be understood as moments in which perception is stylized into controlled patterns. Sometimes the patterns are very rigid, but even when they are not, the provinces represent alternatives to the flux of uninterpreted experience, "paramount" reality. Because they stand alongside and over against paramount reality, one enters finite provinces of meaning by crossing a threshold (p. 343). Because they are not coterminous with paramount reality they may be said to operate according to their own specific rules (pp. 340f). Because they are constituted "cognitive styles," their reality "lapses with attention" (p. 340). These three points together imply a fourth: finite provinces of meaning represent an inherent challenge to paramount reality, calling its basic structures into question, viewing its basic characteristics and textures from different, sometimes fluctuating vantagepoints. Schutz explores this challenge with specific reference to play, to scientific inquiry, and to poetry (pp. 340, 345–7). Art not only represents life, it interprets it. The child at play has entered a world – a province – in which new and special laws apply. The scientist and the poet each in his own way can refract the stuff of experience, and each sort of activity is legitimate within its own frame of reference. It is in this way that the finite provinces of meaning may play the role of "ciphers" by which the ordinary verities of everyday life may be transformed into new and – for those who participate in them – revelatory clues to existence itself.

But all of this is true of stories. Stories *as such* – including consciously historical stories – stand at a critical remove from the unmediated stuff of brute experience, and it is for that reason that they can provide the interpretative resources by which brute experience can be made to yield up its significances. If stories are finite provinces of meaning, one would enter them by crossing a threshold, they would be structured according to their own laws, and their reality would lapse with attention.

The second of these three assertions seems obvious enough, but what of the first and third? We may approach this matter with an observation from that consummate story-teller, J. R. R. Tolkien:

> Children are capable, of course, of "literary belief," when the story-maker's art is good enough to produce it. That state of mind has been called "willing suspension of disbelief." But this does not seem to me a good description of what happens. What really happens is that the story-maker proves a successful "sub-creator." He makes a Secondary World which your mind can enter. Inside it, what he relates is

"true": it accords with the laws of that world. You therefore
believe it, while you are, as it were, inside. The moment disbelief arises, the spell is broken: the magic, or rather art, has
failed. You are then out in the Primary World again, looking
at the little abortive Secondary World from outside.[2]

The essay from which that quotation is taken is entitled "On Fairy
Stories," and indeed, one would be hard pressed to find someone
who would take exception to it *for fairy stories*. What I am here
suggesting is more radical: even the consciously straightforward
reporting of historical event involves the interpretative refracting of
reported details. Even historical reports are "finite provinces of meaning," and as such they stand over against and interpret paramount
reality. There are four factors which make this so. First, as Seymour
Chatman[3] has pointed out, the articulated data of the story are
always selective, they can never exhaust the infinite range of plot
details or descriptions by which the story-world could be made "complete." (Chatman has taken pains to note that the reader is therefore
called upon to infer a great many of the details which are essential
if the narrative is to sustain verisimilitude, and that the telling of a
story therefore elicits the active collaboration of the listener.) Second,
as Gérard Genette[4] has pointed out, the order of presentation is
necessarily qualified by the fact that narrative is ill-suited to the
portrayal of simultaneous events. The narrator is therefore often
obliged to narrate seriatim events which purportedly occurred at the
same time. The resulting distinction between "story time" and "narrative time" is widely noted in literary scholarship, and it provides
an accounting of anachronisms. Third, as Livia Polanyi[5] and Louis
Mink[6] have pointed out, the narrative must be self-contained, must
be coherent, must have a single unifying point (I call this the story's
"core cliché"[7]). For Mink, the act of "following" a story represents
an attempt to grasp it in its entirety. But for that to happen the story
must *be* entire – "held together in a single image" (p. 547). It is an
image built up seriatim, a piece at a time, with memory serving as
the chief architect; nevertheless it is perceived to be a whole, "grasped
together in a single mental act."

Finally, as Boris Uspensky[8] and Robert Weimann[9] have pointed
out, the telling of a story necessarily involves taking a stance, a point
of view, by which its various elements are evaluated. As Weimann
has said, "Without (a point of view) no narration is possible ... It
is the absolute prerequisite of all narrative activity" (p. 246).

The requirement that a narrative be self-contained is directly related to the matter of selectivity. "Real life" is not composed of one plot, but of many, which may intersect in an infinite variety of ways. In the same way, the plot elements which make up "real life" extend forward and backward beyond the boundaries of this or that given incident, and the stream of ramifications which flows from it may continue to complicate things long after we have "closed the book" or "moved on to another chapter of our lives," as we say.

We are now suddenly in a place to understand exactly why an appreciation of literary functions represents a critical and minimal element of any hermeneutic which seeks to do justice to the ways in which we come to understand the meaning of experience. Because it stands at a critical remove from the "world" of brute experience, the contours of the narrative world necessarily differ in significant ways from the contours of unmediated, brute experience.[10] For our exploration of irony in the gospel narratives there are three significant implications of that fact. First, the relationship between the narrative world of the gospels and the "historical" life of Jesus is infinitely complicated by factors inherent in narrativity itself, *and it cannot have been otherwise.* It is precisely because the gospels stand at a critical remove from brute experience that the *significance* of Jesus can be elaborated there. We might couch this point in terms derived from Polanyi and Mink: in the Church's "conversation" with the world and with itself, the gospel stories were preserved precisely because they were understood to be meaningful in some way, and what the narrator has taken to be their significance has influenced and shaped the stories in the telling. Second, the narrative world of the gospels is only "completed" when its details have been articulated against the assumed body of information which comprises the "world" of its hearers. We might couch this point in terms derived from Chatman: the interstices of the narrative will have been filled in by the narrator's projected audience, and our reading of the gospels must therefore be informed as closely as possible with whatever clarifying data we can glean about the contexts in which the stories were *told*. Third, the point of view of the reader/hearer will always be removed in some measure from the point of view of the characters in the story. We might couch this point in terms derived from Uspensky: the articulation of point of view is inherent in the process of composition itself. *The gospels themselves provide their readers with resources of evaluation which are different from those available to their characters.*

The dissonances thus created are potential in virtually any story, as Robert Scholes and Robert Kellogg have suggested: "The narrative situation is thus ineluctably ironical."[11] Scholes and Kellogg continue: "If we push far enough the question of why irony makes the effects it does, we shall end up in the largely unexplored territory of how and why stories play a part in the life of man" (pp. 240f).

With that observation our discussion has been brought round to the question with which this chapter began: what are the functions of the internal narrative elements which make possible this dialectical relationship to actual, brute, paramount reality? In the process of this brief digression we have been given a vantage-point from which we might sharpen somewhat our articulation of that question. We have seen that the narrative world stands alongside or over against the actual world, and that there are good reasons for respecting as inviolable its structural integrity. We have seen that the listener enters the created world of the story by crossing a threshold, and that in the process he leaves or brackets ordinary reality. From within the the story-world he can come to view ordinary reality from a particular point of view. He may pass judgment on the story's characters, or he may sympathetically identify with them. Their behavior or values may come to serve as paradigms or antiparadigms by which the complexities of his own actual experiences can be organized into meaningful and potent patterns.

There is more that is immediately significant for the topic at hand. We have seen as well that the integrity of the narrative world, and the fact that it stands at a critical remove from the actual world, impose upon the story-teller an absolute obligation: he must orient his readers to the critical background information of the narrative world, and to the distinctive structures and laws by which that information is organized. In that obligation there is created the happy possibility of ironic dissonance, which the story-teller may deliberately exploit in order to inform or persuade the reader of levels of significance which the teller takes to be resident in the story itself. In this it has become clear that the disparity which separates the point of view of the story's listeners from its characters is not merely a coincidence of narrative artistry. It is, instead, a critical factor which informs and shapes the narrator's selection and arrangement of his material. So we may re-frame the question of this chapter: by what rhetorical strategies might the narrator guide the listener into and around the world of the story, and into an awareness of its inner significances?

Showing and telling

The fundamental elements of narrative artistry are four: plot development, characterization, setting, and mood. We shall return to these momentarily. The narrator may orient his readers within these in either of two ways: he may *tell* the reader what he needs to know, or he may *show* him.[12]

Showing

We can clarify the distinction between showing and telling by pausing briefly to contrast narrative proper with drama. In drama there is no narrator (except, of course, by the conscious decision of the playwright), and so the playwright and director must structure the play in such a way that the audience is guided automatically into and around its narrative world. Essential information about character development or changes in time or place must be picked up by the listener indirectly, from clues which are sometimes only incidental to the plot itself. Changes of scenery or costume, shifts in lighting or staging or music, may therefore be critical to the elaboration of the story-line, and may be carefully integrated into the dramatic presentation precisely with a view toward informing the audience of the critical details it needs to follow the plot successfully. When this happens, we may say that the audience has been oriented by "showing," since there is no narrator to tell it what is going on.

One aspect of showing which is critical for our purposes has to do with the orienting functions of dialogue. Specific details of information may be placed on the lips of the story's characters precisely so the audience can *overhear* it. On the surface of it − from the standpoint of the character − such information may be merely coincidental, of relative unimportance. From the standpoint of the observer − who must overhear whatever he knows of the play's development − such clues may be critical. The range of such information may be very broad, may be extraordinarily subtle or complex, and may require sensitivities especially attuned to the cultural horizon in which the play is set.

Telling

Narrative proper differs from drama in precisely this: in addition to story elements which have been indirectly shown the reader, there is also a narrator, who may intrude into the story and address the reader directly. When this happens, we may say that the reader has been oriented by "telling." Changes in scenery or costume, shifts in atmosphere, the movement from one scene to the next may be signaled indirectly, by description, *or* they may be told the reader point-blank. Whenever the narrator intrudes into the story-line with interpretative or orienting asides, he must momentarily stop the progress of the story to do so. There may be a slight sense of distance, together with a lessening of the reader's emotional involvement with the story. At the same time, explanatory notes may create for the reader an impression of superiority over the characters, a superiority which he shares with the narrator, and which influences his judgments about the story's meaning.

That the biblical narrators use both showing and telling is a critical assumption of reading which has too often escaped our notice: the details of the biblical narrative may serve orienting functions which are coincidental to the story itself, but which are necessary if the reader is to understand the story's movements and the relationships between its parts. They may establish and deepen the mood of the story by evoking inarticulate responses below the reader's threshold of consciousness. Or they may inform the reader of critical elements or perspectives he needs in order to penetrate the story's deeper significances. Often, then, historical details are included, not out of concern for historical completeness or accuracy, but also − sometimes expressly − because they are required by the exigencies of the telling itself.

Story elements

Plot

We have said that narrative is composed of four constitutive elements: plot development, characterization, setting, and mood. Throughout its long history, literary theory has repeatedly isolated this or that component as primary, and has employed the other three in the service of that one. Aristotle, in his *Poetics*, for example, considered plot to be primary. Characters are significant agents in bringing about event; aside from that they are dispensable. Elder Olsen, writing from a neo-Aristotelian perspective, has articulated this viewpoint in this way:

We have decided that plot governs character ... I suppose a natural instance which is ... clearly parallel to what we are considering is that of finding someone who can fill a certain job. When an executive has a position to fill, the job is the first consideration, and the man to hire is second ... Similarly, if certain actions are to happen in the plot, and produce a given effect, a character must be invented or found who can perform them.[13]

In their broadly ranging essay on *The Nature of Narrative*, Robert Scholes and Robert Kellogg have suggested that the reduction of oral literature to writing naturally involved the retention and adaptation of modes of expression which were critical for oral composition. Thus the earliest Greek literature was the ready inheritor of influences which had shaped the traditional oral epic. Central among these is plot: "In the transmission of traditional narrative it is of necessity the outline of events, the plot, which is transmitted" (p. 12). The point is that Aristotle considered plot primary because that was what was demanded by the exigencies of oral composition. Albert Lord has explored this factor in his study of the oral composition of Hungarian folk narrative.[14] According to Lord, the story-teller must maintain interest in the narrative at all costs, and in the teeth of all distractions. Suspense becomes vital, and for that reason he must withold vital information until it becomes absolutely critical to the developing plot-line. In some sense, his success or failure – not only as a story-teller, but also as a breadwinner for his family – will depend upon his innate sense of timing.

It is customary in literary criticism to explore plot in terms of its wider movements: complication, crisis, and denouement. These terms are quite ancient. Aristotle employed them in his *Rhetoric*. Recently a variety of interpreters – Augustine Stock,[15] Gilbert Bilezekian[16] and Curtis Beach[17] – have revived E. W. Burch's[18] notion that, in its complication, crisis, and denouement, Mark's Gospel is based on the rhetorical patterns of Greek tragedy. The assumption here is that Mark is consciously imitating the tragic literature of his day. This is certainly a fruitful line of inquiry. For now, however, I should like to deal briefly with plot from a somewhat different direction: "plot timing" or "narrative pace." We have noted already Gérard Genette's distinction between "story time" – the time of the "actual" events, as they purportedly happened – and "narrative time" – the time it takes the narrator to report them.[19] The two sorts of time are altogether different, yet they must be correlated in some way or the narrative will not appear plausible. Unlike "story time," "narrative time" is quite flexible. It can expand or contract, can reverse itself, can stop altogether. It can present instances by recollection or antici-pation, and therefore "out of historical sequence." We might illustrate with reference to Mark.[20] In his articulation of the story-line, Mark may stop to make interpretative asides, as we have seen, or he may include detailed descriptions of his characters. His description of the Gerasene demoniac in Chapter 5 covers three full verses. As the description unfolds, the movement of the plot – that is, narrative time – stops briefly. The action freezes while the reader is oriented to the specific circumstances in which the events make sense. At the other extreme, summaries – such as the brief note in 1.28 that "at once his fame spread everywhere throughout all the surrounding region of Galilee" – may speed the narrative time to almost break-neck speed. In the recitation of dialogue, the lapse of story time and the lapse of narrative time appear to proceed at about the same pace.

In the development of narrative time, one major compositional difficulty has called for especially creative resolution: since the nar-rator can describe only one scene at a time, how is he to include events which – in *story* time – happen simultaneously? Perhaps the most straightforward resolutions of the problem are through recollection or through the arrival of a messenger from the "other scene," whose report supplies both the characters and the audience with a full description of the goings on "off-stage." In his *Handbook of Classical Drama*, Philip Harsh has pointed out a particularly interesting Greek variation on the use of messengers in the resolution of the problem of simultaneity: dual time.[21] Because they are com-posed almost exclusively of dialogue, events on the stage progress at a pace which roughly approximates "story time," naturally tucked in a bit around the edges by a bit of condensation. On the other hand, a series of messengers may arrive with summary reports of "simultaneous" events which are unfolding at a completely unrelated pace off-stage. The events on-stage may occupy a couple of hours, while the events narrated by messengers may involve days or even weeks.

Mark's skill with narrative pace is uneven. We may note, for example, the somewhat awkward transition between 1.28 and 1.29. In 1.28 Jesus has just completed an exorcism in the synagogue in Capernaum. The story ends with a summary: "His fame spread everywhere throughout the surrounding region of Galilee." The speed here is breakneck, and the summary appears to move the plot into a new arena. In 1.29 we are back in the synagogue. The pace is regularized, and the reader is brought up short. The effect is startling, even a bit disorienting. On the other hand, there are turns in the narrative which reflect remarkable subtlety. The story of the death of John the Baptist in 6.14–29 is out of sequence, and does not appear to be conceptually related to the events which precede or follow. The story does not move the plot forward, and could be easily removed without loss of continuity. Yet placed here, it introduces a brief pause, during which the mission of the twelve (cf. vv.12 and 30) is carried on. The illusion of simultaneity is clearly a narrative trick, here employed with remarkable effect. Occasionally Mark solves the problem of simultaneity by straightforward intercalation: a story is begun; then a second, related story is told in its entirety; then the first story is completed. It is generally agreed that we should seek some measure of resonance between these "Markan sandwiches."[22]

There is no instance of dual time in Mark, although there are occasional reports from "messengers." When Mark enlists characters in this way, the information they disclose is often critical to the potency of the story. For example, in 9.14–29 there is the story of the exorcism of a lad possessed of a demon. As the story opens, Jesus and the inner circle have returned from the Mount of Transfiguration to a scene of open hostility (v.14). Jesus' question and the father's answer in vv.16f let the reader know what has gone on during his absence:

> And he asked them, "What are you discussing with them?" And one of the crowd answered him, "Teacher, I brought my son to you, for he has a dumb spirit; and whenever it seizes him, it dashes him down; and he foams and grinds his teeth and becomes rigid; and I asked your disciples to cast it out, and they were not able."

The reader – hardly Jesus! – needs to know how long the boy has been in this state, and so that information is included in vv.21f:

> And Jesus asked his father, "How long has he had this?" And he said, "From childhood. And it has often cast him into the fire and into the water to destroy him; but if you can do anything, have pity on us and help us."

The literary functions of these two passages are very clear: they provide exactly that critical information which the reader needs in order to understand the potency of Jesus' cure, and they provide it in a way which the reader can *overhear*.

Character development

Nowadays, literary sensitivities tend toward the appreciation of character development, and that fact may itself be sociologically significant. Eric Kahler has argued that the shift in literary interest from plot to characterization may be calibrated against a growing self-consciousness in post-Medieval European thought about the internal constitution of the human person.[23] In contemporary literature, plot and setting are very often the backdrops against which the structures of character can be brought into relief. The *dramatis personae* struggle against the limitations imposed upon them by the doings of other characters, or against the social or natural laws which are implied by the setting. As they aspire or despair, as they succeed or fail, and – more tellingly! – as they respond to success or failure, the inner workings of their character are developed.

Wesley Kort has suggested that the characters of literature play a paradigmatic role in the understanding of character generally,[24] and a fully formed theory of moral development has been built on a similar foundation by the ethicist, Stanley Hauerwas.[25] But this thinking is not new. Already the ancients understood the social implications of the audience's identification with the protagonist of a tale. The catharsis the audience experienced as it sympathized with the tragic hero was itself considered a social good. The tendency toward identification may represent a basic motivation for idealizing a particular character and for setting him up as prototypical or paradigmatic. In this way, he may be made to carry the weight of a complex configuration of values or behavioral patterns. The villain or antagonist may reflect that configuration on the inverse. A fascinating illustration of this fact is to be found in Livy's *Ab Urbe Condita*, the "History of Rome":

> Here are the questions to which I would have every reader give close attention – what life and morals were like; through what men and by what policies, in peace and war, empire was established and enlarged; let them note how ... morals first gave way ... sank lower and lower, and finally began the downward plunge which has brought us to the present time ... What chiefly makes the study of history wholesome

and profitable is this, that you should behold the lessons of every kind of experience as on a conspicuous monument; from these you may choose for yourself and for your own state what to imitate, from these mark for avoidance what is shameful in conception and shameful in result.[26]

This is true of story-telling generally, not only of historical example. Children may learn from the stories their parents tell them that there are heroes in the world, that heroism is ultimately praise-worthy, that patience or diligence will "out." But they will learn more. In the complex nuances and textures of the story-teller's language, in the attitudes he displays toward his characters, they will learn what it means to be a hero or a villain in the social setting in which the story is told. It is in this way that the expression "development of character" may be made to have a double significance: in developing the character of his stories, the story-teller develops the character of his listeners. There are widely ranging techniques for doing so. A listing here would be nearly endless, and so we may pause long enough only to mention a few which are germane to the evaluation of the biblical narratives.

Seymour Chatman has developed a paradigm of character based on "traits": a trait is a "relatively abiding or stable personal quality."[27] To my mind, what is critical here is that the reader picks up essential clues about characterization indirectly as he evaluates and re-evaluates the various configurations of traits displayed in the character's words or actions. Thus everything is potentially significant: the consistency or inconsistency of the character's words and actions, the texture of his language, the ease with which he is angered and the sorts of things which make him so, the slightly lop-sided way he wears his hat. Mark may *tell* us that Peter stammered out his question on the Mount of Transfiguration "because he did not know what to say" (9.6), but the comment is really unnecessary. The reader can *see* that for himself. Luke may have dropped Mark's note that James and John were called the "sons of thunder" (6.14; cf. Mark 3.16), but he *shows* the reader precisely that impulsive and violent side of their character in their question to Jesus about the Samaritan village: "Lord, do you want us to bid fire come down from heaven and consume them?" (9.54).

Biblical narrators – among them certainly Mark – often judge their characters "good" or "bad" in terms of their relation to the paradigmatic figures in their stories. Very often the appropriate denunciation or affirmation is found on the hero's own lips. Thus, in the story of the death of John the Baptist (Mark 6.14–29), the denunciation against Herod expresses a condemnation with which Mark concurs, but that condemnation gains a measure of potency when it comes from the Baptist himself. The character of the Baptist is also developed here, since these words reflect implacable courage. Something similar is reflected in the potencies of Jesus' denunciations of the authorities in Chapter 12, and in the fury with which he cleanses the temple in 11.15–17. Jesus has already repeatedly indicated to the disciples (and to the reader!) that he knows the authorities are plotting his arrest (8.31; 9.31; 10.32–4). The implicit parallelism between these two men gives the Baptist's story the quality of a sub-plot which reflects, and thereby deepens, the developing horrors of the major plot-line.

Sometimes the narrator may choose to *contrast* two characters, and thereby to underscore the similarities and differences between them. Howard Kee has pointed out the theological implications of the use of blind men as literary foils for the disciples in Mark 8.22–6 and 10.46–52: "Both stories of the blind who see throw in sharp relief the portraits of the disciples who cannot understand even when an explanation is offered them."[28] Mark's skill with the use of such literary foils perhaps reaches its apex in his contrast between Jesus' almost placid responses to the high priest during his trial before the council (14.55–65), and Peter's panic-stricken and stammering fabrications to the high priest's maid during his own "trial" before the rabble in the courtyard below (14.66–72). Perhaps equally potent is the contrast between Jesus and the authorities in the sabbath healing story in 3.1–6. It is significant that this story ends with the extremely heavy ballast-line, "The Pharisees went out, and immediately held counsel with the Herodians against him, how to destroy him" (v. 6). Over against this Mark places Jesus' rhetorical – and unanswered! – question, "Is it lawful on the sabbath day to ... save life or to kill?" By this foil Mark exposes the illegality and the senselessness of the authorities' collusion against Jesus.

As in any story, the biblical narrator is also free to intrude into the narrative and describe his characters directly. There is a variety of situations in which it is natural to "tell" the reader significant background information which explains the behavior of the characters of the story. One method of characterization over which the writer of imaginative literature has a greater measure of control is in the assigning of names. In this matter, clearly the writer of an ostensibly historical account is restricted by the traditions he takes to be accurate. But he is not completely without leverage. Mark, for example, includes notes about Simon's nickname, Peter, and the epithet Jesus had assigned to James and John, the "sons of thunder" (3.16f). There may be touches of humor here, but that would be difficult to establish. Perhaps we shall never know how many of Mark's readers would have heard subtler nuances in the names of the characters in the story, a *Petros* who falls apart at the last crucial moment, a tax-collector named – of all things! – Levi (2.13). But then there are sobering elements, too: Mark's story includes a *Bar-Abbas*, a "son of the father," whose story may be an allegory for what happens to us all.

Alongside proper names and nicknames may be placed the descriptive adjectives the narrator uses to place his characters, and quite often these are included because the proper interpretation of the story hinges on the information they provide. If the critical turning of the exorcism story in Chapter 7 rests upon Jesus' conversation with the possessed girl's mother, that conversation in turn rests upon the information that the woman was a "Greek, a Syrophoenician by birth" (v.26), and therefore a foreigner. The attentive listener will hardly fail to notice the similarities with the story of the raising of Jairus' daughter in Chapter 5, with its note that Jairus was "one of the rulers of the synagogue" (v.22). And is there not an implicit irony in the description of Bartimaeus as a blind man – a *tuphlos* – in 10.46–52, when he is the only person in the crowd who recognizes Jesus for who he truly is?

There are moments in the narrative in which the descriptions run into great detail, and the detail may be a critical factor, carefully woven into the plot-line. This attention to descriptive detail is especially evident in miracle stories, since it serves the apologetic function of establishing beyond reasonable doubt the conditions which obtained before the miracle occurred. A case in point is the description of the Gerasene demoniac in 5.2–5, to which we have already referred:

> Immediately there met him out of the tombs
>   a man with an unclean spirit,
>   who lived among the tombs,
>   and no one could bind him any more,
>   even with a chain;
>   for he had often been bound
>   with fetters
>   and chains,

and the chains he wrenched apart,
and the fetters he broke in pieces;
and no one had the strength to subdue him.
Night and day among the tombs
            and on the mountains
he was always   crying out
            and bruising himself
            with stones.

Clearly this extensive description is intended as a contrasting back-drop to the description of his exorcized state in v. 15:

They came ... and saw the demoniac
            sitting there,
            clothed
            and in his right mind ...
and they were afraid.

What has happened in the meantime? Jesus has dismissed the demon with a *word*. In this way, the word of Jesus is shown to possess greater power over demons than had the desperate prophylactic measures taken by the townspeople. Their fear is explained in this way, as are their eager entreaties that Jesus "depart from their neighborhood" (v. 17). For its part, this request deepens the sense of desperation the reader picks up from the description of their attempts to control the demoniac in verses 3–5.

We have been discussing characterization thus far as a more or less static phenomenon, but, in point of fact, characters change. They vacillate. They face moments of crisis. They may not be entirely true to their convictions. They develop. More than fifty years ago E. M. Forster provided us with a vocabulary for describing the inner vacilla-tions and movements of story characters. Forster introduced into the discussion a distinction between characterization which is "round," "flat" or "stock."[29] A round character is complex or subtle, may have deeply divided loyalties, may behave unpredictably. A flat character is two-dimensional, is less complex and more predictable. What traits he shows are usually consistent, as are his motivations. A stock character is one-dimensional, with a single, consistent, pre-dictable trait.

Forster's categories provide rather a fascinating basis for the examination of gospel characterization. Mark, for example, has pro-vided us with an entirely stock picture of the Pharisees. He fairly spits out the term. As Jesus' antagonists, their motivations are simple, unequivocal, predictable. They do not wrestle with the greater questions of the Kingdom; they simply elect not to be among the elect. Mark seems to like his villains flat: not so his disciples. The disciples in Mark are complex characters, divided in their loyalties, ambivalent about their calling. They preach the Good News of the Kingdom, and carry in their hands the power to heal and to cast out demons, yet we suspect that when the power fails them at that crucial moment in Chapter 9 they almost have it in them to cast out with their hands the scribes instead. Mark's disciples follow Jesus, to be sure, but at the critical turn in the narrative they bleat out their loyalty and scatter like sheep.

Shimon Bar-Efrat has suggested that the indirect approach to character development (by this he intends "showing" rather than "telling") is "close to reality":

> In real life, also, we come to know people through their way of talking and acting. This technique is dynamic, because the qualities of the characters are gradually built up from their appearance, utterances and performances. Each new appearance may bring about a change in our impression.[30]

As correct as this observation is, we must guard against the notion that characterization in narrative derives its basic textures from our perceptions of people "in reality." It is equally the case that our perceptions of real people are shaped by dispositions and patterns we pick up from the stories that we hear and the literature that we read.

In ancient literature, as we have seen, characterization was not morally neutral. Rather, it assumed a specific moral norm against which individual traits and behavior were constantly judged. Theodore Weeden has already made this point in a discussion of the passage from Livy's *Ab Urbe Condita* we noted earlier:

> In our discussion of Livy it was noted that he seldom makes direct personal comment on the lives of the people about whom he narrates. Rather, he comments indirectly by the way in which he portrays the actions and thoughts of the personages in his historical drama. Scholars have often pondered over the fact that Mark never comments or expresses himself directly to the reader (with the possible exception of 13:14). Might he not choose, as Livy did, to comment indirectly to his readers by the way he portrays his characters and the events in which they participate?[31]

That is, we must not permit Mark's remarkable restraint in the use of direct characterization − telling − to blind us to the direct narrative techniques by which he constantly shows us what he thinks of his story's characters. By taking a position, he articulates a "locus of loyalty" about which the listener is forced to make a choice. In this way, the characters of the story become paradigms and antiparadigms of those behaviors and traits which are taken as normative by the group. It is partly in this sense that the narrative acquires socially significant overtones.

Setting and mood

We shall treat questions of setting and mood together, since these two concerns are inextricably related. By "setting" we mean the spatial and physical dimensions of the story, and the furniture which forms its basic properties. By "mood" we mean the elements of the story which evoke tacit emotional responses on the part of the reader − the texture of the story-teller's language, the patterned nuances of vocabulary. To my knowledge there has never been a literary theory which subordinates plot and character to setting. Yet there are stories which function as though that were so.[32] Setting establishes the spatial parameters of the story, and can therefore in some sense regulate the development of character or plot. The parameters it imposes on the action can frustrate or facilitate the intentions of the story's characters, who are thereby channeled by their contexts into one form of action rather than another.

As the spatial dimension of the story, setting enjoys a special relationship to plot, the story's temporal dimension. In a sense, the intersection of these two mirrors the relationship between time and space generally. At any given moment, all of space occupies only a single point in time. Conversely, time passes, moment by moment, for every point in space. Thus time and space are complementary. So, too, are setting and plot. If the narrator wishes to describe the setting in his story he must stop the movement of the plot to do so. By dawdling on details, by diverting attention here or there, by carefully building up and overlaying images and impressions, he can create functional pauses during which the action of the narrative slows. It may stop altogether. If something critical is pending, suspense builds.

On the other hand, there are techniques for building urgency into the story: narrators may provide only minimal description, or none at all, may use a terse vocabulary, may include only summary mention of unfolding events. The effect of "rapidfire" language can be electric, especially if the story is presented orally. It is in this way that setting relates so closely to mood. The textures of the story-teller's language – the modulations of its vigor and the associations with other stories it may evoke – may combine to create impressions of excitement, comedy, melodrama or horror. Sometimes setting and mood are so carefully integrated that the resulting atmosphere contributes to our fascination and keeps us reading on. C. S. Lewis has described the moment at which he became aware of the critical role the appreciation of atmosphere played in his own reading. A friend had described to Lewis a childhood fascination with the alien and enchanting images of American Indians in the writings of Fenimore Cooper. For Lewis' friend, "the 'Redskinnery' was what really mattered. In such a scene as my friend described, take away the feathers, the high cheek-bones, the whiskered trousers, substitute a pistol for the tomahawk, and what would be left?"[33]

Perhaps Lewis' account should serve as a brake on our madcap race to appropriate and render familiar every last vestige of strangeness in the gospel stories. But quite beyond that – and this is more directly significant – we ought to consider the possibility that matters of setting and mood are at least as important for authors as they are for readers.

That this is true for the narrators of biblical stories is a critical factor in reading which has too often escaped our notice. We may illustrate with a discussion of the "texture" of the narrative's language. One aspect of linguistic texture which is frequently noted in biblical exposition is allusion. We seem to have made a science – or perhaps a mania[34] – of ferreting out parallels within our literature and other related traditions. We have not, however, developed anything at all like a systematic appreciation of the role such parallels might play in the inner dynamics of the literature itself.[35] What follows is therefore more tentative and exploratory of a subject which to my mind deserves closer attention.

Allusion may be made in an almost infinite variety of directions, both within the narrative and outside it. Allusions within the narrative may refer either ahead to events yet to come, or back to events which have already happened. In the latter case, they help to deepen the sense that the otherwise disparate parts of the narrative may have some internal connection, and in that way sustain the impression that the narrative parts are elements of a larger whole, that the story-line coheres. In the case that allusions foreshadow narrative elements yet to come, they may serve a basic orienting function of predisposing the reader to respond in one way and not another: that is, the reader's reactions to any event may be shaped by anticipations generated by linguistic elements which appeared earlier in the narrative.

Closely related to foreshadowing allusions are outright prophecies, identified as such. The literary functions of prophetic utterance will be the subject of a section in Chapter 4, but it may be appropriate here simply to note that prophecies may heighten the reader's sense of the inevitability of the story's outcome, and in that way deepen the sympathies he holds for the story's characters.[36]

If allusions are made to information which stands outside the narrative, they may evoke associations with the reader's prior knowledge, and in that way create the impression that the narrative takes place in familiar territory. They may suggest that similarities exist between the narrative world and the outside information, or they may set the reader up for the narrator's ultimate intention of contravening those similarities. If their language is archaic they may create the impression that the narrative world extends beyond the boundaries of the story itself, back into earlier eras. The famous shift in diction between Luke 2 and 3 may function in this way. By casting the opening chapters of his narrative in heavily Semitized diction, Luke evokes in his readers a sense of deep resonance with Old Testament prototypes and patterns, and in that way he suggests that this story has its roots in something ancient and venerable.

It is in this way that allusive language may serve rhetorical functions which are related to the creation and maintenance of the mood of the story. By summoning associations with the hearer's prior knowledge, the narrator may evoke inarticulate, subconscious responses which themselves guide the reader through the inner significances of the story or its world.

This point is critical. It corresponds to the basic notion that the "languaging" of experience is a kind of interpretation, and that the "languaged" event stands removed in significant ways from the brute event itself. For our purposes, what is important here is that the allusive language with which the biblical story is told may widen the distance between the story's characters and its audience.

It is not accidental that the stories of Jesus came to be told in language which is strongly suggestive of Old and inter-testamental themes. Rather, that fact represents the early Christian conviction that the stories of Jesus are only properly told in such a way that the deeper resonances with such themes can be evoked for the listener. Furthermore, there is implicit within such a conviction the assumption that the Church possessed rights over the verbal and literary heritage which it shared so uncomfortably with Judaism.

What has been said about allusive language may be broadened to include the whole range of linguistic skills – the "language-world!" – which the story-teller assumes on the part of his listener.[37] There may be several levels at which the language-world can inform, alter or shape the listener's perceptions of the narrative's structures, movements or significances. At its lowest level, reading itself requires not only sensitivities attuned to the various lexical dimensions of the text's vocabulary, but also a kind of pre-formal intuitive reaction to the textures and biases latent in that vocabulary.

With this, our chapter has been brought full circle. We have suggested a number of ways in which narratives differ from brute, uninterpreted experiences – selectivity, shifts in sequence, the governing presence of the narrator's point of view. We have suggested that it is precisely because narrative stands at such a critical remove from brute experience that it can refract that experience into meaningful and useful patterns, and that it is upon the foundation of those patterns that the group can construct its common life. The process we have described is hardly accomplished by this or that individual story; rather, the group's stories gain collective force in the telling and re-telling, reinforcing and corroborating one another in an ever-widening circle of associations and allusions. Gradually the group's collective vision of reality is built up by the laying and overlaying of the impressions, images, and convictions that the stories convey.

That all of this is linguistic activity does not need mentioning. What is worth noting, however, is that the linguistic character of the story as it is told is largely unavailable to the characters within it (the only exception to this general rule is in the reporting of dialogue). That is, if we could isolate a single factor which distinguishes the "knowledge" of the story's teller and reader from that of its characters, it would be precisely this: the reader has the story itself, structured as it is in a linear fashion, expressed in specific and significant language, with its full range of linguistic nuances, associations, and allusions. The characters do not. That fact makes narrative always – and as Scholes and Kellogg suggest, "ineluctably" – ironic.

In this study we are interested in irony somewhat more consciously worked out. The ironic tendencies naturally inherent in stories are sometimes deliberately exploited by conscious rhetorical strategies, and in that way made to evoke especially potent reactions on the part of the reader. The strategies by which those tendencies are developed and the effects they have on the experience of reading are the subject of Chapter 4, to which we shall shortly turn.

Before we leave Chapter 3, however, we must pause to reaffirm the potencies of the biblical stories *as such*. Insofar as biblical scholarship focuses its attention solely on the question of the story's historical accuracy, or on the theological "information" it may provide, or on the residue of traditions which may underlie it, we shall fail to explore the dynamic movements of the story-line itself. But Mark is a skilled story-teller, and the potency of his tale ultimately leaves the listener in the grip of subtle but engrossing literary forces. To the extent that we have overlooked those forces, or shrugged off the hold they have placed upon us, we have failed even to read the narrative, much less interpret it for another age.

4

TEXT AND SUBJECT: TOWARD A
RHETORIC OF IRONY

In this chapter it is our task to pull the varied material from Chapters 2 and 3 into a single framework. On the surface of it, that framework would not appear difficult to construct. One would need only to show that the assumptions and goals of these two approaches to literature are not incompatible, that their interpretative agendas would be complementary if only their vocabularies could be regularized. And that much would be quite easy to demonstrate, I should think, if only because there is what on the surface appears to be a sequential relationship between them. We may diagram briefly:

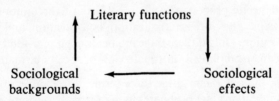

If we begin with sociological backgrounds, we can see that the assumptions which inform the structuring of the community's language-world will serve as the assumptions which underlie the text, against which the details of the text are rendered specific. These are the assumed frames of reference of every articulated sentence in the work, and they are inherent to some degree in virtually every linguistic exchange. As we move on to consider the narrative in its own right, we may note with the literary critics that the articulated details of the text interact with these assumed frames of reference to form new frames, frames which may be said to be constituted by the language exchange as such. But here we are recalled to the observation of the sociologists who concern themselves with the rhetorical effects of stories and story-telling: the information and points of view expressed in the new frames of reference may significantly alter the life-world or language-world of their hearers. With that, we come full circle.

There is a difficulty here which requires attention: while the relationship between the competencies assumed by the text and the competencies generated by the text may be thought of as *sequential*, that model may not be as integrative as the workings of natural reading actually require. Perhaps the movement from the one kind of competency to the other is better thought of as an oscillating movement, in which the competencies assumed by the text and those generated by the text interact with one another dialectically. How is this so? We may turn first to the work of Peter Berger, the sociologist who, with Thomas Luckmann, first popularized the notion that our perceptions of reality are significantly shaped by the dynamic social settings in which we find ourselves. The remarks which follow come during the course of a discussion of the role of religion in creating and sustaining the structures and values which constitute the life-world of its adherents. Berger opens with a general description of the enterprise of world-building which is society in general:

> Society is a dialectic phenomenon in that it is a human product, and nothing but a human product, that yet continuously acts back upon its producer ... The fundamental dialectic process of society consists of three moments, or steps. These are externalization, objectivation, and internalization. Only if these three moments are understood together can an empirically adequate view of society be maintained.[1]

As Berger intends them, these three terms describe the process by which a human product originates in man's consciousness, takes on its own reality, and as such affects directly or indirectly the structures of his consciousness. As a product of human enterprise, language is ineluctably bound by in Berger's "dialectical paradigm": it is both shaped by, and shaper of, the society which uses it. Berger points out that the steps, or moments, of this dialectic process occur simultaneously, rather than sequentially, and that man therefore exists in a dialectical tension between the world he assumes to be given and the world he is calling into being.

If the realities of world-construction and world-maintenance stand in dialectical tension for language in general, we should not be surprised if they do so for narrative literature. Here, as elsewhere, we can discover close and significant parallels between the general phenomena of language and the particular phenomena of stories. An explanation of the reading process which makes that tension explicit is Umberto Eco's superb study of *The Role of the Reader*.[2] What

Berger has said as a sociologist, Eco has said as a student of semiotics: the author must rely upon a specific "encyclopedia" of information, which both informs and limits what the reader can make of the details of the text. Not only is this so, but as the unfolding details of the text are taken in and evaluated, they inform the interpretation of all subsequent elements. The text not only assumes competence, it creates it.

We have dealt with this question at some length because we have needed to establish at the outset that the differences in point of view which constitute the reader's ironic insights may be the result of complex interactions between literary and cultural elements. We have also needed to be clear that an adequate rhetoric of narrative strategies must in some measure account for the competencies the narrator has assumed on the part of his reader, even if it can only do so in a generalized and tentative way. As he writes, a narrator is able to assume an enormous variety of competencies on the part of his "Model Reader" – particular kinds of listening or reading skills, bits or whole worlds of background information, the ability to recognize and respond appropriately to the narrative's implicit points of view.[3] We are therefore left with a problem of organization: how are we to present in a systematic fashion the widely ranging rhetorical strategies by which the story-teller may interact with and shape the linguistic skills of his listener or reader?

From what we have seen, the entire narrative exchange may be understood as an oscillating interaction between two different sources of what we shall call "competencies": competencies *assumed* by the text, and competencies *generated* by the text. The interface between these two represents the working matrix of any given sentence of the narrative text, and the silent background against which it must be read if we are to understand its import. Fortunately, this question has been much discussed in the literature on reading theory. In *The Role of the Reader*, Eco has listed a variety of sorts of assumed background information against which the individual elements of the narrative must be correlated in order to determine their precise textual meanings (pp. 3–43). All these, taken together, comprise what Eco calls an "encyclopedia," and they are composed of a series of "codes," "subcodes," and "frames of reference":

Competencies assumed by the text

1. Basic dictionary meanings
2. Rules of co-reference

3. Contextual and circumstantial selections
4. Inferences by common frames
5. Rhetorical and stylistic overcoding
6. Inferences by intertextual frames
7. Ideological overcoding.

In this listing, Eco has dealt only with what we have called "assumed" competencies. For a listing of the rhetorical competencies *generated* by the text, we shall have to draw on a number of other sources. For clarity, this list may be divided into two parts, one dealing with strategies of "telling," the other with strategies of "showing":

Competencies generated by the text

Strategies of telling
8. Prologues
9. Asides
10. Winks at the reader
11. Foretelling.

Strategies of showing
12. Foretelling. Foreshadowing. Flashback
13. Verbal ironies
14. Exclusionary strategies.

Much of the material introduced in these three lists has been discussed in Chapter 3. Here it is our task to inquire after its significance for the creation of intentionally ironic reactions on the part of the listener or reader.

Irony: a preliminary definition

Before we begin we must pause momentarily and focus our definition of the term irony itself.[4] Sometimes irony is defined quite narrowly. Cicero's definition − "Irony is saying one thing and meaning another" − has served as a guide for many a literary theorist. At other times, the term is extraordinarily broad: "Irony is more than a literary device; it may be said to inhere in [one's] outlook on life."[5] The difficulty of offering a precise definition is suggested by this opening lament from D.C. Muecke's fine study, *The Compass of Irony*. In an opening statement, Muecke lists nineteen different terms for irony or "types" of irony which are discussed in the literature.

Many of these, he tells us, have been invented on the spot by the critic who employs them, with the result that "one never sees any ordered relationship between the kinds and consequently never gets a clear picture of the whole range or compass of irony." (p. 4)

How, then, should we proceed? Muecke has provided us with an accounting of irony's three constitutive elements (pp. 19f):

1. First, irony requires that there be two or more levels of discourse, one available to the victim of the irony, the other to the observer.
2. Irony requires that there be dissonance or tension between the two levels.
3. Finally, irony requires that someone — either the victim or the ironist himself — be innocent of the tension. In this way, the observer is invited to respond on more than a rational basis. The work of irony is ultimately a work of subtlety and shock.

With these three conditions in hand we can begin to develop a simplified picture of the workings of dramatic irony. A story is told in such a way that its plot structures yield two levels of significance. The story-teller or dramatist may take special care to provide the spectator with clues which suggest that there are dimensions of meaning which are shielded from the story's characters. The dissonances between the two levels of knowledge may evoke deep, even subconscious, reactions on the part of the spectator. The incongruities of irony may range from the hilariously funny to the deeply tragic, may be complex or straightforwad, and may be subtle or excruciatingly blunt. Those incongruities will be especially potent when one or another character utters a *double entendre*. A very clever ironist may make the secondary and primary meanings of the *double entendre* diametrically opposed to one another. There are degrees of subtlety here. In tragedy, usually the ironic saying is uttered unwittingly, and the speaker is its victim. In comic irony, the *double entendre* is uttered with the speaker's — the eiron's — full knowledge, while his antagonist — the alazon — is its victim.

There is another subtlety here which should not escape our notice. In tragic irony, often the speech (which doubles back and victimizes its unwitting speaker) mirrors the ironic actions of the plot (which double back and victimize the unwitting actant). Where that synonomy is complex, the ironic speech could easily be mistaken for an implicit allegory of the ironic plot. But there are rhetorical potencies in that synonymy which may not be insignificant in the narrator's strategies. Because the speech mirrors the plot, it represents a major clue to the deeper significances which are to be found there. Oedipus' famous speech is not merely ironic, it signals the movements of the plot in synecdoche:

> This murderer, no matter who he is, is banished
> From the country where my power and my throne
> Are supreme.

Because of the subtleties involved, we should not be surprised to discover irony in places where we least expected it. And that is precisely the point: irony is sophisticated art, a kind of verbal trickery. Sometimes it reflects remarkable subtlety or power. It is not surprising that users of irony themselves tend to be somewhat clever in their dealings with their audiences, setting them up for this or that reaction, then contravening those expectations. A flat view of language misses it entirely. Certainly we should be prepared to look further afield than classical drama in our investigation of the workings of irony. As Muecke might say, the compass of irony has many points. I raise the matter here because it suggests a necessary clarification: in our references to dramatic irony in Mark, we are not suggesting that Mark is consciously or unconsciously imitating Greek *theater*, much less this or that particular play. That suggestion, wherever it might be made, simply oversteps the bounds of the evidence. Instead, we are arguing that the techniques for evoking and sustaining ironic dissonance are widely distributed in ancient literature, and would have been ready to hand in Mark's milieu.

In presenting his three-point model, Muecke was careful to note that ironic nuances are not always clearly articulated in a text, "the upper level need not be *presented* by the ironist; it need only be evoked by him or be present in the mind of the observer" (p. 19). That is, the compass of irony may have many points, but it has two poles: dissonance between the text and points of view already "present in the mind of the observer," and dissonance "evoked" by the ironic plot itself. With mention of these two poles we are returned to the wider arena of competencies assumed by the text and those the text may generate. What they may be, and the strategies by which they may be developed or exploited, is the subject of the material which follows.

Competencies assumed by the text

Much of the material in this section has as its background the discussion of language which occupied our attention in Chapter 2. We cannot overestimate the role of assumed background information in the reading process. In a recent study, "The Theory of Ironic Speech Acts," David Amante has related what we have called the "language-world" to the study of irony as a rhetorically potent language exchange: "Knowledge of the social system, manners, principles governing conversations, shared background and knowledge of speech acts all contribute to our awareness of irony."[6]

As we begin our discussion of background information, we should note that much of the information assumed on the part of the reader is also assumed on the part of the story's characters, and is therefore not, strictly speaking, ironic. There is, however, a critical condition in which this qualification is expected: *when the assumptions are contained in the fabric of the narration as such they may be hidden from the story's characters*; that is, the characters inside the story cannot hear the story, nor be informed by the textures, the allusions or the ambiguities of the story-teller's language. As we shall see, much of irony hinges upon this distinction.

Basic dictionary meanings

It hardly seems necessary to note that reading or listening requires awareness of the basic lexical dimensions of the text and its vocabulary. In point of fact, there may be extremely complex interpretative operations already evident even in this elementary interaction with the text. Here already there are implications of irony and the recovery of ironic nuances. In part those implications are born of the significance the vocabulary of the text holds for guiding the reader into and around the world of the story. In particular, the vocabulary supplied in the text may guide the reader in projecting the background information which the narrator has elected not to supply. This operation of filling in missing details on the basis of those supplied is critical in the reading process, and constitutes a basic preliminary "interpretation" of the text. The following illustration is from Seymour Chatman's study of narrative structure, *Story and Discourse*: "If a girl is portrayed as 'blue-eyed,' 'blonde,' and 'graceful,' we assume further that her skin is fair and unblemished, that she speaks with a gentle voice, that her feet are relatively small, and so on."[7]

Chatman further points out that this activity of filling in interstices and projecting background goes on continuously, and that the reader's ability to do so is virtually unlimited, like that of a geo- meter's "to conceive of an infinity of fractional spaces between two points."

Eco distinguishes between lexical properties which are "virtual" in the reader's encyclopedia of knowledge, and those which are actualized, or made relevant in the course of reading (p. 23). Decisions about which dimensions of the text are virtual and which are actual must be made at every point in the reading process, and may be corroborated or contravened at later stages of the reading.

Analysis of the deep structures of language[8] suggests that native speakers may be tacitly aware of varieties of lexical associations which may be lost on those who have learned the language as adults. This caution may be especially critical in our reading of classical or biblical literature. It is the modern reader's natural tendency to fill in the interstices of the story from language-worlds which are alien to the milieu of the text itself. What is important for the reading of irony is that the vocabulary of the narrative may guide the reader in several directions at once, and the would-be reader of irony must possess sufficient verbal skills to recognize when that is taking place. We encountered this thought before, in Chapter 2, in our discussion of tensive language and in our reading of Philip Wheelwright. We have not space here for further analysis, but it may be helpful if we pause briefly to illustrate.

In the rather ghoulish story of the assassination of the Moabite king Eglon in Judges 3. 15–22, Ehud, the assassin, approaches the king with the words, "I have a message [*dabar*] from God for you" (v. 20). But *dabar* is ambiguous; it may mean "word," "message" or "thing." The story plays upon that ambiguity, the king expecting a spoken message, Ehud intending something more sinister. The reader knows what that is from a narrator's tip-off in v. 16: Ehud had hidden beneath his robes a "two-edged" (literally, "two-mouthed") sword. The king draws close for his "message," the "word" of the Lord draws its swift justice, Ehud disappears, and the action of the story closes on Eglon's utter mortification. The reader is aware of subtleties in language which are easily overlooked: "We watch the scene with full knowledge of what will happen, and we listen to Ehud's cryptic words, double-edged like his sword. The episode is unquestionably gruesome, the irony also gruesome."[9] Similar word- plays may be found in Joseph's interpretation of the dreams of the butler and the baker in his imprisonment in Egypt (Genesis 40; cf. v. 13 with v. 19); in Daniel's judgments over the lecherous elders in the "trial" of Susanna (Susanna 54, cf. v. 55; 58, cf. v. 59); and in Paul's retort to Bar-Jesus ("You 'Son of the Devil!' ") in Acts 13. 6.

Rules of co-reference

As Eco intends it, this concern need not delay us. By "rules of co-reference," he refers to the establishment of lines of relationship between the various parts of the text, the clarification of syntactical relations, and so forth. It may happen in the course of this operation that the reader discovers ambiguities, such as pronouns which could refer to either of two antecedents. Where possible, these must be "disambiguated" (Eco, pp. 18f). Where ambiguities remain, the reader must await further clarifying clues. As we have seen, there are dimensions of irony which are explicitly served by lingering ambiguities. There are moments in which one senses that such ambiguities have been intentionally embedded in the text by the story-teller. When that happens, they may signal that more is going on than meets the eye, and in that way serve as invitations to read more deeply. A classic example is in Shelley's poem "Ozymandias:"

1 I met a traveler from an antique land
2 Who said, "Two cast and trunkless legs of stone
3 Stand in the desert. Near them, on the sand
4 Half sunk a shattered visage lies, whose frown
5 And wrinkled lip, and sneer of cold command
6 Tell that the sculptor well those passions read
7 Which yet survive, stamped on these lifeless things,
8 The hand that mocked them and the heart that fed.
9 And on the pedestal these words appear –
10 "My name is Ozymandias, king of kings:
11 Look on my works, ye Mighty, and despair!"
12 Nothing beside remains. Round the decay
13 Of that colossal wreck, boundless and bare
14 The lone and level sands stretch far away."

Here, the critical ambiguity is in the inscription on the pedestal (lines 10 and 11): "My name is Ozymandias, king of kings: / Look on my works, ye Mighty, and despair!" From Ozymandias' perspective, "the Mighty" have great cause for despair. The leering expression described in lines 2 and 3 suggests a figure of great power, one not easily pleased. The conquering of the Mighty with which lines 10 and 11 resonate seems to be a primary and visceral concern for the bigger-than-life figure − it is for this, and for this only, that he wishes to be remembered. What Ozymandias has built warrants despair because it, too, is "bigger than life." One suspects that he has commissioned a work of such proportions precisely to dwarf those who see it. The size of the sculpture is an indication of Ozymandias' evaluation of his own importance. "Look on my works, ye Mighty, and despair!" is the epitaph of a successful power-monger. From the perspective of the traveler, however, the message on the pedestal suggests failure of colossal proportions. What Ozymandias has wrought has ultimately come to ruin: "Nothing beside remains." The face of the statue lies broken, a "shattered visage" in the desert sands. The message on the pedestal suggests for the reader that the Mighty have reason for despair which is in the end altogether different from that which Ozymandias intended. A look at his "works" makes the bankruptcy of power-mongering instantly evident.

There are examples closer to our own literature. In John 11.50 the high priest Caiaphas utters an unknowing prophecy of the *theological* significance of Jesus' death: "You do not understand that it is expedient for you that one man should die for the people, and that the whole nation should not perish." That Caiaphas is urging a political expediency is clear from the ruminations of the council in v. 48: "If we let him go on thus, every one will believe in him, and the Romans will come and destroy both our holy place and our nation." But there are deeper nuances here, and the evangelist makes certain that they are clear for his reader by adding this interpretative aside in v. 51: "He did not say this of his own accord, but being high priest that year he prophesied that Jesus should die for the nation." What makes the *double entendre* particularly pointed is that Caiaphas prefaces his blind prophecy with these words: "ὑμεῖς οὐκ οἴδατε οὐδέν" − "You guys don't know nothin'!" It is often pointed out that John's entire gospel fairly resounds with this sort of unintended irony.

Contextual and circumstantial selections

By the term "contextual selections," Eco refers to the reader's ability to identify the frames of reference within which the vocabulary of the text makes a specific kind of sense. He describes these as "semiotic systems," and he points out that such systems may shift over time.

An adequate reading of virtually any text must therefore be sensitive to its cultural and intellectual contexts:

> Contextual selections are coded abstract possibilities of meeting a given term in connection with other terms belonging to the same semiotic system (in this case, a given language). Thus, a good encyclopedic representation of "whale" should record at least two contextual selections: in a context dominated by the sememe "ancient," a whale is a fish; in the context dominated by the sememe "modern," a whale is a mammal. (p. 19)

"Circumstantial selections" are somewhat more narrowly conceived. They refer to what Ludwig Wittgenstein described as "language games:"

> Circumstantial selections code the possible co-occurrence of a given term with external circumstances ... Thus "aye" means "I vote yes" in the framework of certain types of formal meetings and "I will obey" in the framework of the navy. (Eco, p. 19)

Clearly a reader's skill in reading could be calibrated against the range and accuracy of possible contextual and circumstantial selections he can readily identify and evaluate. In the study of the gospels there is a correlated concern which has long commanded the attention of the critical historian: here, the material must be related to not *one* context, but *two*. There is the *Sitz-im-Leben Jesu* and the *Sitz-im-Leben der Kirche*. Often the congruence between these two is so close that no distinction need be made. At other times, the movement of external circumstances has introduced significant drift. In the ongoing life of the Church a saying may take on new and more relevant potencies. Occasionally the dialectic between these two *Sitze-im-Leben* is exactly what creates the ironic tensions in the text. One such place is in John's accounting of the cleansing of the temple in Chapter 2. The verses which follow come just after Jesus has made a row in the temple precincts:

[18] The Jews then said,
          "What sign have you to show us
                for doing this?"
[19] Jesus answered them,
          "Destroy this temple,
                and in three days I will raise it up."

Here the saying makes sense only as a prophecy of the crucifixion and resurrection. The evangelist wishes to make certain that the reader understands the irony, so he clarifies with an aside: "He spoke to them of the temple of his body" (v. 21). But this understanding would have been an impenetrable riddle in the *Sitz-im-Leben Jesu*, a riddle the authorities have no way of unraveling. They respond in a way which − for the reader − expresses their failure of vision: "It has taken forty-six years to build this temple, and you will raise it up in three days?" The heavy irony of the scene is made possible by the shifting circumstances, and by the ambiguity in Jesus' expression, "this" temple. If the situation were not so serious, we might consider this a verbal wink at the reader; "rase it and I'll raise it" is a broad joke told at the authorities' expense.

There is another irony here, also made possible by the shift between the *Sitz-im-Leben Jesu* and the *Sitz-im-Leben der Kirche*: in v. 17 the evangelist notes that Jesus' activity in the temple fulfills prophecy: "Zeal for thy house will consume me." In the context of the temple exchange, that prophecy may refer to Jesus' passion for the temple and the sanctity of its precincts. In the context of the Church's later reflection it refers to his death, the result of his passion for the temple: "Zeal for thy house will destroy me!"

Inferences by common frames

By "common frames," Eco is referring to the reader's awareness of what is taken for "common knowledge" in the milieu of the author and his reader. Such matters need not be articulated, since they are assumed by both parties in the textual exchange. There are two sorts: common frames might refer to the reader's knowledge of the practical workings of life, or they might refer to specific cultural knowledge which is assumed and not explained. Homer did not need to explain to his listener the rules of hospitality which were operative in the ancient world; yet everywhere the cogency of his narrative depends upon that knowledge. The parable of the Good Samaritan depends for its potencies upon the reader's prior knowledge that Samaritans are, after all, pariahs in Jewish territory, yet nothing need be said by way of clarification. The omen in Aeschylus' *Oresteia* that "the hare is Troy, destined to fall in the tenth year, just as the hare was to have been delivered in the tenth month" depends for its significance on the information that the gestation period of the hare is hardly ten weeks, let alone ten months. A parallel may be found in Mark's explanation of the cursing of the fig tree in 11.13: "When (Jesus) came to it, he found nothing but leaves, for it was not the season for figs." That explanation depends upon the knowledge that *taqsh* appear on the tree as edible precursors of real figs; if they are missing it means there will be no figs when the time is ripe. There is a certain irony present for Mark's reader in that assumed information, since the fig tree will serve as a type or a symbol of rejected Israel.

Rhetorical and stylistic overcoding

By these, Eco refers to the rules of rhetoric and genre which govern the organization of the contents of the text, and which must therefore govern the reading process as well. Such "overcodes" may involve only the formal characteristics of a work, or they may govern its actual content and verbal structure. Eco's own illustration provides a clear example:

> "Once upon a time" is an overcoded expression establishing (i) that the events take place in an indefinite non-historical epoch, (ii) that the reported events are not "real", (iii) that the speaker wants to tell a fictional story.   (p. 19)

There are several sorts of rhetorical and stylistic overcodes – genre rules, awareness of idiomatic expressions, intuitive awareness of "type-scenes," etc. – but these may be gathered together under the single umbrella term, "convention." Convention is a critical factor in the construction of narrative, since it acts as a kind of verbal shorthand which permits the narrator a certain economy of words. At the same time, convention may signal the reader to expect this or that development in the narrative, and in that way shape his reactions as the story unfolds.

There is a dimension of this problem which has become critical for gospel scholars; we may mention it briefly in passing: we have not yet firmly established what are the parameters of convention within which the gospels function.[10] Yet that there *are* conventions we must not disallow. They are absolutely necessary components of the narrative exchange *as such*.[11] In the latter pages of this chapter we shall try to gain some leverage on this matter of convention from a somewhat more generalized vantage-point.

Inferences by intertextual frames

"No text is read independently of the reader's experience of other texts," Eco tells us (p. 21). And he is right. Intertextual references are potentially present anywhere, and when they are made, they too may govern the reader's perceptions and dispositions. Eco clarifies how that happens by first distinguishing intertextual inferences from inferences drawn from common frames: "Common frames come to the reader from his storage of encyclopedic knowledge and are mainly rules for practical life. Intertextual frames, on the contrary, are already 'literary topoi,' narrative schemes" (p. 21). When Eco defines intertextual frames this way, it is clear that he does not mean necessarily to restrict the term to specific texts: "Intertextual knowledge encompasses all the semiotic systems with which the reader is familiar" (p. 21). This clarification is important. It means that traditional themes and story elements, although they do not derive from specific texts, nevertheless may function as sources of intertextual knowledge. It is also clear that intertextual frames of reference may be more or less precise. A skilled speaker may run the gamut from direct quotation to indirect allusion. What is not so obvious is that indirect allusion may effect reactions in the reader which are less directly conscious, but for that reason more psychologically potent. For the native speaker, allusions in a text may evoke associations which would have been impossible for direct quotation.

This may be even more the case in contexts which preserve traditional literature orally,[12] or which structure the national self-consciousness around national epic literature. Certainly it was so among the Greeks. Here, as elsewhere, the allusions are made, not to this or that particular version of the story, but to the elements they hold in common, which are the common property of the tradition itself. The presence of traditional elements – repeated themes, plots, and characters – throughout the extant Greek literature should itself remind us that such elements were common property. In his introduction to his translation of *Euripides*, Moses Hadas relates the force preserving literary tradition to religion: "... Greek literary art like Greek architecture tended to preserve forms once perfected, and ... the religious origins and associations of tragedy dictates at least formal adherence to traditional usages."[13] There were other factors. Attendance at theater was considered a civic duty; courts were even adjourned and prisons opened during the dramatic festivals so that duty could be discharged. Further, the large size of the chorus would insure that any given audience would have within it a significant number of spectators who had had that experience as training. Thus, in *Agamemnon*, Aeschylus does not need to inform the audience that Agamemnon is to be murdered by Clytaemnestra – the parameters of the tradition have rendered the plot fixed, and the murder inevitable. In *Oedipus the King*, Sophocles does not need to explain to the audience what Oedipus himself did not know – that the man he had killed before the play began was his father, and that the woman he had married was his mother. When the first act opens and the first actor appears on the stage, the spectator knows already how the plot will turn out. With that information in hand, Sophocles has Oedipus utter, at every turn in the play, some deeply ironic comment, all unknowing:

> ... May
> His evil heart beat out its years in sorrow,
> Throughout his life may he breathe the air of death!
> If I give him shelter, knowing
> Who he is, and let him feel the warmth of my fire,
> I live in Laius' palace, my queen was once
> The queen of Laius, and if his line had prospered
> His children would have shared my love.
> But now time has struck his head to earth
> And in revenge I will fight for him as I
> Would fight for my own father. My search will never
> End until I take in chains the murderer
> Of Laius, son of Labdacus.

The point of this brief survey is simply that exactly analogous forces have shaped the intertextual matrix of the gospels as well, and where they are found, they also may evoke ironic reactions on the part of the reader. The linguistic milieu in which the evangelists worked was heavily invested with literary and oral traditions – personal convictions given expression in stories, and national aspirations given voice in apocalyptic visions. It is no accident that the visions and the stories employ the same language, the same characters, the same themes. Nor need the connection between them be strictly literary.

It may be that the vital links between them are made up of oral traditions and now veiled allusions, and if that is so, they may be difficult to trace. Even so, we must remain clear about the potencies allusive language would have had for the evangelists' original readers.

Mark's Jesus claims the title "Son of Man," but Mark does not need to explain because of the lively speculations about such a figure which ran rampant in the ancient Near East. Luke's Jesus, in telling the story of Dives and Lazarus, draws upon and transforms a traditional Egyptian folk-tale which had circulated already for the better part of 3,000 years. John, in his prologue, may play upon the traditional figure of "Lady Wisdom," without whom "was not made anything that was." Matthew, it seems, could hardly resist the tendency to make intertextual allusions explicit; perhaps he does so for apologetic reasons, and perhaps under the influence of Jewish interpretative *middoth*. In either case, however, the very fact that we find such explicit elements in Matthew's redaction of Mark is mute testimony to the potency of Mark's rhetoric. As we shall see, in the gospels – as in Sophocles – the intertextual knowledge assumed by the evangelists may serve the interests of sophisticated and subtle ironic strategies.

One final factor requires attention before we leave this brief discussion of allusions. Often allusions are fragmentary and suggestive, and their elements must be pieced in alongside or on top of linguistic structures which would make good sense without them. The result is that those existing linguistic structures can subtly but quite effectively transform the reader's understanding of the allusions and in that way also the primary sources from which they are drawn. This is no mere accident of association. Instead, it is a fact of language which can be developed and exploited for heuristic purposes. To my mind, that process reaches its acme in the *pesharim* and the interpretative *middoth* of rabbinic Judaism, but as a movement it is already in full flower in the NT literature.[14]

Ideological overcoding

The fact that the story is traditional does not lead necessarily to the conclusion that its elements may not have been appropriated for new and different social circumstances. The language of those new circumstances may be philosophically – and we add, "theologically" – loaded. In another section of his introduction to Euripides, Moses Hadas has already made this clear in a remark, which immediately follows his observation that Euripides' plays regularly criticize the behaviors of their characters in terms of values which are current for the *audience*: "Plays like *Alcestis, Medea, Hippolytus* justify themselves amply as drama; but they acquire a new dimension of meaning if the reader is aware that in each the victim suffers from, and by implication criticizes, disabilities enjoined by current Athenian usages" (pp. ix, x). In this way, Euripides employs the past to gain leverage on the present, but even as he does so, he liberates the present from bondage to values which are no longer current or useful.

We shall see a similar movement afoot in the gospel stories, especially in stories which introduce controversy. In controversy stories, the questions raised often involve challenges against institutions or practices which were crucial in the Church's emerging self-consciousness, and the answers are often couched in terms which would have been theologically loaded for the listener. If in this way, they provide aetiologies for new institutions and practices, those institutions and practices – and the issues surrounding them – in turn form the critical ideological background against which they make a particular kind of sense. It takes no leap of insight to realize that the reader's loyalties may already have been shaped by the position he took in the living controversy in which he found himself: that is, for the evangelists' readers, the controversy stories would have been invested with special potencies.

Gilbert Bilezekian has already shown that those contextual potencies may be deepened by the rhetorical strategies operative within the stories themselves. In some sense, this makes Jesus the supreme ironist:

> By confuting (his opponents), He causes the action to move forward and the tension to increase as the protagonists entrench themselves more firmly in their respective traditions.[15]

Bilezikian's remark makes particularly good sense when we recall that the characters of stories may represent paradigms and anti-paradigms of postures and behaviors considered normative by the group. By sharpening the distinction between Jesus and his antagonists, the narrator can also sharpen the reader's judgments and deepen the intensity of his reactions.

There are, of course, other methods of developing the ideological point of view which is controlling for the narrative as a whole. To my knowledge, the finest discussion of the question broadly taken is Boris Uspensky's brilliant study of point of view in Russian literature, *A Poetics of Composition*.[16] Uspensky points out that the author may speak for himself in the voice of the narrator, or he may assign the actual act of evaluation to this or that character. Often, in Russian literature, the normative point of view of the narrative as a whole is given expression on the lips of some minor character whose presence does not otherwise affect the development of the plot. There are analogies in classical narrative strategy, although these may be somewhat less subtle.[17] Philip Harsh has pointed out that, in Euripides' *Alcestis*, it is the chorus which articulates the author's own point of view (p. 19).[18] As Robert Fowler has suggested in his study *Loaves and Fishes*, the evangelist at times expresses his own ideological point of view on the lips of this or that "reliable" character. The reliability of such characters may be demonstrated by clear narrative strategies, or it may be implied in the consistency between their dialogue and the narration *as such*. With this comment, we have lapsed into the matter of narrative competencies generated by the text, a matter to which we shortly turn.

Before we leave this brief treatment, we ought to pause and reflect on the significance of ideological overcoding for our reconstruction of the social world of the story-teller and his listener. In this question, Eco himself has provided us a measure of guidance:

> Finally, an ideological bias can lead a critical reader to make a given text say more than it apparently says, that is, to find out what in that text is ideologically presupposed, untold. In this movement from the ideological subcodes of the interpreter to the ideological subcodes tentatively attributed to the author ... even the most closed texts are surgically "opened": fiction is transformed into document and the innocence of fancy is translated into the disturbing evidence of a philosophical statement. (p. 22)

Eco's study does not focus specifically on irony, but on the competencies necessary for all reading. We may review those skills briefly by way of summary:

1. The skilled reader must be aware of the various lexical meanings of the words involved.
2. He must be able to recognize ambiguities in those meanings, and where possible, in the light of the context, "disambiguate" them.
3. He must be capable of projecting possible circumstances and contexts in which the expressions make specific sense.
4. He must be able to recognize rhetorically and stylistically informed expressions for what they are, and must be able to recognize their similarities and differences from other

instances of their genre (Eco calls this "rhetorical and stylistic overcoding").

5. He must be able to draw inferences by "common frames" of reference.
6. He must be able to recognize and draw inferences from intertextual frames of reference (Eco calls these "literary topoi," and "narrative themes").
7. And he must be able to recognize and respond appropriately to ideologically loaded expressions.

Even a cursory review of that list suggests that ironic nuances may be constituted in the narrative exchange as such, and that the reader who ignores the historical and cultural milieu in which the narrative originates will be unable to detect them. With this comment we are returned to David Amante's comments about assumed background in his essay, "The Theory of Ironic Speech Acts." Amante goes on:

> The basic structure of all types of irony consists of a set of expectations which are deliberately projected so they later may intentionally be negated ... In addition, the intentions negated, especially if they are complex ones ... need never be stated at any point in the text; such expectation only needs to be assumed to exist by the ironist – many situational or social expectations would fall into this category. What the ironist does expect is that his audience has well-developed sensitivity to and knowledge of language and of social customs of a given country and, sometimes, of a given period. (p. 80)

Herein lies a problem. Perhaps the subtler dissonances in the text have been masked already by the movements of time and culture. Wayne Booth already suggested caution in our evaluation of ironies from a different cultural epoch:

> There is in fact a neat and absolute law here, in a field that I have said presents no absolutes: the more remote a work is from my home province (my century, my country, my family, my profession, my church, my club, my generation) the more mistakes I will make in a given reading period.[19]

To my mind, the matter may be more nuanced than Booth suggests. The rhetorical potencies of hyperbole are always clear to the foreign reader, the subtleties of understatement scarcely ever. (One exception is litotes, a form of understatement which is betrayed by specific grammar, and which may not be unimportant in a narrator's overall rhetorical strategy.) But at bottom, Booth is right. This is a problem which literary criticism shares with biblical studies as a whole. The twentieth-century scholar, working at such a wide cultural and historical distance from the subject of his investigations, runs a somewhat greater risk of reading ironies where there are none, and of violating the text by over-interpretation. But Booth's caution, ironically, cuts both ways. The twentieth-century scholar also runs greater risk of overlooking ironies where they are legitimately to be found, and of violating the text by under-interpretation.

Fortunately, we are not left without guidance. The scholarly enterprise of ferreting out the verbal and conceptual background to our literature has continued unabated since its importance was first fully felt in the nineteenth century. We now have massive tabulations of such parallels, and new developments are being unearthed more rapidly than we can evaluate them. In the texts now available we have a wealth of information which surely represents a significant guide to the traditional conceptual and verbal background of our texts. What remains is for us to ask how the presence of allusions to the traditions would have affected the reading process, and what rhetorical strategies they might have served thereby. Whatever else we may say, the scholar's responsibility to deal with matters of narrative assumptions and rhetorical strategies is an absolute one, however difficult they may be to detect. We must frankly admit that difficulty: reconstructing them is rather like performing an autopsy on a spirit. But in the finely tuned workings of biblical narration, it is often that spirit which gives the text its characteristic vitality and power.

Competencies generated by the text

Much of the material in the following pages has as its theoretical background the discussion of narrative strategies which occupied our attention in Chapter 3. In that discussion I suggested that there are factors inherent in narrativity *as such* which place upon the narrator an absolute requirement: he must guide his reader into and around the world of the story, and in doing so must provide clues by which the reader can penetrate the story's inner significances. Some of those clues he may provide directly, with straightforward authorial comment — what we called "telling" the reader what he needs to know. Other clues he may weave into the fabric of the narrative itself — what we called "showing" the reader. In this section we shall continue to observe that distinction. What is needed here is an exploration of the ways strategies of telling and strategies of showing may be employed in the interest of creating ironic dissonances.

The nearly infinite range of ironic possibilities poses a problem of illustration which is particularly acute in this section. For that reason, and for purposes of economy, we shall draw our illustrations wherever possible from a single richly ironic story: that rather sordid affair between David and Bathsheba which is narrated in 2 Samuel 11. 1–12, 23. Robert Alter once called this story "one of the richest and most intricate examples in the Bible of how ambiguities are set up by what is said and left unsaid in dialogue, of how characters reveal themselves through what they repeat, report, or distort of the speech of others."[20] It is often pointed out that this passage is ironic. Good begins his *Irony in the Old Testament* by discussing it (pp. 35–8). In 1968, Menakhem Perry and Meier Sternberg gave the irony here an extensive treatment in a Hebrew article, "The King Through Ironic Eyes."[21] Alter has discussed them in some detail in his study, *The Art of Biblical Narrative* (pp. 17f, 76). This story is extensive, involving more than half a dozen episodes, each dependent on what precedes for its full plot sensibility. Its details are well known. For that reason, we will not take the space to record them here.

Competencies generated by telling

There is a sense, of course, in which the narrative itself is "told" the reader. Direct address to the audience is an aspect of narration *as such*, and — as we saw in Chapter 3 — is only introduced into drama by the conscious decision of the playwright. There is a kind of irony which is effected by the sustained use of understatement in the narrative itself. A horror story told in clinical and dispassionate language will be experienced as ironic by the listener, if only because the texture of the language is inconsistent with its content. We do not find this form of meiosis in the David and Bathsheba story, but we do find it in Mark, in the matter-of-fact, understated way he reports the macabre events leading up to the execution of John the Baptist (in 6. 14–29). For the most part we must deal with this matter of "telling" in a narrower sense. There is a variety of ways in which a narrator may address his audience – through the title itself; through linking statements, "winks at the audience," and other interpretative asides; and – very frequently in our literature – through the use of a prologue.

Prologues

Prologues are particularly interesting. These are critical in establishing in the reader's consciousness the overarching conceptual frames of reference in which the play or story is to be heard and evaluated. In Greek drama, the prologue may approximate narration, especially when the character who delivers it is protactic, that is, when he delivers his opening monologue and then disappears completely from the remainder of the action. We find this device with special frequency in the plays of Euripides, whose long and complex prologues are necessitated by the freedom he takes with the traditions he is using. Almost always in ancient literature these direct comments to the reader are "reliable"; the information they provide is trustworthy. That fact is not without its rhetorical significances, since it implies a standard or norm against which the developing inconsistencies, hyperboles, and understatements of the text may be calibrated. We may draw an example from the story of David and Bathsheba in 2 Samuel. In chapter 10, the narrator has been describing David's successful military campaign against the Syrians and the Ammonites. In 11.1, he introduces a radical shift of scene, to Jerusalem and David's palace:

> In the spring of the year,
> the time when kings go forth to war
> David sent   Joab,
>   and his servants with him;
>   and all Israel;
> and they ravaged the Ammonites,
> and   besieged Rabbah.
> But David remained in Jerusalem.

In this way, so Alter points out, the narrator "firmly ties the story of David as adulterer and murderer with the large national–historical perspective of the preceding chronicle." It is thus "a brilliant transitional device" (p. 76). It is brilliant, but it is also awkward. The very first line is unnecessary, especially the comment about the "kings going to battle." Why is it here? It is here because it establishes a contrast with the final clause, "David remained in Jerusalem." That final clause is therefore scandalous. It represents in synecdoche all the indulgences which are forbidden or impossible for soldiers in wartime.

I am indebted for this observation to Edwin Good. "It is only a touch," Good tells us. "One might miss it" (p. 35). One might miss it, except that the contrasts between David and Uriah which it foreshadows will deepen in timbre as they resonate through the remainder of the story-line. It is significant and ironic that those contrasts will be enumerated on the lips of Uriah: "The ark and Israel and Judah dwell in booths; and my lord Joab (a subtle touch!) and the servants of my lord are camping in the open field; shall I go to my house, to eat and drink, and to lie with my wife?" (v. 11). With this comment, Uriah will unknowingly refuse on the grounds of its severe impropriety exactly that of which David is already guilty. The developing contrast between the two men is pivotal. The whole episode plays upon it and maximizes it: it is the strength of Uriah's moral character which exposes the failure of David's. It may be worth noting that he will refuse his *own* wife lest his indulgence in what would otherwise be legitimate sexual intercourse reflect betrayal of his comrades-in-arms. It is Uriah, then, who is to be the tragic hero of this tale: in his integrity he behaves as he believes he must, and in doing so sets in motion − at least exacerbates − a series of events which eventually bring disaster down upon his own head. Uriah is the hero, and the prologue establishes David as the villain.

Asides

From time to time in the course of his story, a narrator may pause to address the reader directly. We can usually recognize asides of this sort because they do not move the plot forward. The action of the narrative freezes while the narrator and reader momentarily step aside to confer about this or that critical piece of background information. It may be worth noting that this pause in the action is sometimes important for an ironist's strategy, since it suspends the narrative world, and that suspension creates the impression that the asides contain privileged information. They cannot be heard by the story's characters.

An excellent example is found in the cleansing of the temple in John 2, an irony we have discussed already. In the critical ambiguity about which temple Jesus intends "to raise up in three days," the evangelist pauses to tell the reader that Jesus "spoke to them about

the temple of his body" (v. 21). But this comment the authorities do
not, indeed cannot, overhear.

In our story of David and Bathsheba, there is an irony which
depends upon the knowledge that the note Uriah is carrying to Joab
contains directions for his murder-by-proxy. The contents of the
note are disclosed to the reader, but – as with all asides – hidden
from Uriah: "Set Uriah in the forefront of the hardest fighting, and
then draw back from him, that he may be struck down, and die"
(2 Sam 11.15). Here, the king's treachery depends upon the trust-
worthiness of its victim! The contrast between David and Uriah
deepens. Joab understands only too well, and without delay sees that
Uriah is dispatched.

Alter points out that there is in biblical literature a particularly
subtle narrative strategy related to these asides. In their evaluation
of the actions of the story's characters, the biblical story-tellers sometimes even speak on God's behalf: "It is a dizzying epistemological
trick done with narrative mirrors ... the self-effacing figures who
narrate the biblical tales, by a tacit convention in which no attention
is paid to their limited human status, can adopt the all-knowing,
unfailing perspective of God" (p. 157).

An aside of this sort appears in our story of David and Bathsheba:
"But the thing that David had done displeased the Lord" (2 Sam
11.17). Sometimes God Himself is cast as a character inside the story,
and his comments make him out to be the supreme ironist. We find
in Job 38 this splendid example of irony by sarcasm:

[4] Where were you
    when I laid the foundation of the earth?
    Tell me, if you have understanding.
[5] Or who determined its measurements –
    surely you know!
    Or who stretched the line upon it?
[6] On what were its bases sunk,
    Or who laid its cornerstone,
[7] When the morning stars sang together,
    And all the sons of God shouted for joy?

Winks at the reader
I am not certain where the expression "winks" entered the scholarly
vocabulary. Robert Fowler uses the term in *Loaves and Fishes* (pp.
161f). Max Eastman used it to describe an element of tragic irony

in his 1936 study, *The Enjoyment of Laughter*: sometimes the playwrights "exchange with the audience a gruesome wink at the expense of their doomed hero."[22] In *Oedipus the King*, Sophocles has a messenger arrive with a message for Oedipus. The response of the chorus is an ironic wink at the reader:

στέγαι μὲν αἵδε, καὐτὸς ἔνδον, ὦ ξένε,
γύνη δὲ μήτηρ ἥδε τῶν κείνου τέκτων

Here is the palace and he bides within, O stranger,
But here is his wife and (the) mother ...

The subtleties of the remark are difficult to translate, since English requires a definite article before the word "mother." In Greek, however, the definite article is lacking. Μήτηρ stands in apposition to γύνη, and introduces an ambiguity: "Here is his wife and mother ..." In actual delivery, the qualification − "of his children" − could be separated by a momentary pause, and in that way the audience tipped off to the *double entendre*.

There is a particularly subtle wink in the story of David and Bathsheba in v. 4:

[4] So David ... took her;
     and she came to him,
     and he lay with her.
     (Now she was purifying herself)
     from her uncleanness).

Clearly, the "uncleanness" is a reference to her menstrual cycle. As a narrative element, it is puzzling. It does not move the plot forward, and what it tells us about Bathsheba is purely coincidental to the development of her character. Why then is it here? First, it positively establishes paternity.[23] Second, and more subtly, it deepens David's culpability by showing him not only morally, but also ritually defiled. David makes himself ritually unclean by defiling Bathsheba at the moment of her purification. This, too, is not much. It could be easily overlooked, especially since the urgencies of the narrative move on to the murder of Uriah which follows. I have not said it is central. It is only a wink, after all, only to be seen by the reader who has his eyes fully open to it.

At other points, the winks are not so subtle, but they may depend for their potencies on the reader's background and verbal skill. In v. 12, David says to Uriah, "Remain here today also, and tomorrow

I will 'let you depart.' " But the translation "let you depart" masks
the potency of the *pi'el* form of the verb. We can gain some sense
of its secondary significance by adopting an English idiom for our
translation: "Remain here today also, and tomorrow I will do away
with you!" Perhaps the *double entendre* can be preserved this way:
"Remain here, and tomorrow I will dispatch you." But this is
ominous, the more so since it comes hard on the heels of Uriah's
refusal to have relations with his wife. "The armies are in the field,
shall I be sleeping with my wife?" he asks David. And then he
answers his own rhetorical question: "Not on your life!" (v. 11).
The threat in David's remark is barely hidden below the surface of
his sentence. It is masked from Uriah by its ambiguity, and by the
soldier's unhesitating trust of his superior.

Foretelling
Sometimes the winks become broader, and turn into full-scale
disclosures. When that happens on the lips of one of the story's
characters, the reader is oriented by "showing." Sometimes, however, they are embedded in the framework of the narrative, and in
those cases we have foretelling by "telling." The line between these
two is necessarily very thin, especially when the character who fore-
tells the fate of the protagonist is protatic, and stands outside the
structures of the plot. Because of this close relationship, we may
mention foreshadowing here, and reserve fuller treatment for the
discussion which follows in the next section.

Competencies generated by showing

As we noted in Chapter 3, essential information about character
development or changes in time or place may be picked up by the
reader indirectly, from clues which are sometimes only incidental
to the plot itself. Often those clues are found on the lips of the
characters, and are included expressly so they can be overheard by
the listener or reader.

Foretelling. Foreshadowing. Flashback
What we heard from the lips of David – "Tomorrow I will dispatch
you!" – is an example of foretelling. Foretelling may be found on
the lips of virtually anyone in the story – the speaker in the play's
protasis, the chorus, a prophet or prophetess, a divine figure. In
Euripides' plays, the prologues are often spoken by deities, who

address the spectator directly. In the prologue to his *Hecuba*, the prologue comes – aptly – on the lips of the ghost of Polydorus. Sometimes – as in *Oedipus the King* – the protagonist unknowingly announces his own catastrophe. Here, the irony lies in a dramatic reversal:

> If I can drive out this corruption and make the city
> Whole, I shall do more than save my people,
> Who are my friends, but still my subjects –
> I shall save myself.

Sometimes the foretelling may contain only partial or contingent information. In the prologue of Euripides' *Bacchae*, Dionysus ends his speech with the threat that, if Pentheus leads the armies of Thebes against his devotees the Maenads, he will himself personally lead the Maenads into battle:

> He thrusts me away from his offerings, and in his prayers nowhere makes mention of me. Therefore I mean to reveal myself to him and to all Thebans as a god indeed. When I have settled things here to my satisfaction I shall direct my steps to another land and manifest myself. If the city of the Thebans becomes enraged and tries to drive the bacchants from the mountain by force of arms, I shall lead my Maenads into battle against them. That is why I have assumed this mortal form, changing myself to look like a man.

As Harsh has said of this passage, "there is no omniscience here. Pentheus' decision is left entirely to Pentheus" (p. 30). Yet the contingent possibility of disaster lingers on in the spectator's mind. He does not know what Pentheus will do, but he does know that, should Pentheus choose this course, it will spell catastrophe. Apparently Euripides is quite fond of exercising the poet's control over the deities. In these plays, often only the playwright is omniscient. In *Ion*, he even has Hermes close his opening monologue with the note that he is going to slip away and watch the action from a neighboring grove of trees, "to learn what will be done." The fact that Euripides' audiences permitted such a thing is implicit evidence that, at least in their theater, they remained sanguine about their deities!

Foreshadowing is more subtle than foretelling, since it depends upon the reader's skill in establishing relationships and anticipations which the text does not make entirely explicit. There are a number of techniques for foreshadowing, and some of them are quite subtle.

They may depend upon the power of innuendo and ambiguity. We have seen already in the story of David and Bathsheba that the opening verse foreshadows the judgment the narrative will later place upon David. In the *Iliad* the death of Hector is repeatedly foreshadowed by this or that double-edged narrative comment.

Flashback is much like foreshadowing and foretelling, except that it may provide insights *after* the events they interpret. In his comparison of Homeric and biblical narrative techniques, Erich Auerbach has called attention to an extensive flashback in Homer's *Odyssey* (Book XIX).[24] In this aside, the story-teller explains the presence of the scar by which Odysseus' old nursemaid Eurykleia recognizes him after his arrival home. Penelope has instructed Eurykleia to wash the feet of this erstwhile stranger – in fact her long-awaited husband – who has lately won her admiration. Eurykleia complies, and takes Odysseus' feet in her hands. That action exposes Odysseus' scar, and in that way his identity. But the scar is a new element in the narrative, and its origin must be accounted for. There is therefore a long, involved accounting of how Odysseus had been gored by a boar in his childhood. The flashback, which lasts for better than seventy-five lines, occurs in its entirety before the recognition fully dawns on her. When she picks up his identity, she drops his foot. There is an urgent and whispered exchange, and a pact is established between Odysseus and the maid: she is not to disclose who he is. In the meanwhile, Odysseus has been carrying on a long and endearing conversation with Penelope, who, unaware that it is her husband who sits beside her, utters simple and eloquent ironies, all unknowing:

> If only this word, stranger and guest,
> were brought to fulfillment,
> soon you would be aware of my love and many gifts given
> by me, so any man who met you would call you blessed.

Before we leave this section, we may pause for a moment and ask after the rhetorical potencies of such devices. On one level, the foretelling may create or sustain the reader's sense that the catastrophe is inevitable, and in that way deepen his sympathies for the tragic hero. On another level, they may drain the catastrophe of its "purely theatrical thrill," and in that way distance the reader enough so that he can recognize and deal with the intellectual and moral dilemmas resident there. The intellectual distance involves a subtle narrative trick: the fact that the characters are fulfilling prophecy represents a blind spot in their perceptions, and therefore exactly that hinge-pin upon which the ironies may turn. These are subtle and confusing movements, and the interaction between them is an acknowledged part of the ironic experience. In this way, the ironic crisis on the stage is mirrored by a corresponding dissonance within the spectator's own consciousness. As the plot resolves its complications, the spectator experiences relief and a personal catharsis. As he identifies with the protagonist, as he faces parallel circumstances in his own experience, the observer may be lead to some small resolution of the catastrophes which inevitably attend his own life.

Verbal ironies

Along the way we have encountered a number of elements which involve ironies of expression, ambiguities uttered unknowingly by this or that character. Not all ironies of expression are uttered unknowingly. There are four forms of verbal irony which may be uttered with the speaker's full consciousness: deliberate ambiguity, sarcasm, hyperbole, and meiosis. The possibility of deliberately ironic speech calls for a special word of clarification: in such instances, the irony which is spoken is not ironic *for the speaker*, although its secondary nuances may be hidden from the other characters and disclosed to the reader. When David tells Uriah, "Stay the night, tomorrow you will be dispatched," Uriah has no inkling of the sinister overtones in the saying. But David does. When Ehud says to Eglon, "I have a word from God for you," Eglon does not hear the secondary nuances which lie closer to Ehud's intent.

Secondary nuances may be hidden from the other characters, but that is not always the case. In sarcasm, the speaker *intends* that the others hear as his meaning the opposite of what he says. When the soldiers in the gospels humiliate Jesus before they string him up to die, there can be no question about what they intend. There is no confusion about the crown of thorns, the spitting, the purple robe, the placard which declares him "King of the Jews." This is sarcasm cultivated to the point of savagery: it is barbaric and brutal. As verbal *sarcasm*, it is not dramatic irony. But there is a level of irony here which turns the sarcasm back upon itself, a double significance of which the soldiers are completely unaware. They have no way of knowing that this is, in fact, the "King of the Jews," and that this can be his only appropriate coronation. When the scribes in their sarcasm deride him on his cross − "Let the Christ, the King of Israel, come down from the cross, that we may see and believe" − they utter exactly that declaration which seals their own damnation.

Exclusionary strategies

Very much of the irony we have been discussing is effected through sophisticated narrative tricks, ambiguities and winks at the reader, subtle but potent allusions, and the dropping of orienting information on the lips of this or that unsuspecting character. In point of fact, however, irony is most often brought about by the simple expedient of excluding the victim of the irony from some part of the story and placing the critical information on the lips of another character. Uriah does not know the content of David's letter to Joab (2 Sam. 11.14f), but the reader does. There are several techniques for effecting irony in this way; I call them "exclusionary strategies."

The simplest exclusionary strategy is simply to have the person exit the stage momentarily while the critical orienting information is disclosed. Something similar is easily done in narrative; one simply notes that the victim is not present, or describes the victim as being elsewhere. A classic example is a rather poignant irony in the apocryphal story of Tobit. In this story, Tobit has suffered a series of reversals, in his misfortune he has been blinded, and he expects the end very soon. Before he dies, however, he utters a prayer for help (3.1–6), and then prepares to set his affairs in order. Those preparations require that he send his son, Tobias, to collect money he had invested in Rages (4.20f), a journey of some distance. Meanwhile, as the narrative tells us, God has sent the angel Raphael, disguised as the stranger Azarias, to answer Tobit's prayer. Raphael agrees to accompany Tobias on his journey. Tobit's sister Anna weeps at their departure, but Tobit reassures her with this promise, made ironic by Raphael's disguise:

> Take no care, my sister; he shall return in safety, and thine
> eyes shall see him. For a good angel will keep him company,
> and his journey shall be prosperous, and he shall return
> safe.   (5.21)

In our story of David and Bathsheba, the use of an exclusionary strategy has been reversed to form an ironic trap in which David can be impaled. We have noticed that part of the reciprocating dynamic between David and Uriah is the treacherous shrewdness of the king, contrasted with the trusting innocence of his subject. But there is an intermediate irony here, one to which the king is entirely blinded. That irony is clarified and carried forward in the report of David's encounter with Nathan the prophet. When Nathan tells David the famous parable of the ewe lamb (2 Sam. 12.1–6) the surface details of the story disguise from David the deep allusions and parallels which the attentive listener to the story can scarcely avoid. In his ignorance, David passes a deeply ironic judgment on the villain of the parable: "As the Lord lives, the man who has done this thing deserves to die" (v. 5). David is unaware of the irony until it is too late, until Nathan's accusation "You are the man!" indicates that he has been tricked into self-imprecation. The exclusionary trick lies in Nathan's subtlety, in his intentional use of nuanced language to cloak the allusions in the story under the guise of another, shallower, significance. In this way, the parable points up a deeper contrast between David and Uriah, a contrast which devalues David's shrewdness and makes him out to be the undiscerning one in the story: that is, the fact that David was deaf to the synonomy between Nathan's story and his own is itself an ironic reminder of the moral obtuseness with which he has committed this act of violence against Uriah.

We are told only in the briefest form what was David's reaction to the prophet's judgment; the deeper significances of his repentance the narrator has left unsaid. Instead he describes the king's grief over the illness of the child born to him by Bathsheba:

[16] Then David besought the Lord for the child;
and David fasted,
and   went in
and   lay all night upon the ground.
[17] And the elders of his house stood beside him,
to raise him from the ground;
but   he would not,
nor   would he eat food with them.
[18] On the seventh day the child died.

We should note about this description that it retains a rather delicate air about it. It does not intrude upon David's inconsolable silence, it simply describes it, from the outside, as it were. This, too, is exclusionary. But it is not irony. It is a way of asking the reader to discover within himself the sympathies which will permit him to penetrate the inner recesses of David's grief.

We must begin our summary by recalling the point with which this chapter began: while the relationship between the competencies assumed by the text and those generated by the text may be thought of as sequential, that model may not be as integrative as the workings of actual reading require. Perhaps the movement from one kind of competency to the other is better thought of as an oscillating movement, in which the two interact with each other dialectically. We have discussed in some detail the points upon which that dialectic turns, and it remains for us here to ask what they mean for the reading process.

It is now possible to clarify how it is that these two sorts of reading skill can be so closely integrated. On the one hand, assumed competencies are never virtual until they are summoned to the reader's consciousness by elements which are actually articulated in the text. On the other, generated competencies require a specific kind of background and verbal skill in order to be decoded properly. At the same time, the linear quality of language suggests that the competencies *generated* by the text are continually slipping over to become the assumed competencies of the episodes which follow. The oscillating relationship between these two sources of information is therefore critical, not only for scholarly reading, but also for "reading naturally." By playing upon that oscillation, an author can deepen their resonances, and in that way clarify for his reader what he takes to be the underlying ironic significances of his story-line.

All of this has implications, of course, for our reading of Mark. If he has appropriated the Jesus traditions in the service of his own community, they must also be read in the light of the circumstances in which the community found itself. Information of that sort – e.g. knowledge of the historical events between the closing of the narrative and the moment of its reading, information about the cultural or linguistic nuances which inform the narrator's presentation – will have been available to the reader from sources which lie outside the narrative, from the language-world of the community in which the story was given expression. Unlike that disclosed by the narrative itself, information about external circumstances will inform the reader's perceptions from the very beginning of the reading. The interaction between these two sorts of context – internal/literary and external/sociological – creates the functional matrix in which each element of the narrative can be said to make a specific kind of sense. We must therefore at each turn of the narrative ask certain leading questions: what information from outside the narrative would have shaped the reader's perceptions of the significance of what is inside it? What has been disclosed thus far to the reader, and what to the characters? Are there signals here that more is going on than meets the characters' eyes – ambiguities, intertextual allusions, exclusionary strategies at work, issues which would have had special potency for the reader? How do the differences in point of view influence the reader's perceptions of this particular pericope? This or that character? This or that event or behavior or character trait? Finally, what about this pericope prepares the reader for the developments which will appear later in the narrative?

In this chapter we have discovered an answer to a challenge which has frequently been brought against our discipline: how can we expect to draw legitimate conclusions about the text when our tools and techniques of study are so different from the free-floating habits of reading naturally? What we have seen is that "reading naturally" is an extraordinarily complex affair. It involves skills, habits of mind, and background competencies that are sometimes so subtle that their operation escapes the reader's conscious notice. The task of the scholarly interpreter requires that he make those operations explicit so he can – at least theoretically – reproduce their configurations and interpret their significances for readers who are distanced from the narrative by the movements of time and culture.

In much of his myopic scrutiny the scholar is painstakingly retracing steps which in point of fact inform the native reader's easy sweep through the text. That is to say, scholarly reading is very much like natural reading, slowed to a snail's pace. When the scholar "explains" the text, he sometimes points out levels of significance which would not have appeared obvious to the native reader, but that in itself is no criticism. The native reader would have picked them up intuitively, without being fully conscious of the reactions they evoke in him. Natural reading is much like scholarly reading, accelerated to a gallop. It has its own validity, of course. It does not require the scholar's validation. Done well, it is a thing of beauty, a complement to the artistry of the author and his text. But it is a thing of beauty only if it is done well. It is here that the scholar's myopic exegesis can be finally validated: in the training of his mind and his reader's eye he may gain some small measure of the agilities and precisions which naturally grace the skilled native reader's art.

5

THE EVIDENCE OF IRONY IN THE GOSPEL OF MARK

To you has been given the secret – the *mystery* – of the Kingdom of God, but to those outside everything is in riddles; so that they may indeed see but not perceive, and may indeed hear but not understand; lest they should turn again and be forgiven.   Mark 4.11–12

In more than one sense the project in which we are engaged meets its most critical challenges in this chapter. Here we shall present a thoroughgoing reading of Mark's Gospel, pointing out and elaborating the ironies which appear along the way. But Mark is massive, and any interpreter who attempts to explore its details or its strategies of composition exhaustively is bound to suffer the fate of Sisyphus. One can live out one's days on an inexhaustible mountain of tedium. At the same time we shall want to engage in dialogue with those scholars whose views in one way or another impinge upon that reading, and to answer in our discussion the challenges they may raise. If the Gospel of Mark is massive, the literature which treats it is more so. The scholarship on Mark is enormous.[1] It is enormous, but it is not monolithic, and one can take little comfort in the fact that it is riddled with cracks and fissures. Would Sisyphus have welcomed an end to his tedium if it came at the bottom of an avalanche?

The sheer volume of material requires that we take steps to keep our focus narrow. Thus we are faced from the beginning with a problem of selectivity and organization, of treating the relevant material with economy and order.[2] At the same time we must continually balance what we make of the parts against what we know of the whole. In the interests of balance we shall treat the material – block by block – in the order in which Mark presents it. The reasons for this procedure are rooted in the nature of narrative itself. The narrative text unfolds word by word, sentence by sentence. The activity of reading requires that the reader construe the narrative world – its plots and sub-plots, its characters and its settings – as parts of a whole, yet it is a whole which is peculiar in that its parts appear in a linear fashion, one after the other. As the narrative unfolds before him, the reader must constantly anticipate undisclosed possibilities, and then correct his anticipations against each disclosure. Even though the meaning of the narrative may only become entirely clear in its *telos*, it is in the unfolding encounter with the parts that the reader's perceptions are informed and his reactions shaped.[3] And that is the stuff of irony. At its root, the ironies of the text are created in the narrative exchange itself, one element following another.

A primary issue for organization, then, is this: how is the text itself organized? Where do the blocks of material begin and end? A study of Mark's use of transitional elements – temporal and chronological transition, summary, ballast line, and *inclusio* – yields somewhere in the neighborhood of 105 pericopae in Mark, many of them heavily laden with irony, many others less so. Some are directly ironical, while others prepare the reader for later ironies by generating competencies which will form the background of the narrative material which follows. We cannot treat the whole of Mark in equal depth, and will reserve detailed comments for those pericopae in which the ironies are pronounced or extraordinarily complex.

The 105 individual pericopae break down into perhaps a dozen major blocks of material. There are two ways in which these larger blocks are critical to our study of Markan irony. In the first place, they disclose important information about Jesus' identity, and they do so selectively, in a specific sequence. With reference to the narrative itself the reader will at any point know only what he has been told *thus far*. Secondly, these blocks are the result of editing, and they may therefore represent the deliberate appropriation of traditional material for new and different circumstances. Paul Achtemeier has expressed with special clarity what scholarly study has long assumed to be an operative principle of exegesis: the context in which a story is found may be a critical indicator of what the author/redactor takes to be its essential significance:

> By juxtaposing traditions to one another [Mark] was able to allow them to interpret each other in such a way that further comment was unnecessary, or so at least he seems to have thought ... Much of what Mark wanted to say, he said by means of the way he ordered the traditions at his disposal.[4]

This assumption is critical, not only for scholarly reading, but also for "reading naturally." By drawing various elements into close proximity to one another, an author can deepen their resonances, and in that way clarify for his reader what he takes to be their overarching significances.

The prologue Mark 1.1–15

We may begin, as would Mark's reader, with an encounter with the superscription and prologue. Thus far the scholarly discussion has largely dwelt on matters related to the prologue's details, and the question of how far it extends. Our concern is with the literary question of the role these verses play in the overarching narrative. If indeed they are a true prologue, rather than merely a device for beginning the narrative, we should expect that they will prepare the reader in significant ways for what follows. And that is precisely what they do. Here, in barely a dozen sweeping verses, the greater movements of the later action are already anticipated. What we must notice is that those movements are different for the reader from what they are for the story's characters, and that that difference is critical to their ironic significances. We may begin with the superscription.

Mark 1.1 – The superscription

[1]   The beginning of the Gospel of Jesus
                                                Christ
                                                Son of God.

Scholars are agreed that it is significant that Mark begins with a superscription, but what that significance may be has been a matter of debate. Thus far the discussion has focused on this or that detail of its text or vocabulary – the meaning of ἀρχή, the historical or cultural antecedents of εὐαγγέλιου,[5] the omission of υἱοῦ θεοῦ from certain of the earliest manuscripts and Fathers,[6] or, more broadly, on the relationship of the superscription to what follows.[7]

For our purposes, however, all that is somewhat beside the point. Our concern is with the verse's literary function: at the very beginning of the narrative it discloses to the reader the critical information that Jesus – the protagonist of the story which follows – is both

"Christ"/"Messiah" and "Son of God." We shall discover reiterations of both of these titles at crucial turnings in the narrative, and by introducing Jesus in this way, Mark makes certain that the messianic reverberations which appear later will be heard for what they are. William Lane anticipates this observation on the inverse: "... Mark's superscription affords an indication of the general plan of his work: Peter's acknowledgment of the messiahship of Jesus in 8:29 has its Gentile counterpart in ch. 15:39, where the centurion confesses that Jesus is the Son of God" (p. 41, n7). What he has failed to note, and what is critical to an appreciation of Mark's ironies, is that the superscription from the very beginning places in the reader's hands interpretive keys which are denied the story's characters until very much later in the narrative.

This point is crucial for whatever we finally make of the significance of the Messianic Secret. Robert Fowler has already pointed this out: "Inasmuch as the reader knows from the very beginning that Jesus is the Christ, the Son of God, there is never any question of a Messianic Secret *for the reader of the gospel.*"[8] Fowler goes on: "... Mark 1:1–3 is the cornerstone of the irony in Mark" (p. 159).

The rhetorical implications for an ironic reading of Mark's Gospel Fowler leaves unexplored. We may elaborate them here briefly. In the first place, the insight the reader enjoys will naturally place him at an advantage over the characters of the story, and at virtually every point he will be called upon to pass judgment on them for their blindness or obtuseness. Secondly, as the reader passes judgment on the characters in the story, he does so in a manner which is consistent with the story-teller's point of view. He is convinced, it seems, by narrative factors of which he may be only dimly aware. But there is a certain subtle irony in all this: the reader, too, may have begun with inadequate or inappropriate expectations. As he reads, if he does so with any level of skill or sympathy, he may discover that his own points of view have been blind or obtuse, that the narrative is in its own way passing judgment on its readers. How that happens will become clearer as we proceed.

Mark 1.2–11 – John the Baptist/Baptism of Jesus

This opening material is extremely important in Mark's narrative strategy, since it establishes at the outset both the prophetic context and the eschatological orientation of everything that follows. The opening of the second half of the book (esp. the story of the trans-figuration in 9.2–13) will have a similar tenor. We should not be surprised that these verses are particularly heavy with allusive language, or that they foreshadow much of what follows later in the narrative. Mark is setting the scene of this story, and while the action begins immediately – and on a sparsely furnished stage – the entire rest of the narrative will depend for its direction of movement on the character of its beginning.

The evidence for this observation is not difficult to find. The deeply seated enthusiasm of the crowds for John's message antici-pates the enthusiasm they will later show for Jesus, during his early ministry, certainly,[9] and during the triumphal entry (11.1–10). It is important that "all the country of Judea and the people of Jerusalem" come out to see John, just as later there will come to Jesus people from "Judea and Jerusalem, and from Idumean, and from the trans-Jordan, and from about Tyre and Sidon" (3.7f). It is also important that John preaches a baptism of repentance (1.4), for that demand will form a critical factor in Jesus' own preaching (note: the summary in 1.15: "Repent! And believe the good news!"), as well as in the preaching of the twelve in 6.12: "They went out and preached that men should repent." It is no accident that word of this preaching will reach Herod, and that it will prompt confusion between Jesus and the Baptist (6.14–16; cf. 8.28). This is an ominous association, and the execution of John which is narrated in 6.14–29 will anticipate the passion of Jesus, who follows in John's footsteps.

But perhaps there are reverberations of this catastrophe already in the prologue. Jesus is described as one who comes "after" – ὀπίσω μου – the Baptist, and at the moment Peter declares him "Messiah," Mark's Jesus will describe discipleship as willingness to follow one's master into martyrdom: "If any man would come 'after' me – ὀπίσω μου – let him deny himself and take up his cross and follow me" (8.34). It is significant in this regard that Jesus only begins his preaching ministry after the Baptist has been "handed over" (1.14a). There is debate about the meaning of the unqualified παραδίδωμι here, and it is sometimes suggested that the reference is to John's execution. Willi Marxsen has argued on this ground that Mark is deliberately creating the impression of successiveness here (and in 6.14 and 8.28).[10] It appears to me that the narrator has in-stead indicated that Jesus' ministry cannot properly have begun until John's was completed, and in that way has created an *association* between Jesus and John. But even if in 1.14 he refers only to John's

arrest,[11] it would be catastrophic, and would in its own way anticipate the arrest of Jesus,[12] and thus ultimately the arrest of all who
would follow Jesus (see 13.9–13).

The reader, we must suppose, knows nothing of the elaborate
foreshadowings here. What he has instead is a rich lode of eschatological and messianic allusions embedded in the descriptive language
of the narrative: in John's heraldry (in vv.7f), in the associations
evoked by John's appearance and behavior (in v.6), in the opening
reference to the prophet Isaiah, and in the conflate quote which
follows it (in vv.2f). It is significant that we do not actually begin
the narrative proper until the appearance of the Baptist in verse 4.
Verses 2 and 3 are part of the interpretative framework around the
story, and they make explicit for the reader an aspect of the Baptist's
identity which the characters in the story must infer for themselves
from other factors: John is indeed the messenger who prepares the
way of the Lord. His appearance fulfills OT prophecy, and that fact
stands him – and Jesus as well! – squarely within the prophetic
tradition.[13]

That John is a type of Elijah will later be made explicit for the
narrative's characters (9.13), but that typological reference is implicit
here already in a way which is readily apparent to any reader who
can recognize the linguistic allusions in verse 6. Here is an example
of what we called "intertextual competence" in Chapter 4. John is
described in terms which recall Elijah exactly. It is no accident that
the language of verse 6 parallels so closely the descriptions of Elijah
in 2 Kings 1.8.[14] The narrator might have used synonyms, or might
have presented the details of his description in some other order.
This is not customary language for Mark.[15] If the allusion to the
LXX here is intentional, it can only mean that the identification of
the Baptist with Elijah had been explored already in the tradition,
and that fact lends its support to the possibility that Mark would
have expected that the allusion would have been clear for his reader.

The impression that John stands within the prophetic tradition
is even more broadly developed, however. The reference to his mantle
of camel's hair (1.6) recalls the association of the garments of hair
with which the lying prophets disguise themselves in Zechariah 13.4
(LXX), and the narrative itself recalls the Martyrdom of Isaiah, in
which Isaiah withdraws from Jerusalem as an act of symbolic judgment, settling in the wilderness, on a mountain (2.8), clothing himself with garments of hair (v.9) and eating wild herbs (v.11). John,
too, has appeared "in the wilderness," for Jerusalem, the symbolic

center toward which the plot moves, will ultimately prove to be exactly that place which rejects the eschatological figure who is the subject of John's heraldry.

On the surface of it, there has thus far been no sign of Jesus. But that is not exactly so. The very fact that John is not the Messiah but only his harbinger has implied Jesus' presence already. Is Jesus not anticipated by the heraldry itself, by the identification of the Coming One as one "mightier" than John (v. 7a), as one whose sandals John is not worthy to untie? Is he not anticipated by John's promise – or threat – that when he comes he will immerse the crowds in the Holy Spirit (v. 8)? Is he not, after all, the "Lord" whose way John has come to prepare (v. 3)? Were this a drama, we might say that Jesus is an actor standing in the wings, patiently awaiting his cue. But standing there, a silent figure, his shadow looms already across the stage. The implied presence of the Messiah is critical. Everything that has appeared thus far has pointed to it. The reader expects a messianic figure of gigantic proportions, what Thomas Howard has called "a towering and furious figure who will not be managed." [16]

It is only a shadow, to be sure, but that looming shadow, and the Baptist's self-effacement, such critical factors in vv. 8f, set up the reader and the story's characters for a terrific disappointment. We are hardly prepared for the understated way Jesus finally makes his appearance in verse 9: he simply appears, without fanfare, like everybody else who has come to be baptized by John in the Jordan. The verbal similarities with verse 5 have often been noted. We may diagram them briefly:

[5] And there went out to him
        and all the people of Jerusalem;
    and they were baptized
        by him
        in the river Jordan,
      confessing their sins.

[9] In those days Jesus came
        from Nazareth of Galilee
    and he was baptized
        by John
        in the   Jordan.

Lane observes these parallels correctly, but the inferences he draws from them seem to me entirely misguided:

> By this correspondence and contrast Mark suggests that all
> those from Judea and Jerusalem who came to John prove
> to be yet rebellious and insensitive to the purpose of God.
> Contrary to expectation, only the one from Galilee proves
> to be the unique Son who genuinely responds to the prophetic
> call in the wilderness. In doing so he identified himself with
> a rebellious generation in need of redemption.   (p. 55)

The point here is much simpler: Jesus appears incognito. No one
inside the story has any reason to suspect that this particular figure
is any different from the others. To be sure, the verbal parallels
between verses 5 and 9 are inexact. In particular, the final clause of
verse 5 – the confession of sins – has not been carried forward to
verse 9. But that information is part of the interpretative framework
of the story. The *crowds* have no way of guessing Jesus' motivation
for baptism. On the surface of it, Jesus is so unlike John's "Coming
One" that he is able to conceal his identity from the crowds entirely,
and it remains hidden from the disciples until well into the narrative.

It is the same with the voice from heaven. Mark has been very
careful to show that the voice in verse 11 has been concealed from
the story's characters. The verbs here are all singular, and the voice
addresses Jesus directly. Everything about the baptism which might
represent a clue about Jesus' messianic identity has been systematically
shielded from the story's characters. Walter Bundy already pointed
this out in 1942:

> The Jordan vision is also dramatic in its technique. Into the
> prosaic scene depicted in verse 9 it introduces, with startling
> suddenness, the unseen forces actually operative in the
> destinies of the actors on the stage of history. It gives the
> reader a glimpse behind the scenes. He is allowed to see what
> the action itself does not disclose until later. It is a sort of
> dramatic aside which, at the very beginning, lets the reader
> in on the secret of the hero's true nature and identity.[17]

So although this is a private experience, something heard only by
Jesus, it is overheard by the reader, and is carefully shielded from
the crowds. This is an example of a rhetorial technique we designated
"exclusionary strategy" in Chapter 4. It will appear surprising and
puzzling to the story's characters when Jesus returns shortly after
John's arrest, preaching, calling disciples and performing miracles.
Speculations will abound about who he might be, but it is important

that no one guesses that he is the "beloved Son of God" in whom God is "well pleased." At best he is the Baptist *redivivus*, or Elijah, or another of the prophets (6.14; 8.28).

There is one other point which requires comment before we leave this section: Mark's language in the baptism account continues the messianic and eschatological imagery introduced in his description of the Baptist in vv. 2–8.[18] We have seen already that allusive language forms a particularly potent narrative strategy. It evokes in the reader certain kinds of subliminal reactions by drawing up alongside the primary frame of reference secondary and tertiary frames, frames which shape the reader's reactions and in that way aid him in discovering the story's deeper resonances. All of this, too, is hidden from the story's characters. The reader has the advantage in precisely this: he has the story itself. Whatever else we read in Mark, we must bear this constantly in mind. The reader and Jesus have been told something which is carefully shielded from the story's characters. The ironic tensions in the points of view which are later all developed in one way or another play off this central distinction. The reader and Jesus know that he is "Son of God" and "Messiah;" the other characters do not.

Mark 1.12–13 – The temptation

That that information is disturbing to Jesus is clear from the force of Mark's language in verse 12: "The Spirit immediately drove him out into the wilderness." It is common to see in this brief story complex allegorical or typological allusions to the First Adam.[19] The beasts are diminutive beasts, and therefore hardly antagonistic. The ministry of angels in verse 13 recalls the *Life of Adam and Eve* (4.2, and 2 *Enoch* 22.6), in which Adam is said to have eaten "angel food." The eschatological implications are clear: Jesus, like Adam, does battle with Satan, only – unlike Adam – he does so successfully. The eschatological overtones of this event are perhaps clearest when we recall Frederick Borsch's discussion of the imagery of the Son of Man as a *primal* figure in the ancient Near Eastern literary traditions.[20] This insight can hardly have been available to the story's characters. It is, however, mediated to the reader through the use of carefully nuanced and allusive language. At the same time, the double significance here is not quite clear enough for the temptation to be classed as ironic. Probably it is safest to see it in the service of other ironies in Mark, ironies which depend upon the knowledge that Jesus indeed functions as the Son of Man.

Mark 1.14–15 – The ministry in Galilee

There are times when Mark's transitions are so smooth that they create difficulties for interpreters who require that their outlines be tidy. Perhaps nowhere is that fact so clearly in evidence as here. On the one hand, the break at v. 14 appears radical. Certain of the reiterated elements are dropped – the desert, the heraldry, the crowds, the Spirit. The Baptist disappears altogether, and the scene shifts to Galilee. Verses 14 and 15 mark out important differences between the preaching of Jesus and the preaching of his harbinger. John's message has to do with the preparation for the "Coming One;" Jesus' with the arrival of the Kingdom. John's proclamation is accompanied by a demand for repentance; Jesus' demand for repentance is accompanied by a summons to belief "in the good news." But at the same time, there are close verbal ties which continue to link these verses to the opening verses which precedes. It has sometimes been argued, for example, that the presence of the term "gospel" – εὐαγγέλιον – in v. 15 ties it to the superscription in v. 1. If this brief pericope *is* a transition, it has links now with what precedes, now with what follows. This is quite subtle. In its similarities and differences with what precedes and follows, it links the ministry of Jesus to that of John, and at the same time it shows Jesus embarking on a mission which is distinctively his own.

What Mark has accomplished in the superscription and prologue could scarcely be called eloquent, but there are rhetorical skills here which to my mind have not yet been fully appreciated. Through the careful piling up of adjectives and allusions in his interpretative framework, through the preaching of John the Baptist, through the composite quote in vv. 3f, he has built into his narrative a moment of urgency which is particularly pregnant for the story's reader. In the baptism he has announced to the reader that that urgency finds its fulfilment in the character of Jesus, lately come to John, like everybody else, for baptism. This clear identification he has carefully shielded from the story's other characters, whose bumbling and blindness will later evoke constant reactions of judgment on the part of the story's reader. In this way, the textures and understructures of the prologue reinforce for the reader the overarching eschatological implications of Jesus' arrival on the scene of history, and they lay the foundation of the Messianic Secret which will later play so central a role in Mark's developing narrative.

Opening Events   Mark 1.14–45

The events of the next eight stories introduce a number of themes which will recur throughout Mark's narrative. All of these in one form or another revolve around issues of Jesus' identity and character: he is shown to be teacher (1.16–20, 21–8), preacher (v. 39), healer (vv. 29–31, 40–5), and exorcist (vv. 23–6).[21] Most significant of all, in the heart of the series, he is identified again as "the Holy One of God" (v. 24). The disclosures of Jesus' identity unfold unevenly – not everyone is equally aware of them – and they evoke responses of enthusiasm (vv. 28, 30, 45) and puzzlement (vv. 27, 35–7) on the part of the story's characters. Thus already, before the controversies actually begin in earnest, there is the necessity of secrecy (v. 45).

Jesus is not the only character introduced here. If you will, we are still moving actors and props on-stage. The call of the first disciples in 1.16–20 introduces four characters who will later play individual speaking roles, and it establishes at the outset the conditions and paradigms of their discipleship. The events in the synagogue in Capernaum in vv. 21–8 introduce the crowds, whose questions and puzzlements will form a significant portion of the dialogue in the remaining narrative, as well as the human scenario within which many of Jesus' pronouncements are given expression. The demon in the synagogue plays a role not entirely unlike the figure of the divine messenger in Greek drama, and in this it anticipates other demons whose voices will later punctuate the narrative.

This section also begins to develop the story's plot complications. There are tensions in the perceptions of these various groups, tensions which will prove to mirror in a minor way the tensions in the larger story. Thus, although there is little about these stories which is directly controversial, there are intimations and anticipations of controversies yet to come. As we shall see, this complex is therefore strategically placed. It enhances and consolidates the readers' perceptions of Jesus, and in that way prepares him for the controversies which first appear in Chapter 2. The reader's perceptions and predispositions are already nearly shaped by the time those controversies begin. For their part, the controversies will serve to deepen those intimations and predispositions into fully formed commitments. In that preparation, the cleansing of the leper in verses 40–5 may play a special transitional role. This story is riddled with difficulties, but even the most casual reader will note a shift of stress – the presence of unexplained anger; cautions against saying too much, to the wrong people; hints of the developing controversies which lurk just out of sight in the wings. All of that will burst full-blown on the reader when the curtain rises on Chapter 2.

Mark 1.16–20 – The call of the first disciples

In these twin-call narratives there is nothing which is directly ironic. Jesus simply appears and calls four fishermen. All four will later prove to be central figures in the disciple band, and as such will play individual roles which are largely denied the other disciples.

The fact that the stories are truncated is often noted. We are not told whether the four had any previous encounter with Jesus, nor are we told whether they made any sort of preparation for this journey. What we *are* told is that the fishermen responded to the call immediately. From the stand-point of an ironic reading, what makes that response particularly noteworthy is that these four men drop everything to follow Jesus *without knowing who he is*. Nothing yet narrated could have prepared them for this moment. Thus, when they respond so readily, they do so on the force of the call alone. In this way, the focus is shifted slightly from the fishermen's immediate and unquestioning response to the authoritative personality who can evoke such a response. As readers we are left with more unanswered questions: what is there about Jesus which gives him this power over men? Or what is there about the disciples which gives them the power to respond to Jesus' call? We are not told. Even the words of the call itself are suppressed in the story of James and John (vv. 19f), and the effect is that the immediacy of their response is somewhat heightened.

The words *are* included as the single elaborated detail in the call of Simon and Andrew: "Follow me and I will make you fishers of men" (v. 17). It is not entirely clear what Simon and Andrew would have heard in such a promise. A clever word-play on their vocation, perhaps? A hint of missionary adventures? Perhaps something more ponderous was in view. Wilhelm Wuellner has presented evidence which suggests that the expression was an allusion to an OT metaphor for salvation and judgment.[22] The fishers of men are those who sort the catch, in the process deciding whom to keep and whom to discard (cf. Matt. 13.47–50). In any case, the reader would have heard more than Simon and Andrew, since at this point in the narrative they know nothing of Jesus' messianic identity. It may be worth noting that – the mission of the twelve in 6.6b–13 notwithstanding – this prophecy is not fulfilled within the narrative itself.

What is its function? Here I may venture what I intend as only a tentative hypothesis. The calling of these disciples is important from a narrative stand-point, since they will later play developed and complex roles as characters in Mark's drama; they must be introduced somewhere, and in such a way that their paradigmatic significance is made evident. The call is therefore also important as a paradigm of conversion, of response and responsiveness to the call that Jesus places on all disciples. If that is so, the truncated quality of both stories makes perfect sense. When Peter later claims that they have "left everything" to follow Jesus (10.28), Jesus' generalized response (in vv.29f) indicates that his question is placed on behalf of all disciples, and not the twelve only. It is the same here. The necessity of "leaving everything" is a generalized theme, a paradigm. This much is scholarly commonstock. What is often overlooked is that the promise — "I will make you to become fishers of men" — may be an integral and indispensable part of the paradigm. This is particularly so, if Wuellner is right that there are overtones of eschatological judgment here. Certainly the overtones latent in that promise would have had special reverberations for Christians who were experiencing suffering, and whose social status had left them impotent in the face of the world's judgment against them. If Mark's Church envisioned itself as the eschatological community, that promise would not have been so distantly removed as we might at first suppose.

So this is a story about four fishermen, but it is also paradigmatic, a call to the reader. If he is to recognize the call as a general one, and the response of the fishermen as a paradigm, if he is to empathize with the story's characters and claim as his own the promise they have been given, then he, too, must respond to a mysterious figure for which nothing in the narrative has yet prepared him.

Mark 1.21–8 – Teaching and an exorcism in the synagogue at Capernaum

What had been a pivotal concern of the call-narrative in verses 16–20 is here carried into a new arena: Jesus' authority to *teach*. This pericope betrays evidence of editing, and the account of the exorcism in verses 23–6 appears to be intrusive. The editing has produced the rather strange identification of an *exorcism* as "teaching." The teaching itself is the heart of the narrative. Notice that, although they are bare of extraneous details, these verses stress repeatedly, and from a variety of angles, the potency of Jesus' teaching ministry:

"He taught ... they were astonished ... he taught with authority, and not as their scribes ... and they marveled, and questioned among themselves, saying ... this is new teaching, with authority."

If this reiterated marveling over Jesus' authority forms the heart of the narrative, we can see how it is that the introduction of the exorcism accords with that stress. Folded into the center of the story, the exorcism clarifies that the authority evident in Jesus' teaching was also extended over the demonic world, and it suggests in this way that he is possessor of a kind of teaching which is potent because it is supernatural: that is, the exorcism provides a graphic illustration of the arenas in which Jesus' authority is operative. Verse 22b therefore contains a barb which will later prove to be important: "Jesus taught with authority, *and not as their scribes.*" That is, the scribes are impotent in such matters. I suspect Mark is setting the reader up for the conflict in 3. 22–30, in which the scribes object that Jesus' power to exorcize demons derives from collusion with Beelzebub. If they are powerless in such matters as this, then their authority to teach is suspect as well!

The possibility of collusion with Beelzebul appears to be a very real one, however, and Mark takes pains to provide his readers with critical resources which will shape their responses later on. What those resources are is the subject of a brief excursus, to which we now turn.

Excursus: the cries of the demons

With the introduction of the demons we encounter a compositional problem which recurs in Mark's narrative: they constantly cry out Jesus' name and title, yet no one except Jesus appears to notice. Is it the case – as John Meagher has recently argued[23] – that Mark is simply guilty of slipshod work? There are three such places, and to answer Meagher's argument we must look at them individually.

The first is in the pericope we have been examining in 1. 21–8. The scene is the synagogue in Capernaum. The exorcism is understood as an illustration of the authority of Jesus. The cry of the demon provides significant clues to the source of that authority: Jesus is "the Holy One of God, who has come to destroy" the demons (v. 26). On that basis the demon asks, rhetorically, and to negative effect, "What have you to do with us? Have you come to destroy us?" Yet the murmuring of the people in v. 27 indicates that they know nothing of this disclosure: "What is this? A new teaching! With authority he commands even the unclean spirits and they obey him!" (RSV)[24]

As it stands, the story appears to be internally inconsistent. Second, there is the cry of the Gerasene demoniac in 5.7: "What have you to do with me, Jesus, Son of the Most High God? I adjure you by God do not torment me." One notes immediately the close parallel with the question placed by the demon in 1.26f. Here, however, the cry is somewhat more carefully integrated into the story in which it is found, since it provides occasion for the explanation that Jesus had commanded the demon to depart in v. 8, and for the conversation about the demon's name in v. 9. Yet even so it is awkward. The fact that it is retrospective is startling, and reflects the common Markan habit of explaining narrative elements in retrospect. We ought also to notice that the reaction of the local people is parallel to that of the crowd in Capernaum. They have no inkling of the content of the exchange with the demon. If vv. 7f were excised, the narrative would read smoothly. Finally, the summary in 3.7–12 contains this note: "Whenever the unclean spirits beheld him, they fell down before him and cried out, 'You are the Son of God'" (v. 11). The saying is abbreviated, as we would expect in a summary. It is generally agreed that the entire section is a Markan construction.[25] There is recorded no reaction of the people, but it is not insignificant that the scribes who accuse Jesus of collusion with Beelzebul in vv. 20–30 know nothing of these confessions. And it seems strange that Jesus, when he responds to their charges, does not mention the cries of the demons, even though the content of those cries would have significantly furthered his case.

Thus the cries of the demons are problematical. Meagher is right that they introduce incongruities into the stories in which they are found. Our question is somewhat differently posed: if the cries of the demons introduce incongruities, why are they found here? What *literary functions* can they have been expected to serve? The obvious response is that they constitute disclosures of Jesus' identity which the reader can *overhear*. As such, they function exactly like the voice from heaven in 1.11. Overheard in this way, they clarify and reinforce the reader's perceptions of Jesus' identity, and at the same time they predetermine his reactions to the judgments leveled against Jesus at various places in the narrative. The demons have told us in various ways that Jesus is "The Holy One of God," and "Son of the Most High God," who "has come to destroy – or to torment – the demonic powers." For what it is worth, I think it a delicious coincidence – but not an intentional irony – that the demons in the narrative, in all their attempts to master Jesus, simply further his cause against them.

Meagher is right that they introduce difficulties. But when he carries that observation into the conclusion that Mark does slipshod work, he is himself guilty of handling his material clumsily. A modern reader would expect a disclaimer — "no one heard this but Jesus," or some such thing. Mark is more subtle. Is not the fact that no one seems informed by the cries of the demons a way of signaling that these are private exchanges after all? There are other signals. In 3.12, Mark says that Jesus strictly prohibited the demons from disclosing his identity. When they do blurt out Jesus' name, the titles they use are clear confessions of his authority, and are told in such a way that the demons are made out to have radically dissociated themselves from him. He has come, after all, to destroy them. Yet the scribes in 3.22 are blind to that fact. Their accusation that Jesus is in league with Beelzebul is also blind to the irony that, if they are his antagonists, and if he is, as the demons confess, the Holy One of God, then they are themselves "in league with Beelzebul": Jesus has come to destroy them, too![26]

If Mark signaled that the characters in the story had not heard the demons' declarations about Jesus' identity, what can that fact mean for our reading of his narrative? It indicates to the reader that he is possessor of privileged information, information which has come from a supernatural source, and while it is a source which is antagonistic to Jesus, it is one which nevertheless recognizes his true identity. The cries are ironic affirmations — on the surface of it, attempts at mastery, but from the reader's point of view, desperate confessions which in their very content reflect their basic impotence. As such, they serve the developing dramatic ironies in Mark's story-line. This is a kind of information which has been systematically denied every other character in the story except Jesus himself. The result is that Jesus, the demons, and the reader stand together in a kind of occlusion, such that their common knowledge separates them from the remaining characters in the story. This is an example of plot manipulation to exclude certain characters from significant information, just as we have seen it at work in the development of irony generally in Chapter 4. With this comment we may return to the discussion of the demon in the synagogue at Capernaum we had momentarily left behind.

Here we need say only very little, by way of summary: if the cries of the demons serve as ironic disclosures, they also ironically invalidate the objections raised later about Jesus' power. As we have seen, this is quite subtle, a matter of preparing in advance the reader's dispositions and attitudes. Here, that preparation takes the form of an absolute repudiation: the demons repeatedly dissociate themselves from Jesus, in the process indirectly affirming his messianic character and identity. Here again, the narrative's stresses are deepened as they reiterate themes which had been introduced earlier in the narrative:

> 1.24 "What have you to do with us,
> Jesus of Nazareth?
> Have you come to destroy us?
> I know who you are,
> the Holy One of God."

In his 1973 dissertation, Robert Fowler explored the rhetorical effect of unanswered questions:

> Although in a sense unanswered or rhetorical questions do not provide reliable commentary *per se* for the reader, they do serve to guide the reader's thoughts into the proper channels. Even if they do not furnish the reader with the correct answers, as it were, they at least furnish the correct questions ... Confronting the reader with unanswered questions is without doubt a shrewd rhetorical ploy, for it encourages the reader to seek out the answers.[27]

Fowler goes on to quote Stanley Fish: "A question, after all, implies the availability of an answer; and to ask it is always to create a psychological need for its completing half."[28]

So unanswered questions are important. Here there are two. The first is the semitism, τί ἡμῖν καὶ σοί; (literally: "What to us and thee?"). Mark often translates semitisms, but here he does not. Perhaps that is because the tenor of the question is so obviously hostile, perhaps because the second question − "Have you come to destroy us?" − clarifies the import of the first. In any case, the movements of the narrative have generated subtle reactions on the part of Mark's reader, and while they are subtle they are nevertheless clear. The characters in the synagogue who place and then answer their own rhetorical question − "What is this? A new teaching with authority!" − ultimately declare more than they can know.

Before we move on we must ask ourselves where all of this has led us. We have traced through the narrative the development of two quite different perceptions of Jesus. For the characters in the story he is an enigma, a figure of power, to be sure, but a figure whose power is manifest in unusual, sometimes disturbing ways. It has not dawned on them that his miracles must point beyond themselves to something significantly different from anything they yet expect. The reader has been given a different picture: Jesus is the Christ (v. 1), the Son of God (vv. 1, 11), the "Holy One of God" (v. 24), fulfiller of the prophets, perhaps even the "Lord" of Isaiah 43.1 (vv. 2f). Whatever else, he is one "mightier" than John (v. 7). Thus far, there has been very little hint of trouble. The eschatological implications of Jesus' character have dominated the foreground of the story, and we cannot know for certain how aware the reader would have been that this story is to issue in tragedy. In the next two major sections we shall discover hints that the narrator can assume a certain competence about such matters. Yet he has not made much of them here. Instead, he has consolidated the perceptions of his readers by focusing on the overwhelming evidence that in the person of Jesus we have, in fact, encountered the long-awaited Christ.

A series of controversies Mark 2.1–3, 6

As we move into the controversy stories of Chapter 2, we should pause briefly to note the rhetorical effect of debate and argument on the Gospel's reader. This is a matter which has already received a good deal of attention in the scholarly literature, since it represents one of the primary concerns of form criticism. In his massive study, *The History of the Synoptic Tradition*, Rudolf Bultmann has already described in meticulous detail the social and religious contexts in which controversy dialogues were given their final form in the Church.[29] Although our discussion here will depend upon Bultmann, it will differ from his treatment in fundamental ways. He was interested primarily in showing how living controversies in the experience of the Church found their expression in these "products of Christian imagination" (p. 41). We are interested in their final rhetorical impact on the reader. He dismantles the pericopae in an attempt to discover within their component parts earlier strata of the tradition, and in that way to identify the forces which effected their evolution. We are interested in discussing the controversies as they stand, in the contexts in which we find them.

Nevertheless, Bultmann's pioneering work provides a measure of guidance in its clear affirmation that the Church grew more skilled and more forceful in its use of controversy dialogue to further its own apologetic interests. As he has shown, this tendency is evident throughout the literature of the ancient world (pp. 39–61). With this study in hand, we can set forth some preliminary anticipations of the ironic significances at work in Mark's controversy dialogues.

The evidence is clear: when the dialogues are subjected to form-critical analysis they often appear simpler or less sharp in their earlier forms. The movement of the tradition sharpened the controversies in ways which increased their usefulness to the Church. For this reason Bultmann notes "the increasing tendency of the Church to clothe its fundamental beliefs in the form of controversy dialogue" (p. 51). The assignment of concrete situations to the apophthegmata which form the core of the dialogues is one evidence of this tendency. As we shall see, what Bultmann has said of the concatenation of parts may often be said of the controversy stories as wholes: in their inner movements and dynamics they represent Jesus traditions consciously appropriated for new and different circumstances. The rhetorical strategies by which that appropriation takes place are straightforward: a question or challenge is raised; Jesus' response provides an authoritative answer. What is significant for our discussion of irony is that the questions often involve challenges against institutions and practices which were crucial in the Church's emerging self-consciousness, and the answers are couched in terms which would have been theologically loaded for the listener. If in this way they provide aetiologies for the Church's own institutions and practices, those institutions and practices – and the issues surrounding them – form the critical linguistic background against which they are to be interpreted. That is, the reader's position will have been shaped already by the position he takes in the living controversy in which he found himself.

We have discussed this matter already in Chapter 4. Here we must recall Eco's requirement that perceptive reading requires sensitivities attuned to the possible circumstances and contexts in which the language of the text makes sense (Eco termed this "circumstantial and contextual selection"). It requires the capacity to recognize and respond appropriately to ideologically and theologically loaded expressions (which Eco termed "ideological overcodes"). As we saw in that discussion, shifts in context and the use of overcoded language create the possibility of irony based on the assumed competencies of the reader.

They also *generate* competencies, as the reader encounters the material of the narrative, unfolding, as it does, one word after another. If we ask what role these controversies play *vis-à-vis* the narrative itself, we shall be led to a somewhat different sort of inquiry.

To my mind, the answer to that question lies in the ballast line which forms their conclusion in 3.6: "The Pharisees went out, and immediately held counsel with the Herodians against him, how to destroy him." That is, these pericopae prepare the reader for the trial. They do so well in advance because Mark wished to signal that the decision against Jesus came early, without a trial, and that it came as an act of collusion. There is a subtle strategy here. In the trial itself, Jesus is silent (this is expressly true, in both the sanhedrin trial [14.61] and the trial before Pilate [15.5]). Yet in the controversies which range throughout his narrative, Mark raises and answers challenges in a kind of running preliminary hearing. In this way, he prepares the reader with the responses Jesus gives, and thus predetermines the reader's reaction to the trial itself. We should not be surprised to discover trial language running through these controversies.

Mark 2.1–12 – The healing of the paralytic

We have seen with Rudolf Bultmann that controversy dialogue provides authoritative responses to critical issues in the life of the Church. We have also seen that the controversies prepare the reader in advance for Jesus' silence at the trial. These concerns merge in the question of Jesus' authority itself. Each of the stories in this first major section will deal with that authority in one way or another; here it is Mark's primary articulated concern. More specifically, this story addresses a matter which would have been crucial in early Christianity: by what right does anyone (Jesus? Mark's Church?) pronounce sins forgiven?

There are three major strategies by which Jesus' authority is established here. Two of them are part of the story, and would have been accessible to its characters. The third is a narrative strategy which establishes Jesus' reliability by a confirming word from the narrator. The most obvious strategy of the three is the result of an interpolation of material in vv. 5b–10a. It is clear that the pericope is composite.[30] By the addition of the interpolated material in verses 6–10, it has been transformed from a straightforward miracle story into a controversy dialogue. We should note, however, that it is the element of controversy which accounts for the presence of the complex here, and that therefore Marx probably considered this to be the story's core. Although there are details which have long puzzled Mark's interpreters, the general strategy of the story is clear: Jesus' ability to heal the man, which can be empirically demonstrated, confirms his right to forgive sins, which cannot (vv. 9–12). There may be a subtle turn of phrase here, since ἀφιέναι – "to forgive" – also means "to remove, to take away." In the semitic mind there is no sharp distinction between sin and illness.[31] Thus Jesus' instruction to the man in v. 5 maintains a certain tantalizing ambiguity, and its secondary significance parallels v. 11:

> [5]   "My son, your sins are forgiven."
> [11]   "I say to you, rise, take up your pallet and go home."

If these two sayings are parallel, it may help explain the way in which they are brought together in v. 9:

> "Which is easier,
>   to say to the paralytic,
>   'Your sins are forgiven,'
>   or to say,
>   'Rise,
>   take up your pallet
>   and walk'?"

As Thomas Brudesheim has pointed out, "in fact, the question 'Which is easier?' virtually identifies the two."[32] But this is a trick question, with a number of rhetorical implications.[33] Jesus has not asked what is easier *to do*, but only what is easier *to say*. The opponents have supposed that Jesus' act of *pronouncing* forgiveness is blasphemy, we are told, because it usurps the authority of God. Jesus is speaking empty words, things easy to utter, but impossible to perform. The *act* of healing the man therefore has a subtle ironic overtone: "It is ironical in the sense that the opponents will be forced to admit that the one who *does* such things as healing the paralyzed man must have more than human authority," Jónsson tells us.[34] Morna Hooker gets at this strategy more forcefully: "It would be incredible that a man with blasphemy on his lips should be able to effect such a miracle,"[35] and that, we add, with a word. We may also bring into this discussion a comment by Joanna Dewey, which brings the matter back to v. 2: "The fact that this healing is by word alone confirms that the emphasis in this pericope is on the power of Jesus' word."[36] The fact that the scribes are silent is therefore extremely significant. It establishes a sharp contrast between Jesus and his antagonists, a contrast which deepens as the controversy stories progress.

The focus of attention brings us the second narrative strategy by which Jesus' authority is developed here. This is extremely subtle. The narrator anticipates in vv. 6f the words of Jesus in v. 8:

[6] Now some of the scribes were
      sitting there
      questioning in their hearts,
[7]   "How can this man speak thus?
             It is blasphemy!
             Who can forgive sins but God alone?"
[8] And immediately Jesus,
         perceiving in his spirit
            that they thus questioned
            within themselves,
      said to them,
         "Why do you question thus
          in your heart?"

The reader knows that the narrator is both omniscient and reliable. When Jesus in v. 8 repeats what the narrator has already established as truth, the result is that his reliability is confirmed: that is, he is shown to be reliable by anticipation. In the actual act of reading, this effect will probably lie somewhere just below the threshold of the reader's consciousness, but it should not be overlooked on that account. The potencies of such strategies have already been established by Robert Fowler and Robert Tannehill.[37]

There is another subtlety here which is also largely overlooked in the scholarly literature. Mark reports inside views only sparingly, and only at those strategic points in which the potency of the story would depend upon them. Here he reports two of them: "... the scribes were sitting there, questioning in their hearts ..." (v. 6); "Jesus, perceiving in his spirit that ..." (v. 8a). But notice the way v. 8 concludes. What Jesus has perceived in his spirit is that "they thus questioned *within themselves*." That is, Jesus reads their thoughts. Jesus' capacity to read thoughts is perhaps the most significant of the three narrative strategies precisely because it is so subtle. The reader is hardly aware of the effect it has upon him, perhaps because he has been prepared already by the series of messianic titles which appeared in the opening events in Chapter 1.

There is a critical hint of an underlying theme here which deserves closer attention. A measure of clarity is to be had if we turn aside briefly to explore this phenomenon in Luke, and then ask if something similar is not operative here. In Luke, the idea that Jesus is able to read thoughts has been developed into a full-scale theological motif. Note especially Luke 2. 34f, which appears to be programmatic:

"Behold, this child is set for the fall and rising of many in Israel, and for a sign that is spoken against ... that the thoughts of many hearts may be revealed." In 6.8, Luke adds to the report of the sabbath healing of the man with the withered hand the note that Jesus "knew their inner thoughts." Something similar is afoot in 9.47, in which Jesus reads the thoughts of the disciples, and in 7.39f, in which he reads the thoughts of Simon the Pharisee. This last story may provide us with a clue to the rhetorical "trick" in our own pericope. The occasion is a dinner at Simon's house. Jesus' feet have been washed by a neighborhood prostitute, much to Simon's disgust. Luke takes pains to note that Simon did not challenge Jesus openly, only that he "said to himself, 'If this man were a prophet, he would have known what sort of woman this is who is touching him, for she is a sinner'" (v.39). It is Jesus who broaches the subject, openly answering Simon's silent charge (vv.40–2). By reading off Simon's thoughts and by effecting the woman's redemption, Jesus implicitly demonstrates that he can, in fact, act the part of the prophet. Because of the significance of this motif throughout Luke, I.H. Marshall has seen exactly the same rhetorical strategy at work in the Lukan parallel to our story here (Luke 5.17–26): their question, if only implicitly, represents an unspoken challenge to Jesus' claim to be playing the role of prophet, and in that capacity to be functioning as God's agent.[38] It is as prophet that Jesus pronounces the man's sins forgiven. A loose parallel is to be found in 2 Samuel 12.13, in which Nathan the prophet pronounces David forgiven for his sin against Uriah.

There are good reasons for transferring this observation to the Gospel of Mark. The first is that Mark displays an ongoing interest in Jesus' prophetic ability, as Howard Kee has shown.[39] In point of fact, the demand that Jesus prophesy as proof of his messianic identity forms a central issue in the trial (14.65). Secondly, Mark never directly identifies Jesus as "God alone;" instead, Jesus is simply "Messiah," and "God's Son."

He is also "Son of Man," but Mark's use of that term here certainly cannot be a divine title.[40] Gilbert Bilezekian has argued that it functions as an ironic "wink" at the reader, although this may be too subtle to carry full conviction. Bilezekian is right that "the reader knows that Jesus is referring to Himself, but (that) this identification does not become clear to the personae of the Gospel until the momentous confrontation with the high priest."[41] It is often suggested that v.10 is addressed to the reader directly, as an authorial aside, but this is difficult. The story would not cohere without it. To my mind, it is better to think of the verse as an element which the reader *overhears*, that it is available to the characters in the story as well, but that it is placed here primarily for the reader's sake.

We have seen with Bultmann that controversy dialogue provides an authoritative response to critical issues in the life of the Church. There are two rhetorical advantages which are evidenced here with special potency: in the first place, Jesus' antagonists – in this case the scribes – are set up as foils for Jesus, and the point of view of the reader is in this way disposed against them. In the second, the listener is permitted to overhear the objection raised, and then, hard on its heels, Jesus' response. If the objection is still a live one in the reader's own context, Jesus' answer may serve as an authoritative basis upon which he can establish his own.

Before we leave this pericope we must comment briefly on the close relationship it has with the trial. There are close verbal parallels worth mentioning, particularly in the accusation of blasphemy (v. 7, cf. 14. 64), and in the reference to the title "Son of Man" (v. 10, cf. 14. 61f). We have seen that the issue of Jesus' prophetic identity, implicit here, becomes explicit in the trial (14. 65). There are subtler parallels, which also warrant our attention: it is no accident that the scribes are sitting, ruminating, or as Mark says, "questioning – διαλογιζόμενοι – in their hearts," (v. 6). If the fact that they are sitting suggests something like a tribunal,[42] that suggestion is deepened by the recurring διαλογίζεσθαι which in these verses might be translated "deliberating."[43] Διαλογίζεσθαι is usually qualified in some way, by "among themselves," which is unambiguous, or by "in their hearts" (as here, in v. 8), which leaves open the question of whether they were deliberating silently – within themselves – or verbally – among themselves. Mark, however, has not left the question to chance: they are deliberating "in their hearts" (vv. 6, 8b). They are in this way set over against Jesus, who not only openly announces forgiveness, but also – quite deliberately and openly, as a kind of "testimony against them" (cf. 1. 44) – effects the man's healing. There are rhetorical potencies in this comparison, potencies Mark has also chosen to exploit. The literary foil between Jesus and the scribes is developed in the *contrasts* in the parallelism between vv. 6 and 8. Jesus (and with him, the reader!) "knows" while they "deliberate." The shift in tenses is significant here: they were "deliberating," imperfect, while he "knew," aorist, and knew immediately, what they were thinking. Their deliberations call Jesus' word of forgiveness into question; his reaction in v. 8 calls their thoughts into question. In this way the reactions of the reader to the accusations at the trial are clearly and deliberately orchestrated in advance by anticipatory narrative strategies in the text itself.

Mark 2.13–17 – The call of Levi/tax collectors and sinners

We have mentioned already in Chapter 1 the ironies inherent in the final verse of this pericope: "I came not to call the righteous, but sinners" (v. 17). In those remarks we pointed out the incongruity of this sort of response to – of all people – the scribes. Thus far, it has been chiefly the scribes who have represented Jesus' primary antagonists, and the guardians of a form of righteousness that Mark's Jesus rejects out of hand. If they wish to be among those called, they, too, must reckon themselves "sinners."[44] We also suggested in Chapter 1 that this saying would have gained considerable potency in Mark's own context. There are a number of places in which Mark will address the question of the Gentile in the economy of salvation, and to my mind, this pericope provides a significant backdrop for those later discussions. To be sure, the issue here is somewhat more highly focused – Jesus is dining with "tax collectors" and "sinners." There are good reasons for broadening out the issue here to include the Gentiles, even though the terms Mark uses are quite precise. In the first place, the term "sinners" does not stand in apposition to "tax collectors." Rather, it refers to the *amme ha-aretz* with whom Jesus was accustomed to dine; in that sense, it simply means "commoners." The cultural background would hardly have required clarification. It can be seen in the multiplicity of parallel witnesses in rabbinic literature (M. *Demai* II.2; TB *Berachoth* 43b; TJ *Shabbat* 3c). Each of these in one way or another prohibits the scholar from dining with the "people of the land." The dating of rabbinic material is difficult, yet it is not difficult to see how some such objection might have been raised already in the first century, after the gospel had been carried to the Gentiles. How can anyone who claims to be a bona fide teacher freely eat with tax collectors and sinners? For his disciples to eat with Gentiles – and in his name! – is to carry the scandal to a new level. (Even a cursory reading of Paul's letter to the Galatians will reveal just *how* scandalous [esp. Gal. 2. 12ff, cf. Acts 11. 2ff in context!]) If Jewish tax collectors and laymen are suspect, how much more Gentiles of any stripe! For this reason, Mark's response to the question here may represent a preliminary step in the direction of the fully developed mission to the Gentiles in 6.1 to 8.30. Secondly, and more importantly, this is not simply an ethnic question. It is for Mark a matter of fundamental theological significance, and that significance has implications not only for tax collectors and sinners, but also for "the scribes of the Pharisees" on the one extreme and for Gentiles on the other. The question is in fact universal: on what basis is salvation to be found?

If the pericope is fundamentally theological, the calling of Levi and the ensuing dinner at this house may have overtones of *teaching* which are critical to Mark's intent. This is a parabolic act, and, at least as Mark sees it, it is loaded with parabolic overtones. In the terms we developed in Chapter 4, the reader may miss those overtones if he is unwilling or able to recognize the presence of ideological and theological overcoding here; that is, in the calling of Levi and the dining with tax collectors and sinners Jesus has acted out what Mark takes to be a fundamental theological truth. That truth he places in the ballast lines of the complex in v. 17:

> And Jesus, when he heard it, said,
>   "Those who are   well
>   Have no need of a physician,
>   but those who are   sick;
> I came not to call the   righteous,
>   but   sinners."

If it is the overcoding which gives the final verse its peculiar ironic twist, it is the final verse which retroactively interprets the whole story and gives it its own subtle ironic nuances. Here again, the "teaching" of Jesus stands him – and the reader with him – over against the scribes, whose right to teach is thereby called into fundamental question. At the same time, the pericope deepens the tensions which have begun to develop in this second of the controversy stories. The challenge here is no longer silent; it is framed up and given expression, although not to Jesus himself. That remains to come. Here the challenge is leveled against his disciples.

All of this shifting movement – the nuanced contrasts between the two sorts of piety – requires that the narrator provide some clear standard or base against which the ironies of the story can be calibrated. That clear standard is provided by the lines with which the complex opened: "He went out again beside the sea; and all the crowd gathered about him, and he taught them" (v. 13). By his calling of Levi Jesus is continuing that activity. This is teaching. This is teaching that accepts, categorically, the outcast and sinner, and rejects, categorically, those who think themselves righteous. The exchange with the scribes here therefore has its special twist: they are themselves blind to the significance of that teaching, and unable to hear the demand it places upon them. How strange that *they* should question *him* for his failure to behave with proper scholarly decorum!

If we are right that this pericope has gained potency in Mark's congregation, we may ask how that deeper potency has come about. Any response to that question will be somewhat hypothetical, but we are not without a measure of clarifying evidence. We shall see in Chapters 7 and 8 a complex of material in which the benefits of salvation are extended to the Gentiles. The fact that this story has survived in this form is itself implicit evidence that rejected people – tax collectors and sinners – had been accepted into Christian table fellowship. What is explicit in Acts and Galatians is implicit here. If this scenario is correct, the question put to Jesus' disciples here in v. 16 must have been a live one in Mark's own congregational life. Jesus' answer in v. 17 provides theological justification for the practice of accepting such people into Christian table fellowship.

This is teaching which stands Jesus at conceptual odds with the scribes, and it does so also for the reader. The narrative passes implicit judgment against the scribes, and it is a judgment which the reader is called upon to share. As he does so, as he accepts as his own the point of view from which that judgment proceeds, he is led to make his own declaration of "unrighteousness," and in that way to come under the aegis and urgency of Jesus' call.

Mark 2.18–22 – The question about fasting

As with the other controversies, the irony in this story depends upon assumed background information, information which would have been important for the reader, but which is not contained in the story itself. We know from other sources that the Church practiced periodic fasts,[45] and that it did so largely in imitation of Jewish custom.[46] The question raised in v. 18 is therefore a potent one: how is it that the Church no longer practices what was practiced by her Lord? Clearly the question is raised here to provide occasion for an answer. Evidence of that rhetorical purpose is indirectly provided by the fact that the questioners simply disappear after asking their question. The fact

that we have no record of their reaction to Jesus' response indicates
that the response itself is the narrator's primary concern. The epigrams
which form that response are only loosely related; they gain their force
not from a building logical progression, but from the articulation and
then the reiteration of two quite different elements.

The first of these is ironic: that is, it is significant for the reader
in a way which would be lost on the story's characters. "The days
are coming," Jesus tells his questioners in vv. 19f, "when the bridegroom will be taken away, and in that day they will fast." In this,
Jesus' response functions as a clear aetiology for Church practice:
we fast, just like the Pharisees and the disciples of John, and unlike
our Lord, but we do so for very different reasons.[47]

Whether or not v. 20 contains a *vaticinium ex eventu* is a serious
question from an historical point of view, but however it is resolved,
we shall want to be careful to note that Mark's *reader* would not
have perceived it as such. Instead, it appears in the narrative as an
anticipation of the coming passion, and in its own minor way functions like the passion predictions in Chapters 8, 9, and 10: Jesus acts
deliberately, knowing what the result will be. We should also note
here a subtle shift in the challenges brought against Jesus. On the
surface of it, their accusation is brought against the *disciples* for their
failure to practice the spiritual discipline of fasting. Nothing is said
about Jesus. But that is only on the surface. Instead, the *implied*
accusation is that Jesus has failed to require of his disciples adequate
discipline, and that for that reason his teaching is faulty. There is
therefore something of a parallel between this pericope and the one
which immediately precedes. Here it is given a special twist: what role
have such disciplines in fostering true spirituality? To the implied
accusation there is an implied answer:

[19]   Jesus said to them,
              "Can the bridegroom fast
              while he is with the wedding guests?
              As long as he is with the wedding guests
              He cannot fast."

In this way Mark has subtly defended Jesus' behavior for its differences from that of the Church and from Judaism. That dimension
of the response is picked up and developed in the reiterated elements
of vv. 21f, at bottom: "New wine is for fresh skins." So the in-
compatibility of Jesus' ministry with the old order is clarified and
reinforced.

Mark 3.1−6 − The man with the withered hand

We may begin by noticing that this pericope forms an *inclusio* with the story of the paralytic which opened the section of controversies in 2.1−12. As such, it concludes the section. We might have guessed as much from the extremely heavy ballast line in v.6: "And the Pharisees, when they had gone out, immediately held council with the Herodians against him, how they might destroy him." We have seen the antagonisms of the authorities mount, at each step of the way becoming sharper and more directly pointed at Jesus. The authorities thrust. He parries. In this story, they grow tired of the verbal sparring. They are silent, and in their antagonism instead execute a death-thrust, and Jesus is impaled upon it.

Or is he? There is a rhetorical counter-defense here which is so subtle that it has almost universally escaped the notice of Mark's interpreters. We may bring it to the fore by focusing momentarily on the effect of the rhetorical question in v.4:

> And he said to them,
>   "Is it lawful on the sabbath
>   to do good
>   or to do evil,
>   to save life
>   or to kill?"

Jesus' question is informed, of course, by their intention of bringing legal charges against him in v.2: "They watched him to see whether he would heal him on the sabbath, that they might have cause to accuse him." They cannot answer his question because they have colluded already against him. Their silence is therefore ominous, an indication that they are unwilling or unable to answer positively, and that their intention − about which they have also been silent − cannot be reconciled with the principles of justice which the question implies. We might state this matter differently. From the stand-point of the reader, the authorities have violated justice in their attempt to defend their sabbath blue laws. There is a kind of subtle irony in this: they break the spirit of the law to prevent Jesus from breaking into letter. Their subsequent collusion with the Herodians makes that irony especially poignant: it is on the *sabbath* that they hand down the decision that Jesus must be destroyed. Mark hardly needs to point out the irony of that decision. The second couplet of Jesus' unanswered question strains the irony almost to the breaking point: "Is it lawful on the sabbath ... to kill?" he asks.

To all of this the miracle must be viewed as something of a back-drop. Yet previous miracles in the narrative have established its secondary and tertiary frames of reference, frames which superimpose themselves on this one: the miracle is proof that the "Son of Man has authority on earth" (cf. 2.10), and that he is "Lord of the sabbath" (2.28). In this it stands – like the cleansing of the leper in 1.40–5 – as a "testimony against them" (v.44).

There is a subtle congruity between this narrative movement and the final irony which punctuates the ballast line in v.6: "The Pharisees went out and immediately held counsel with the Herodians against him, how to destroy him." William Lane has come close to a clear appreciation of the irony here: "The rejection of Jesus entails the rejection of life and redemption and leaves men prey to distress and death" (p.126). For Mark's reader, that element is characterized by dramatic reversal, in which the act directed at Jesus on the level of the narrative plays back upon its actant on the level of the reader. For the reader, the Pharisees' damnation of Jesus is self-damnation. Mark's Greek is overcoded here, especially in his use of the rather loaded term ἀπόλλυμι, "to destroy," as Albrecht Oepke has shown.[48] In his discussion of ἀπόλλυμι, Oepke has demonstrated that the term came to have theological potencies, potencies having to do with not temporal, but eternal, verities. Some of these acquired overtones "which cannot be explained in the light of what has been said (about the background of the term in Hellenistic and Jewish literature)" (p.395). That is, in the Church the term came to reflect the destruction of the soul, either by a demonic agent, or by God acting as righteous judge. This may be the meaning of as many as five of the ten occurrences of the term in Mark.[49] To that irony the authorities are completely blind. Their "hearts were hardened," or, as Vincent Taylor prefers, they were guilty of "blindness of heart" (p.223, *re*: v.5).

It is therefore no accident that the story is heavy with the language of jurisprudence. By the judicious use of accusation and rhetorical counter-question, and by the inconsistency between their actions and the principles of justice implied in Jesus' question, Mark has indicted Jesus' accusers. In the process he has summoned the reader – as jury – to hand down a verdict which is far different from the one for which the accusers watched.

Summary events   Mark 3.7–19

Over against the developments of the last few pericopae we must place
the summary events in these two. The authorities have categorically
rejected Jesus (3.6); the crowds will wildly endorse him (3.7–12).
Representative Judaism has rejected him; he will appoint a new
patriarchate, twelve men, to represent the New Judaism. But all is
not well, as we shall see. In these pericopae and in the further
controversies which follow it, we learn of treachery among the insiders, and of Jesus' rejection by his closest intimates, even his own
family.

Mark 3.7–12 – The multitudes by the sea

If Mark intends to set the reader up for some understanding of the
rejection from "within the ranks," this initial pericope appears as a
master-stroke. The tensions and confusions of the text reach a kind
of peak here. The scene is wild affirmation, and in that way a backdrop against which that rejection will appear especially vivid, as a
general impression of commotion is forced upon the reader. The
piling-up of place names – people came from Galilee, Judea,
Jerusalem, Idumea, the Trans-Jordan, and Tyre and Sidon[50] – and
the piling-up of references to the enormous size of the crowds (πολύ:
v. 7; πολύ: v. 8), the large number of sick people he had healed
(πολλούς: v. 10), and the demons he had exorcised (πολλά: v. 12)
combine to create a scenario which is turbulent, even in its very
language. That impression is deepened by the descriptions of the press
of the crowds (ἐπιπίπτειν: v. 10) and the demoniacs (προσέπιπτον:
v. 11), which are parallel to one another, and which are difficult to
translate into English with adequate force.

The scenario proceeds in two movements, the first (vv. 7f) a general
summary, the second (vv. 10–12) an elaboration of the expression
"whatsoever things he did" with which the first concludes. Between
these two, v. 9 appears at first unnecessary, or at least intrusive.
The preparation of the boat is not directly "plot significant." Why
is it here? It provides occasion for the reiterated expressions about
the crush of the crowds, and they in turn provide the occasion for
the mention of the unclean spirits in v. 11. In literary terms, we
might say that the movements of the plot have been suppressed here
so that the atmosphere can predominate. What we have, then, is a
piled-up scenario which has been calculated to reinforce by deepening

reiteration a sense of Jesus' swelling popularity. If, as Ulrich Mauser insists, "Mark wants to state a withdrawal from the public throng to the solitary scene of the lakeside,"[51] that intention is abandoned or disrupted from the very start. It becomes very difficult, then, when the pericope closes with this strict prohibition to the demons: "He sternly charged them that they might not make him known."

We have mentioned already the ironic strategies served by the cries of the demons. Here we may examine those strategies with greater care. Something of the incongruity of Jesus' prohibition can be had if we modify slightly our customary rendering of φανερός, "manifest." After piling up descriptions of the size of the crowds that came to Jesus, virtually from all over, Mark has Jesus casting out the demons with this stern rebuke: "See that you do not make me famous." On the surface of it, the prohibition is wonderfully understated. The demons and the reader understand perfectly well that he is referring, not to his abilities, but to his identity, and yet here, in the context of such commotion, his remark is almost humorous.

There is a further reason why he should silence the demons, a reason which lies rather deeply embedded in the narrative. Was not "all that he did" in v. 8 − healing and exorcism − itself understated testimony to his identity? If, as is widely noted,[52] this pericope is a summary and transition, we might do well to ask why Mark elected to highlight Jesus' ministry of healing and exorcism. Is it not that these are two primary elements of the messianic expectation?

So the demons are silenced just as Jesus' popularity attains a feverish new pitch, and at the precise moment that his opponents have committed themselves to his destruction. Yet, for the characters inside the story, it is the silencing and the control over the demon world which ought to have constituted a primary attestation of his messianic authority. The rhetorical effect is very subtle: Jesus' prohibition comes only after the reader has overheard the affirmation of Jesus' true identity. Here, then, the declaration of the demons can be said to serve a particularly acute narrative function. It makes explicit, if only for a brief moment, the subtle messianic implications and nuances inherent in the story itself. The demons, by declaring Jesus "Son of God" have interpreted for the reader the true significance of the signs, the "whatsoever things he did" in v. 8.

As we have seen, that information is reserved for the reader and is shielded from the story's characters. Jesus' response to the demons is instant: "he strictly ordered them not to make him known" (v. 12).

The point of the irony, of course, is that they have made him known, have made him known to the reader who has been permitted to overhear what are apparently their cries, not of recognition, but of attempted mastery. It is a subtle touch that the *demons* should be made agents of revelation, that they are themselves used in a broader scheme in which Jesus — and Mark — are their greater masters.

Finally, it is important that they make this declaration here, since, within this chapter, the question of Jesus' authority over the demons is given concrete expression in the opposition of the "scribes who came down from Jerusalem" (vv. 22–7). We shall reserve our further remarks for our discussion of that pericope, and stop here only to note that Mark has here anticipated a question which will later prove to be critical in his developing Christology. By anticipating their challenge, Mark has predisposed his reader to hear the story in one way, rather than in another.

Mark 3. 13–19 — The choosing of the twelve

This brief report requires only passing comment. The identification and fate of the twelve has of course fascinated historians, and has long engaged the lay reader's active imagination. In terms of Mark's own interest, however, the fact that these twelve are named here is perhaps less "plot significant" than those speculations can sustain. Except for Judas Iscariot and the inner circle — Peter, James, John, and Andrew — they are not mentioned by name elsewhere in Mark.[53] Instead, they are described as a group, usually with the technical designation "the twelve."

On the other hand, it is critical that the twelve are constituted a specific group, with a special call and special responsibilities. The twelve represent the establishment of the New Israel, if only in synecdoche, and while its number is fixed, its movements and activities in Mark are representative of the movements and activities of the Church as a whole.[54] What those movements are in signaled — also in synecdoche — in v. 14:

> And he appointed twelve
> that they might be with him
> and that he might send them
> to preach
> and to have authority
> to cast out demons.

There may be subtle reverberations here. The comment about the disciples' authority over demons establishes the backdrop of the criticism of the scribes in vv. 23–30. The implied criticism of the authorities will hinge upon the assumption that they are impotent in such matters (see esp. 1. 22, in which that impotence has been made explicit!). If Jesus has redefined the community of God, he has done so in such a way that the claim of the older "community of God" is called into question. He does so at precisely that moment that its representatives have declared their intention to see him destroyed. We have seen that their decision is an ironic self-damnation. In effect, then, the calling of the twelve follows naturally, inevitably. If traditional institutions cannot bear the weight of this sort of messianism, then others must be set in place to supplant them. We must bear this factor in mind when we move along to v. 23. "If a kingdom is divided against itself, that kingdom cannot stand," he will tell them, and "if a house is divided against itself, that house will not be able to stand." In the context of the self-damnation the Pharisees have pronounced in v. 6, this saying will take on secondary or tertiary levels of meaning which are subtly but significantly ironic: on the surface of it, the saying refers to the kingdom and house of Satan. In this context, it may contain a kind of secondary overcode: Judaism itself is also "divided against itself," and will not be able to stand.

Further controversies Mark 3. 20–35

We shall treat these pericopae as a distinct new section, although it should be pointed out that they are related rhetorically to what precedes. The wildly enthusiastic crowds in 3. 7–12, and the establishment of a new representative "people" in the calling of the twelve in 3. 13–19, together form a backdrop against which these renewed efforts at controlling Jesus appear particularly strident. There are internal backward references here as well. The reference to the crowd "coming together again" in 3. 20 recalls the description of the crowd in 3. 7–12; the consideration that Jesus had become insane depends in part for its intelligibility on the uncontrollable fervor of that crowd on the one hand, and the mounting antagonism of the authorities on the other (3. 6). The decision of the scribes about Jesus' ability to exorcise demons recalls the summary statement in 3. 11f. All of this may be stated on the converse: the decision of the Pharisees and Herodians in 3. 6, the wildly enthusiastic crowds in 3. 7–12, the symbolic establishment of the new patriarchate in 3.13–19 are, in their own ways, "plot significant." Together they prepare the reader for the deepening of the antagonisms against Jesus which will occupy his attention in the next pericopae.

A few words are in order about the structural relationships between these three stories. The reference to Jesus' family frames the accusation of the scribes, and the intercalation suggests that the complex should be read as an interconnected whole. Jan Lambrecht[55] has already argued that the structure here is chiastic:

vv. 20–1 – Jesus at home
The initiative of the relatives
v. 22 – The accusation of the scribes
vv. 23–9 – Jesus' apology
v. 30 – Repetition of the accusation
vv. 31–5 – The arrival of the relatives and the
and the proclamation of true kinship

There is a rhetorically significant link between vv. 20f and v. 22. The repetition of the introductory formula ἔλεγον γάρ, "for they were saying," here ties the second explanation to the first: that is, the declaration of Jesus' family[56] that he was insane provides occasion for the declaration of the scribes that he was working in collusion with Satan. Each deepens the other, and in part the answer to the one accusation corroborates the answer to the other.

Mark 3.22–30 – On collusion with Satan

We have discussed already two levels of irony in this pericope. On one level, by opposing Jesus the scribes have actually aligned themselves with the demons Jesus has "come to destroy." In that way they have set themselves up for the secondary nuances of Jesus' rhetorical question in vv. 23b–26: their own kingdom is divided against itself, it is their house which will fall, they dwell where the stronger one has come to plunder. The silence with which the chapter opened is a factor here as well. We are not told their response to Jesus' apology, and the silence of the scribes here – like the silence of the Pharisees and Herodians in 3.2 – reinforces in the reader's mind their inability or unwillingness to respond.

In a sense they have been set up by the exclusionary strategies of the unfolding narrative. They could not hear that the demons had dissociated themselves from Jesus, or that they had announced to the reader that Jesus had come as their destroyer (1.24). They can see plainly enough his authority over the demons, but they cannot conceive of the source of that authority. Their inability to see, just as their impotence in matters of exorcism, undermines their authority to teach, and it is therefore understandable but ironic that they accuse Jesus of heresy and collusion with Satan. He is, after all, a violator of the sabbath, and a friend of the ritually impure – tax-collectors and sinners, the *amme ha-aretz*. His concept of piety and their convictions about purity are incompatible, and that his power over demons would derive from an impure spirit is a natural enough conclusion. It is natural, but it is for precisely that reason that it is wrong. It is blind to the deeper spiritual significances which are resident in the exorcisms. It is intended as a righteous judgment, a decision which is theologically judicious. That it is ironic becomes clear when Jesus condemns it categorically as an act of blasphemy (vv. 28–30).

The converse of the binding of Satan is also an operative element here, if only implicitly: the Spirit by which Jesus exercises control over the demons is not "unclean," it is "holy." The arrival of the Holy Spirit is, in fact, a pressing expectation of the eschaton, and the binding of Satan is its direct evidence. This hope has widely distributed parallels in the literature, but we need note only the Testament of Levi and the Testament of Judah as evidence:

> *Testament of Levi 18. 10–11*
> [10] And he shall grant to the saints to eat
> the tree of life.
> [11] The spirit of holiness shall be upon them.
> And Beliar shall be bound by him.
> And he shall grant to his children
> the authority to trample on wicked spirits.

> *Testament of Judah 25. 3*
> [3] And you shall be one people of the Lord,
> with one language.
> There shall no more be Beliar's spirit of error,
> because he will be thrown into the lake of fire.

It is therefore extremely serious that the scribes have set themselves in direct opposition to Jesus. In that act, they align themselves with the demons and set themselves up for the fate of Beliar:

Mark 3. 28–30

[28] "Truly, I say to you,
       And sins will be forgiven the sons of men,
       and whatsoever blasphemies they utter;
[29]   But whoever blasphemes against the Holy Spirit
       never has forgiveness,
       but is guilty of an eternal sin" –
[30] For they had said,
       "He has an unclean spirit."

Parables (and a miracle) of promise   Mark 4. 1–41

There is very little in the parables of Chapter 4 which could be classed
as directly ironic in the sense in which we have been using that term.
The fact that this chapter is almost entirely composed of discourse
militates against it, since the extended monologue slows and simplifies
the movement of the plot. We may, however, note two aspects of this
section which serve the ironic movements of the book as a whole.
First, there is ample evidence that the parables were appropriated
in various ways for the ongoing life of the community.[57] The clearest
evidence in this regard is the allegorical interpretation of the parable
of the sower in 4. 13–20,[58] and the presence of Marcan transitional
formulae is often noted. The fact that the chapter is composite would
be adequate evidence in its own right. The notion that the parables
were appropriated for Mark's community does not in itself imply that
they would have meant something different or ironic in the community's consciousness, but it does make it possible that the en-
couragement to Jesus' beleaguered disciples would be more deeply
felt in the context of distress in which Mark's community surely
found itself. The contents of the parabolic discourse would have been
especially appropriate in such circumstances.

There is another side to this discussion which also warrants attention. Much of the discussion currently going on in parable research
has shown that the element of mystery – therefore confusion –
which characterized the reception of the parables is critical for Mark's
understanding of their intent.[59] That interest brings us to the second
implication of this discourse for an ironic reading of Mark. For our
purposes this concern is the more important of the two: the distance
between ὑμῖν and οἱ ἔξω, between those "on the inside" and those
"on the outside," here acquires its clearest articulation. This is a

matter which has implications for the Gospel of Mark as a whole, and for our reconstruction of the esoteric knowledge which defined the boundaries of Mark's community.[60] We shall focus our discussion entirely on this question, and shall leave for another study the somewhat peripheral matter of ironic and secondary nuances in the parables themselves.

Mark 4.10–12 – The reason for the parables

We may begin with a diagram:

[10]   And then he was alone,
       those who were about him with the twelve
         asked him concerning the parables.
[11]   And he said to them,
             "To you
               has been given the secret
                 of the kingdom of God,
             but
             for those who are outside
               everything is in riddles[61]
[12]   so that
               they may indeed see
               but   not   perceive
               and may indeed hear
               but   not   understand;
             lest they should turn again,
                 and be forgiven."

We have placed these verses at the mast-head of this chapter because they are important for our understanding of Mark's ironic nuances. But we must establish at the outset that, as Mark understands them, they are not ironic in themselves. This is critical. A number of scholars have recently used that suggestion in an attempt to alleviate the rather vexing problem of the obduracy mentioned in v. 12. That resolution of the problem of the obduracy is extremely tempting. This may well be the most difficult *crux interpretum* in the entire gospel of Mark.[62] We cannot hope to resolve all of its difficulties[63] here. But whatever else we say, we must insist that in Mark's understanding the saying is straightforward.

Three scholars have defended the view that this is irony. In 1974, Carey Moore took this position in an article which appeared in the

Festschrift for Jacob Myers.[64] Moore argues that the saying is authentic (because difficult), but intrusive. Its original context is lost, and where context is lost, irony may be difficult to recognize. But there is little chance that Jesus intended that this saying be taken literally. Probably, then, he intended something more sarcastic (p. 341):

> Why do I teach in parables?
> Why, I tell them so people won't see.
> I tell them so people won't hear.
> After all, I wouldn't want to instruct people
> or save them.

In 1980, Jerry Gill argued something similar in his study "Jesus, Irony and the 'New Quest'."[65] In this study, Gill suggested that the sarcasm in v. 12 – which is addressed to insiders! – is consistent with Jesus' general attitude toward "thick-headed" questions from the disciples: "After all, we wouldn't want such people (as the Scribes and Pharisees) to repent and be converted, now would we?" (pp. 144f).

The third article, published in 1983 by Bruce Hollenbach,[66] is the most sophisticated of the three. Hollenbach begins with a discussion of the antithetical levels of meaning which generally characterize irony, and on that basis argues that Isaiah 6.10b was ironical in its context in Isaiah. "If it can be granted that Isaiah 6.10b is an ironical statement, it should not be difficult that Mark 4.12b is also, if it be remembered that the Old Testament was much more present and vivid to Jesus and the Jews of his time than to us" (p. 317). Here, then, is Hollenbach's paraphrase: "... so that they may indeed see but not perceive, and may indeed hear but not understand; because the last thing they want is to turn and have their sins forgiven!" (p. 320).

None of these suggestions is entirely adequate for our understanding of the meaning of the saying here. Here, "all things," τὰ πάντα, in v. 11 refers not to the parabolic teaching only, but to the whole of the story-line. There are two points which make this clear. First, it is noteworthy that the term "parable," παραβολή, is feminine, while the expression "all things," τὰ πάντα, is neuter. The one cannot simply represent the other. Rather the "all things which are in riddles" stand in a kind of juxtaposed contrast to the "mystery of the Kingdom of God which is given," like this:

To you	To those who are outside
has been given	
the mystery	all things are in riddles
of the Kingdom of God	

The one is mysterious – given, not taken: it is an act of grace; the other is the posture of the outsider – blind, unwilling or unable to see. But there is more. Verse 13 makes it clear that the disciples and "those who are with them" do not, in fact, understand the riddle of the parables. How then can it be said that they have been given the mystery if they do not understand the parable? Everything works much more easily if we understand the reference in v. 11 more broadly. The inability of the outsiders to comprehend the parables is of a piece with their inability to grasp the deeper significances resident in the miracles, the exorcisms, and the general movement of the story-line itself. For that reason, the explanation given in vv. 11f serves the rather critical rhetorical function of explaining the blindness of "those outside" in the book as a whole.

We have seen already in Chapter 1 that Mark may have understood the whole of Jesus' ministry – and therefore his Gospel as well – as parabolic or polyvalent. In a recent article, Priscilla Patten has presented evidence that the tendency toward the esoteric was overwhelming in Jewish apocalyptic movements, and has suggested that the esoteric elements of Mark as a whole are based on affinity with apocalyptic urgencies.[67] The cogency of Patten's argument depends in part on her observation that the events in Mark hold deeper, esoteric significance, significance which is reserved for the community of faith.

Here is a bit of narrative trickery. Mark frequently has the disciples waiting until they are "in the house" or alone with Jesus to ask about his teaching or miracles. The three verses we have been discussing are a primary example, although this narrative technique is widely distributed throughout Mark's gospel.[68] The rhetorical effect is that the reader is permitted to overhear the question raised and Jesus' authoritative response, and in that way he is made a *de facto* member of the disciple band, one of those "inside." As the narrative later turns against the disciples, as the reader with Jesus is called upon to judge the disciples themselves for their blindness (cf. .14–21), he becomes closer than the disciples, closer even than the inner circle.

It seems clear that Mark 4.11–12 is not ironic *for Mark*, then, because it functions as the explanation, the standard, against which the blindness of the story's characters can be calibrated. The converse of that statement is also critical for what we make of these verses: the source of the reader's ability to see, to comprehend, "the mystery of the kingdom" is indirectly attributed to God himself. It is an example of the "giftedness" of the community of faith, and as such functions as a sociologically potent factor in the community's self-definition. Mark's rhetorical strategies therefore also come close to the surface here. By use of this rather sharp word of judgment he has reinforced and deepened the reader's sense of superiority over the story's characters, and has done so in such a way that the reader identifies his deeper insight with the "mystery of the kingdom of God."

Mark 4.35–41 – The stilling of the storm

It is not usual in outlines of Mark to link the stilling of the storm with the parables. Almost always it is linked with the miracles which follow in Chapter 5. But when the rhetorical movements of this pericope are examined, we shall discover that they parallel and deepen what precedes as closely as what follows. I therefore consider this pericope transitional. We have already discussed the notion that the narrative itself may have been understood as a parable of God, as a nuanced and double-edged message. In the last section we examined briefly the thesis that the "hardening of hearts" explained in 4.11f extends to the whole of Jesus' ministry, and cannot be restricted solely to the parables *as such*. And the content of the parables, which we did not examine, appears to encourage the disciples – and thus, indirectly, the Church – in its moment of crisis. So, apparently, we are to take the sower (vv. 3–9), with its extended interpretation (in vv. 13–20): failure comes, there still will be a bumper crop. So, also, the parable of the candle (vv. 21f): does God light a candle merely to snuff it out,[69] or to cover it up? The parable of the grain growing "automatically" may – at least at its root – suggest something similar (vv. 26–9): the earth produces of itself, automatically, without visible cause.[70] In spite of everything to the contrary, the Kingdom is breaking in!

With that background – and we must remember that it is the immediate background of the reader as well! – we may turn to the stilling of the storm. A careful reader can scarcely avoid the ways Mark has underscored the befuddlement of the disciples in this pericope. The fact that they are terrified by Jesus' power is paradoxical: they are more afraid of the peace in the boat than they were of the storm in the sea. That the disciples do not understand the power of the peace is evident from their final question: "Who then is this, that even the wind and sea obey him?" (v. 41). In this way, Mark makes it clear that their reason for waking Jesus in v. 38 reflected a purely practical urgency: they wanted him to bail water, or some such thing. The language in v. 38 makes that especially clear.[71]

From their perspective, that urgency is exactly right. The sea is their territory, not his. Besides, Jesus is exhausted. Who in his right mind would expect miraculous help from one whose powers are so exhausted that he sleeps in a storm such as this? Thus the disciples are set up for a second paradox: the exhausted Jesus is instantly the most powerful figure in the boat. The sea – and with it the wind! – are in fact his "territory." With that realization, the confusion of the disciples is brought full circle. One's habituated reality sense, what one would "normally expect," has been made the backdrop against which the details of the miracle have been described.

In a sense, Jesus' rebuke to the storm – "Peace! Be still!" – subtly balances his words to the disciples: "Why are you afraid? Have you no faith?" Their terror-ridden response – "Who then is this? – indicates the reason for their unwillingness or inability to deal with the storm more appropriately. They simply do not know who this man is who is in their boat. In Mark's telling of the story, their question is the final note, and is therefore left unanswered. Or is it? Is it not rather directed out of the disciples' frame of reference and put to the reader? We have seen already the rhetorical effect of unanswered questions: they force the reader to supply answers of his own. Mark has already suggested before who Jesus is, and the reader's spontaneous response here helps to secure his agreement: Jesus is the Son of God.

With his question in v. 40 – "Why are you afraid? Have you no faith?" – Jesus indicates that he shares the enlightened perspective of the narrator and his audience. Or rather, the narrator and audience may be said to share the divine perspective of the protagonist. The question of the disciples – "Who is this?" – stands them over against that occlusion. The narrator has in this way exploited their befuddlement to achieve a theological end. It is an end which confronts the reader in a decisive way: only he who truly understands Jesus' identity can have the presence of mind to sleep in a sinking boat.

To these considerations we must add another. It is often pointed out that the language by which Jesus stills the wind and sea parallels the technical language of exorcism. Have we mastery over not only nature, but demonic forces as well? That suggestion has been made by Paul Achtemeier,[72] and if it can be sustained we would have a close tie to the exorcism of the Gerasene demoniac which immediately follows in Chapter 5. The difficulty lies in the question of whether the sea can be said to harbor demons, but to my mind the evidence is not quite decisive. There is a reference in the Testament of Solomon (5.11; cf. also 11.6), to the effect that demons abhor water,[73] but the rather late date (possibly third century C.E.) makes it possible that this has been subject to Christian influences. The parallel passage in the Testament of Solomon 11.6 has almost certainly been modified to reflect Christian interests. Howard Kee has presented evidence that the term "he rebuked," ἐπιτιμᾶν, found here (v.39) and in eight other places in Mark, may represent an underlying Aramaic technical term for exorcism.[74] Of particular significance in Kee's discussion is his background survey of traditions which use that term for the "rebuke" of the waters of chaos, and therefore for the primal assertion, and the eschatological reassertion, of God's mastery over whatever forces would thwart his purposes (pp. 236f). Kee has also shown that in the post-Exilic period the identity of those hostile forces became "more sharply specified," that is, came to be identified with Satan and his minions (p. 237). And it is in keeping with this identification that Achtemeier's position has been set forth. If we take it seriously, the stilling of the storm would follow loosely but powerfully on the heels of Jesus' saying in 3.27 that "no one can enter a strong man's house and plunder his goods unless he first binds the strong man." Mark could hardly have created a more fitting bracket around the parables in Chapter 4!

Even so, the fact that the elements of exorcism are not more explicit should give us pause. Perhaps Mark means to broaden his inferences. We cannot know for certain, and to my mind it is probably safest to see here the reassertion of the Kingdom over cosmic opposition in whatever form it comes, and – with Mark – to leave beneath the surface of the story the matter of the presence of specific demons. With the mastery of cosmic opposition, we see the reassertion of the Kingdom if only the watcher is able to comprehend its significance. It is perhaps in this way that the miracle resonates most deeply with the parables. On the other hand, the "cosmic opposition" reaches the level of personified evil – frighteningly so, violently so – in the story of the demoniac at Gerasa which follows, and to which we now turn.

Miracles   Mark 4.35–6.6

We shall not comment on all of these miracles, and so summary observations are in order about the section as a whole. First, the section both begins and ends with stories which focus on Jesus' identity and the authority by which he exercises his miraculous power. The parallels are conceptual, rather than verbal, but they function in very similar ways. Note that both involve unanswered rhetorical questions:

4.41 "Who then is this,
            that even the wind and sea obeys him?"
6.2 "Where did this man get all this?
            What is the wisdom given him?
            What mighty works are wrought
                by his hands!"

Second, both the opening and closing pericopae are transitional, directing attention backward and forward in the narrative. They function largely as hinge-pins between three large blocks of material, but they do so in a way which links them together, rather like a narrative triptych.[75] We should not be surprised to discover themes which run throughout these three blocks. The rejection of Jesus of Nazareth, for example, formally closes the section of miracles, and by means of its rhetorical strategies resolves in the reader's mind the question – "Who is this?" – with which the section opened in 4.35–41. Yet that question is only provisionally resolved, and it recurs with deepening urgency as the narrative progresses. We shall find it in 6.14f, and then again, in a kind of apex in the book, in the opening of Peter's confession in 8.27f: "Who do men say that I am?" The third section of the triptych drives home the legitimacy of the movement of the gospel to the Gentiles, and does so by reiterated stories which bear that thrust in their core clichés. There are hints of that movement already in the exorcism of the Gerasene demoniac in 5.1–20.

There is also a link between these miracles and the parables in Chapter 4, although it is of a somewhat looser kind.[76] There Jesus proclaimed as potent the word of the Kingdom. Here the potencies of the word of the Kingdom are demonstrated graphically. We saw already in our discussion of the stilling of the storm that that story picks up and then reiterates a basic theme of the parables – nothing can stop the gospel! The reiterated fear which ties together the miracles appears to parallel the unspoken anxiety which motivates the parables. If that link is established it would serve a specific, identifiable rhetorical strategy. The authority which guarantees the promise inherent in the parables is the same authority which Jesus exercises over the cosmic forces (4.35–41), over the realm of the demonic (5.1–20), and over the sphere of illness and death (5.21–43). Just as the parables are selective and representative, so also the miracles are representative, and their basic thrust is to reflect in sweeping terms the breadth and depth of Jesus' authority. We shall see that authority deepen as the narrative moves toward the declaration that Jesus is the Christ. In this, the miracles of Chapter 5 are central. The potency of Jesus' word reaches a kind of apex in the raising of Jairus' daughter from the dead in 5.35–43.

The hesitation in Jesus' hometown is particularly striking following this miracle, so much so that it will break the march of the miraculous and deflect the narrative to other things. Are we to understand that the extension of the gospel to the gentiles is even more of a miracle than that? In any case, along the way, the reader will be privy to dimensions of the miracles which are lost on the story's characters, will be permitted to overhear the demons, and to attend the resuscitation of a corpse. At every turn his reactions to the miracles will be orchestrated by the narrator's conscious strategies, so that when he follows along into Jesus' hometown his reaction to the crowds will be exactly like that of Jesus: the reader, too, will "marvel because of their unbelief."

We saw in our discussion of 4.10–12 that the parables effectively divide between those who are on the inside and those who are on the outside of the Kingdom. The listener is placed in a position superior to that of the story's characters, wherever their disposition is to reject the claim that the kingdom places upon them. The miracles here consolidate that superiority by moving the conflict to a cosmic plane, in the process demonstrating the authority by which Jesus can make the radical claims he makes in the parables. We may state this somewhat differently: the battleground for the Kingdom is shown in the miracles to have cosmic dimensions. The clear confusion in all these stories also graphically illustrates Jesus' words: to those who are outside, everything is in riddles. Thus it is not insignificant that the miracles have been placed just before the rejection at Nazareth in 6.1–6, and the commissioning of the twelve in 6.7–13.

Mark 5.1–20 – The Gerasene demoniac

In this story the ironies are of a special kind. They have to do with the difference not of knowledge, but of reaction. The reaction of the characters reaches its clearest expression in v. 17: "And they began to beg him eagerly to depart from their neighborhood." On the surface of it, Jesus' presence has exchanged one catastrophe for another, and the loss of the pigs is frequently cited as the reason for the desire of the townspeople to be rid of him. But there is another reason, one which to my mind is closer to Mark's narrative strategy. Verse 17 here parallels a pivotal verse in the stilling of the storm story: they wish to be rid of him because they are terrified. Both the loss of the pigs and the shock of the demoniac seated – as Mark says, "clothed and in his right mind" – are evidence that Jesus has tremendous power over demonic forces. His power certainly exceeds theirs, as we shall see, but they do not know from whence it proceeds, or what its disposition is toward them. From their point of view, the loss of the pigs suggests that the power is in some way malevolent. The fact they are Gentiles who keep pigs, while Jesus is a Jew, for whom pigs are offensive, only deepens their confusion and fear.

From the reader's perspective, this is entirely wrong-headed. If to all of this he reacts differently, it is in part because the entire preceding narrative has taught him that Jesus' mastery over demonic forces is evidence of his redemptive activity. Just as the reader would have found incredible the terror of the disciples in the stilling of the storm, so here he is expected to react to the fear of the townspeople with utter disbelief. Note the reiterated contrasts which deepen the resonances between the two stories: the storm is described as a "great storm of wind" (4.37), and the peace as a "great calm" (v.39). It is the calm which provokes the terror of the disciples in 4.41! In the same vein the violence of the demoniac occupies three full verses (5.3–5), to which the description of his sanity stands as a sharp contrast. The calm of the demoniac parallels the calm in the sea. Here, too, the calm is met by expressions of terror, by a desperate effort to be rid of one who can bring peace so readily (v.17).

Yet the reader realizes that Jesus is not malevolent. That realization is reinforced here in various ways. Scattered throughout the story are signals to that effect. Most obvious, of course, is the description of the demoniac in vv. 2b–5:

[2]   There met him out of the tombs a man
          with an unclean spirit

[3]   who lived among the tombs;
              and no one could bind him any more,
                      even with a chain;
                      for he had often been bound
                              with fetters
                              and chains.
                      and the chains
                              he wrenched apart,
                      and the fetters
                              he broke   in pieces;
              and no one had the strength to subdue him.
[5]   Night and day   among the tombs
                      and on   the mountains
              he was always   crying out
                      and bruising himself with stones.

Along with this description we must note the catastrophe of the
demons' headlong plunge into the sea, a clear and indisputable sign
that it is *their* disposition which is malevolent. Against this backdrop
the exorcism will obliquely establish the redemptive character of the
exorcist!

We must remember that Mark has had to stop the movement of
the plot while he describes the man's condition. We might call this
"aggravated pandemonium." That the demoniac is uncontrollable
is important. It highlights the impotence of the townspeople, and sets
that impotence over against the power and authority of Jesus. Jesus
can dismiss the legion of demons with a word. That radical contrast
in power is effected by the narrative contrast between vv. 2b–5 and
the description of the demoniac in v. 15:

[15]   They   came to Jesus,
              and saw the demoniac sitting there
                      clothed
                      and in his right mind.
      And they were afraid.

Thus there are two primary lines of tension here – tension between
Jesus and the townspeople, and tension between Jesus and the legion
of demons. There is also tension between the demoniac and the
townspeople here, and because of that tension the atmosphere is
already fully charged when Jesus appears on the scene. What will
the demoniac do?

The fact that he prostrates himself before Jesus and that he cries out "with a loud voice" (v. 6) presents a mixed image which may itself be significant. There are elements here which appear to be threatening, even spectral – the blurting out of Jesus' name and title, the claim to be named Legion, "for we are many." Co-mingled with these are elements of submission and humiliation, the prostration before Jesus, the desperate pleading not to be sent out to the country. The demon recognizes that Jesus is "Son of the Most High God," the latter phrase an expression now well documented in pagan literature.[77] In the demon's urgency he blurts out a double irony: "I adjure you by God, do not torment me!" (v. 7). The most obvious irony is that the demon should so address the exorcist. We have examples of this formula – ὁρκίζω σε – on the lips of other exorcists and magicians,[78] most notably in Acts 19.13. Obviously this is an attempt to exercise some sort of power over Jesus, but it appears strangely convoluted and difficult that such an expression should come from one who is himself under the exorcist's control.[79] That irony is deepened to another level by the fact that the adjuration is in God's name: "I adjure you by God, do not torment me!"

As the tension between Jesus and the demoniac finally resolves itself, it is replaced by a corresponding tension between Jesus and the townspeople (vv. 14ff). The reader can hardly avoid the parallel between v. 17 and v. 10:

[10]   And he   begged (παρεκάλει)
                         him   eagerly
                         not to send him out
                         of the country.

[17]   And they began to beg (παρακαλεῖν)
                         Jesus   eagerly
                         to depart
                         from their neighborhood.

With these verses compare the plea of the now-recovered demoniac in v. 18:

[18]   The man who had been possessed with demons
                         begged (παρεκάλει) him
                         that he might be with him.

Clearly this is the appropriate response. The narrator has made that clear with a variety of hints. The very fact that this is Christian language – the language of discipleship (cf. 3.14) – would predispose the reader to recognize the appropriateness of the man's request. But Jesus does not. Instead he refuses, and sends the man home. Why? Perhaps it is because he wishes to affirm the legitimacy of this man's openly proclaiming the good news of his liberation from bondage. The narrator does not tell us. He leaves that matter to the reader's speculation. But he does offer guidelines. Here, too, the language is clearly Christian. The message is to be proclaimed in the Decapolis, that is, among the Greeks. This is only a hint, and to my mind it does not do to make this a full-scale affirmation of the Gentile mission, as Kelber has attempted to do.[80] There are too many details against it, most notably the urgent plea in v. 17 that Jesus leave. Still, this pericope does affirm the beginnings of Jesus' activity on Gentile soil, and does so in such a way that his authority over demons is established there as well. The reaction of the crowds is entirely understandable, but, from the point of view of the narrative and the reader, is also entirely without foundation.

Mark 5.21–43 – Jairus' daughter/The woman with the hemorrhage

The narrative strategies at work here are quite subtle. Commentators are fond of pointing out the similarities between the two stories – both involve females, the number twelve is repeated, both involve the touch of Jesus in effecting the cure, and both involve ritual impurity. There is a good deal of speculation about whether the interpolation is a Markan creation, but of course that is beside the point for our purposes. We are interested in the rhetorical strategies evident in the stories as we actually have them. Clearly the interpolation reflects a good deal of narrative skill. It creates a pause in the movement of the Jairus story, a pause during which the tension mounts perceptibly. It also suggests a relationship between the two stories which may lie deeper than the similarities between the woman and the girl. For one thing, the true foil for the woman is not the little girl, but her father Jairus. It is the woman's faith which "makes her well" in v. 34, just as it is Jairus who must "merely believe" (v. 36). Both Jairus and the woman fall at Jesus' feet, although the effect of that gesture is somewhat different in each case. The woman falls at Jesus' feet out of fear of repercussions for her unseemly act of having touched Jesus. Jairus falls at his feet at a way of expressing deference in a moment of extreme crisis. Yet the reader senses that Jairus – the ruler of the synagogue – must learn from the woman, must be prepared by the healing of the woman, for the raising of his daughter which follows. His request of Jesus in v. 23 is ironic in the sense that Jairus asks for more than he knows. The reader is presumably unaware of that irony until the story's climax. But there is good reason for that in Mark's overall narrative strategy. When these two stories are taken together they comprise the longest, most complex *Novelle* in the synoptic tradition. It is long, but it is not tedious. Rather, the painfully slow march toward Jairus' house, the interruption, the report of the servants that the girl has died in the interval, all combine to make this also one of the most suspenseful episodes in the tradition. The fact that the reader does not know the outcome makes him a participant in the suspense as well, prepares him, sets him up for the virtual realization of Jairus' ironic request:

> [23]   And he besought him,
>   saying
>   "My little daughter is at the point of death.
>   Come
>   and lay your hands on her
>   so that she may   be made well
>   and live."

All of this takes place in a context of deep turmoil. Whatever its historical accuracy, in the story the hubbub reinforces in the reader's consciousness a sense of the desperation Jairus must have felt. The arrival of the woman on the scene slows the progress of the crowd toward Jairus' house. In that way the suspense is considerably heightened. The disciples feel it. The dialogue is terse, blunt, almost accusing: "You see the crowd pressing around you, and yet you say, 'Who touched me?'" (v. 31). When Jesus appears to dawdle, the suspense becomes almost tangible.

Jairus' servants arrive. There is an urgent exchange. The story has by this time reached the level of frenzy. Jesus leaves the crowd behind and makes his way to Jairus' house. The hubbub changes quality in vv. 37f. The crowds on the way have − presumably − been left behind (is such a thing possible?), and their place has been taken by the mourners. Note the reversal in vv. 38–40a. The mourners wail and lament; then, with the word that Jesus pronounces in v. 39 − "The child is not dead, but sleeping" − instantly change to derision. Jesus' words here may perhaps be understood as a subtle peirastic irony. Of course the girl was "dead," the whole movement of the story depends upon it.[81] Jesus is not rejecting that notion, but rather is superimposing upon it a secondary – or, as Mark sees it, a new primary – frame of reference. Death is not final, not ultimate. The fact that Jesus puts the mourners out may well be symbolic, a parallel with 4.11f, but in the narrative it also serves a simple exclusionary tactic. Because of their disbelief they are prevented from viewing a miracle of immense significance. Here we encounter Mark's eschatological interpretation of the story at the point at which its personal implications are closest to the surface. For those who are outside (literally here, but also figuratively), everything is enigmatic. Jesus' words are true, but only for those who are on the inside, who have the insight to recognize, with the eye of faith, that the movements of the *eschaton* are embodied in the person of Jesus the Messiah.

Mark 6.1–6a – The rejection at Nazareth

I have indicated that this pericope is transitional, a bridge between the major section on Jesus' miraculous authority (4.35 – 6.6a) and the extensions of the blessings of salvation to the Gentiles (6.1 – 8.26). On this basis, we may say that it has two directions of reference. From the reader's perspective, the significant thing here is that the story consolidates the elements which precede. He cannot yet know that it anticipates what follows. The miracles will continue in the next section, and will continue to provoke the question with which the preceding section began: "Who then is this?" (cf. 6.14f, 49f; [7.37]; 8.27f.) But they will take on a new tenor. Hereafter they slow considerably, and will become the occasion for symbolic teaching. Jesus' movements become more pensive, and he appears more "self-protective." The sheer drama of the preceding miracles gives way to miracles interspersed with teaching.

It is the rejection of Nazareth which makes that transition possible. Here we are brought up short. It is no accident that this pericope should come just after the momentous and suspenseful events surrounding the raising of a dead girl. Jesus has stilled the storm with a word of rebuke, has faced death and banished it with a touch of his hand. The feverish pitch of the preceding narrative has produced in the reader a deep conviction about Jesus' miraculous power, and in that way has set him up for the unbelief evident here. In the face of that unbelief, Jesus is left impotent, unable to do "any mighty work." In the face of unbelief, Jesus' hands are tied. In the contrast with the raising of Jairus' daughter, the reader is left with the implicit conviction that unbelief is more deadly than death itself.

There are also a number of exegetically significant details. The fact that Jesus "marvels because of their unbelief" in 6.6 is a terrific twist in the story-line. Usually the crowds marvel because of his miracles. Taylor calls this "a realistic human touch" (p. 301), but surely it is more than that. For Mark the story functions as an aetiology which explains how and why Jesus' own people were unable to grasp the truth of the gospel: they were scandalized (v. 3), and for that reason Jesus was unable to produce corroborating miracles. He is scandalized in turn. This is astonishing for the reader as well. The reader's astonishment is built upon the preceding demonstrations of Jesus' miraculous power, and upon the reassurances given throughout the narrative that he is, in point of fact, the "Holy One of God," and "the Messiah." It is deepened here, however, by rhetorical elements implicit in the narrative itself. In particular, note the rhetorical questions in v. 2: "Where did this man get all this? What is this wisdom given him? What mighty works are wrought by his hands?" At first the questions appear positive; the reader does not suspect antagonism until that is made explicit in v. 3. Yet the questions, now understood to be antagonistic from the character's point of view, evoke a very different reaction in the reader. He knows where Jesus "got all this," and "what wisdom is given him." That silent reaction − evoked in the reader by these unanswered challenges − prepares him for the further challenge that Jesus is only a craftsman, a "τέκτων" (v. 3).

The issue of Jesus' background as a craftsman is a curious one, one which apparently troubled the Christian apologists.[82] There may be significant background in Sirach 38. 24 − 38. 11, in which the craftsman's skill is contrasted with that of the scribe. Note especially 38. 24 − 8:

> How can he get wisdom that holdeth the plow, and that glorieth in the goad, and driveth oxen, and whose talk is of bullocks? ... So (it is with) every carpenter (τέκτων) and workmaster (ἀρχιτέκτων) that laboreth night and day.

Yet the preceding verse points out the marvelous doings of Jesus' hands! The contrast between the scribe and the workman is therefore a deep one for Mark, one which runs in two directions, and which in its deepest significances implies the impotence of those who call Jesus' authority into serious question.

The blessings of salvation extended to the Gentiles
Subtheme: who is this man? Mark 6.1–8.30

With the rejection at Nazareth we are brought to a section which combines two apparently unrelated themes – the continued probing over Jesus' identity and the movement of the gospel to the Gentiles. There are further ironies interwoven through the narrative, but they are subtly woven into the woof and warp of Mark's narrative tapestry. As such, they are subordinated to other agendas.

We may begin by surveying the material dealing with the Gentile question. This is important, if only because it reflects conscious editorial activity on Mark's part. The section begins with Jesus' rejection at Nazareth in 6.1–6a. The reader will listen as the ominous implications of that rejection are repeated for the disciples in 6.1: "If any place will not receive you, shake off the dust of your feet as a testimony against them." He will follow Jesus on a tour of Tyre and Sidon – Gentile territory – in 7.24–30, and then, by an awkward, contrived route to the Decapolis (in 7.31); finally, he will attend the feeding of the 4,000, also apparently in the Decapolis (8.1–10).

The second theme is most evident in the eucharistic overtones in this last story. They are apparently significant for Mark, who prepares us for this symbolic act by touching lightly on the matter of table fellowship with Gentiles in Jesus' repartee with the Syrophoenician woman in 7.24–30, and rather heavily with Jesus' blunt denunciation of the authorities for the notions about defilement which inform their objections in 7.1–23.

This is a widely ranging concatenation of stories, but they are not so disparate as at first appears. All of them have to do with bread, and with defilement, and with the matter of Jewish legal piety. But they also have to do, implicitly, with the matter of Jesus' identity. Jesus' exchange with the disciples in 8.14–21 (and Mark's aside to the reader in 6.52!) will make that clear: there is something about the bread which represents a kind of key to these stories as a group, something having to do with Jesus' identity. This is no mere "hook-word" by which stories are organized and remembered. It is instead a cipher for something much deeper and more significant.

It is therefore the cipher in 8.14–21 which joins the first theme with the second. Rhetorically, the cipher focuses attention on the blindness of the disciples – indeed, of all the characters – about Jesus' true identity. The miraculous activity continues. The enthusiasm of the crowd mounts. But that enthusiasm is accompanied by speculation that Jesus may be John the Baptist *redivivus*, or one of the prophets. Again the reader's disposition is shaped and informed by elements within the framework of the story, elements hidden from the story's characters. It is in this context that we encounter the cipher about the bread. The reader's knowledge of the eucharist may be a key, especially if the element of breaking, of immolation, is conspicuous in his consciousness. Although the eucharist stands outside the narrative, I would argue that it is one of Mark's "assumed competencies," and would have significantly influenced the reader's perceptions. This is the stuff of irony. By drawing these stories into close proximity to one another, Mark deepens their resonances, and by relating them to a cipher, he suggests that they all, in one way or another, point beyond themselves to a deeper level of significance, a level of significance to which the characters inside the story are blind. There is a sense in which an ironic perspective permeates the narrative here, since the reader is invited to see beneath the surface of events to more primary significations. That difference of perspective creates incongruities, and those incongruities develop from time to time into full-scale ironies. In this discussion we shall largely confine our comments to these, recognizing that verbal ironies signal the presence of narrative ironies which are at once more widely distributed and more subtle.

Mark 6.1–6a – Jesus is rejected at Nazareth

We need not treat this pericope again in detail, but we must pause here to notice the forcefulness of the rejection motif which leads to the material which follows. Commentators are fond of pointing out the vivid detail in this story, the verbatim quotation from the townsmen, the astonishing admission that he "could do no mighty work there" in v. 5, and the equally astonishing remark that Jesus "marveled because of their unbelief" (v. 6). Yet there are also significant omissions. What role did the disciples play, we should like to know? What exactly did Jesus preach? How was his family disposed toward these developments? What were the "mighty works" to which the townsmen refer (in v. 2), if Jesus "could do no mighty work" (in v. 5)? We can hardly avoid the conclusion that this is a story rubbed bald of elaborating details. But that suggests the observation that the details, which are included, are there because they are important in some way. In turn, that observation is all the more striking because the story reiterates from a variety of directions the theme of rejection. There are the disparaging rhetorical questions in vv. 2f, the narrator's remark to the reader that they were "offended" − scandalized − at him in v. 3, and their disbelief in v. 6. Here the rejection of Jesus is nearly complete, and the significance of the rejection is given concrete expression: "A prophet is not without honor except in his own country and among his own kin, and in his own house!" (v. 4).

In this way the reader is prepared for Jesus' abandonment of Galilee for Gentile territory. This is a rejection which cuts both ways. But this is subtle. Jesus claims to be suffering rejection because he is functioning as a *prophet*, at the very least within the prophetic tradition. We have seen already that Jesus' prophetic identity is significant for Mark. Thus, when the Jews reject him, also in that act they reject the truest elements of their own tradition. It is not that they reject Jesus, so much as that they reject their own identity as Jews!

Mark 6. 14−29 − The death of John the Baptist

We may wonder why this story is included in Mark, and why it is included here. The story appears to have very little direct connection with Mark's wider narrative. There are no chronological links, and the story appears to be analeptic. It stands as a discrete whole, with a beginning, a complication, and a denouement. The characters are unfamiliar, and − except for Herod and the Baptist − they are not mentioned elsewhere in Mark. The language is somewhat more cultivated than is usual for Mark, and the story is therefore more ponderous. Walter Wink has expressed the sentiments of more than one interpreter: "What is really significant is ... the fact that this rambling, unedifying account of John's death is included at all."[83]

What, then, is it doing here? There are straightforward suggestions, which may each contribute to an adequate solution. Mortised here, the story creates a subtle chronological pause between the commissioning of the twelve (in 6. 7−13) and their return (in 6. 30). Mark introduces the story as an explanation of the speculations about Jesus' identity (vv. 14): people confused Jesus with John. There is a subtlety in this confusion which can easily escape notice. Jesus and John are in fact *Doppelgänger*,[84] not in their appearance, but in their fates. John, as Elijah, prepares the way for Jesus not only on the plane of the story, but also on the plane of the narrative. John is a foil for Jesus, and this brief narrative is a sub-plot which mirrors the main plot in synecdoche.

There are three ways in which this story may reflect the movements of irony. The first is in the designation of Herod as King. Mark repeatedly uses this term of Herod (vv. 14, 22, 25, 26, 27), but this is historically difficult. Herod was no king, but a tetrarch. Is Mark intending ridicule? Josephus (*Ant.* XVIII.vii.2) indicates that Herod was deposed by Caligula for monarchical pretensions. Mark provides no internal support for this possibility, and it may be instead that his reader will recognize the sarcasm without prompting. We cannot know for certain.

The second possible element of irony here has to do with the role of the Baptist *vis-à-vis* Herod. In comic irony the dissembler − the *"eiron"* − is pitted against the pretender − the *"alazon."* The two stand as foils, the *alazon* trumped up to be more than he really is, the *eiron* understated but powerful. So it is between John and Herod. The self-effacing character of the Baptist has been established already with reference to Jesus. He plays only a passive role in this story as well. His only spoken part is a retrojected condemnation of Herod's adulterous relationship with Herodias. Yet here the Baptist is a moral giant, and in contrast Herod is undone by the moral judgment of the reader. This is not comedy, of course, The subject matter is much too serious. But the dynamic movements of comic irony appear here in almost unmistakable form. It is a twist on an old theme, but even in its differences from comedy it is not without its parallels. (We need note in this regard only Socrates' dying charge to the citizens of Athens in Plato's *Apology*.)

The third form of irony here has to do with the tenor in which the story is told. Wink called this "rambling and unedifying," and that impression is exactly correct. What Wink does not note is that a horror story told in a rambling style is ironic in its impact on the reader. The primary ironies lie in the dissonance between the content of the story − which is horrifying − and the tenor of the story − which is understated and dispassionate. To my mind, the understatement here is the story's most outstanding feature. It is this tension between text and subtext which creates the story's underlying dynamic movement. It is this tension which establishes the backdrop of John's execution, in the process assassinating the character of Herod. The old king has been out-foxed, it appears. He executes John to save face, but in that act exposes his debauchery. The head on the platter is a burlesque of the feast. It is the king's own head, blood-splattered, ghastly, gagging on the monstrosity he has created. The actual details of John's execution may have been more horrible than Mark cares to write about. The story is gruesome enough as it stands, and the reader's reaction is deepened by the rambling, unedifying language in which it is told.

Mark 6.30−44 − The feeding of the five thousand

This is a long story, simply constructed. For our purposes there are three basic thrusts, which need only be mentioned before we hurry on. The first is the fact that the story is here embedded in the middle of a section about Gentiles. Clearly this is a paradigm of the messianic banquet.[85] It is an undeniably Jewish gesture, with overarching Jewish symbolism, in Jewish territory. Why is it here? We must look at the details. In the first place, the comment in v. 34 − "they were like sheep without a shepherd" − represents an implicit condemnation of the Jewish obligarchy. There may be an allusion to Ezekiel 34, in which false shepherds do not protect the sheep, they devour them. But the allusion need not be explicit. Verse 34 has the complexion of a folk-saying, which would have been generally meaningful without requiring intertextual competencies. In any case, the adequacy of the standing Jewish authority structure is implicitly called into question here.

In the second place, this story is a foil for the feeding of the 4,000 − this is Jewish and that Gentile[86] − and the second feeding derives a significant new dimension from the contrast between them. We may state this differently. The second feeding requires the preparation of the first feeding to make its peculiar kind of sense. Were this excised, the second feeding would lose a good deal of its underlying significances.

That leads us to our third concern, the presence of eucharistic language.[87] The parallels are very close between the feeding narratives and Mark's report of the Last Supper in 14.22:

[6.41]   And taking the five loaves
              and the two fish
         he looked up into heaven
              and blessed
              and broke   the loaves
              and gave them to the disciples
                  to set before the people.

```
[8.6]   And he took the seven loaves
             and having given thanks
                 he broke        them
                 and gave them to his disciples
                     to set before the people.
[14.22]  And as they were eating,
                 he took                 bread,
                 and blessed
                 and broke it,
                 and gave        it      to them.
```

All of this focuses the reader's attention on the bread. The similarities between the feeding stories and the Supper point to a deeper level of meaning, not immediately apparent on the surface of the narrative. Jesus' instruction in v. 36 carries a double significance: Jesus is the bread, and this is a command to mission. The response of the disciples is natural, but undiscerning: "Shall we go and buy 200 denarii worth of bread and give it to them to eat?" (v. 37). Mark here anticipates − by showing − what he later tells us directly: the disciples "did not understand about the loaves." We are once again confronted with the cipher in 6. 52.

In its context, the cipher makes clear the direct eschatological implications of these two feedings − the eucharist is the eschatological meal which unites in one Body those two warring factors in Christendom − the Jew and the Gentile.[88] In Mark, this is more an impression than a point, but it is an impression deepened by the Gospel's nuanced and suggestive language, its constant allusions, and its collocated arrangement of stories each of which in some way touch upon that question in their core clichés.

Mark 7.1−23 − Ceremonial and real defilement

The stories gathered together here call into serious question traditional conceptions of piety. It is this concern which has prompted the insertion of vv. 9−13, and therefore this conception which Mark takes to be central. The explanation of Jesus' denunciation of the Pharisees and scribes is given in v. 15, which is apparently enigmatic and in need of clarification. As often happens in Mark, the disciples are provided with a special explanation in vv. 17−23, in a manner which the reader can overhear. This private teaching is exclusionary. In these verses Jesus declares the rules of kosher a violation of the law, and in their place substitutes an internalized ethic which is remarkably like a famous passage on the evil *yetzer* in Qumran's Manual of Discipline (1 QS 3.13 – 4.26). The language is particularly subtle in vv. 20–3, a matter of an oscillating ambiguity between the physical and the spiritual possibilities for "what comes out of a man." We are ourselves so accustomed to seeing v. 15 in the light of vv. 20–3 that we miss the obviously crude impression it would at first have made upon the listener. There is little wonder that the crowds are confused.

The spiritualized explanation in vv. 20–3 ties the entire section together into a relatively coherent whole: "From within, out of the heart of a man, come evil thoughts, fornications, thefts," and so forth. The seat of such evils is the *heart*. In the Manual of Discipline, it is the heart which is the battle-ground of the spirits of Truth and Perversity. Mark's reader will remember that the scribes and Pharisees have just in the opening pericope been condemned for the alienation of their hearts (v. 6). This deepens that, and builds upon the reaction evoked already in the reader. It is a subtle narrative allusion, and its potencies may not have been consciously recognized by the reader. That it is potent nonetheless is important, if only because it deepens the reader's suspicions about the sort of piety represented here.

It is v. 6 which must command our closest attention. This language is unusually strong, even for Mark. By drawing the reference to Isaiah into the picture, Jesus indicates that the Pharisees and scribes have abandoned a true perspective on the law, and have in its place substituted a shallow, hypocritical posture. There may be an irony in the language here; perhaps "word-play" would be the more appropriate term. Jesus calls the authorities "hypocrites":

[6] Well did Isaiah prophesy of you hypocrites,
    As it is written,
      "This people honors me with their lips
      But their heart is far from me,
[7]   In vain do they worship me,
      Teaching as precepts the doctrines of men.
[8]   You   leave   the commandment of God,
      and hold fast the tradition   of men."

This is a new term in the Jewish religious vocabulary. Richard Batey has recently suggested that it derives from the introduction of theater into Jewish life, and that the actor was looked upon disparagingly from the stand-point of traditional Jewish piety.[89] Jesus turns that opinion back upon itself: "The use of ὑποκριτής in the Synoptics presents a rather consistent critique of religious leaders who like actors put on a performance for public adulation" (p. 564). The description of the scribes and Pharisees as hypocrites is therefore consistent with the quotation from Isaiah. This is piety which dresses up and plays a part. It is script, but not scripture, a masque of true piety. The cross-examination of Jesus about the behavior of his disciples in v. 5 is a mock-trial. What it reflects in intensity it lacks in conviction.

The second word-play here is in v. 9: "You have a fine way of rejecting the commandment of God, in order to keep your tradition!" That this is ironic was pointed out more than eighty years ago by E. W. Bullinger:

> Here the irony is beautifully brought out by translating καλῶς "full well." καλῶς means *with propriety, suitably, becomingly.* It suited the people to set aside the commandment of God, and make void the Word of God by their tradition. This exactly suited and corresponded to the action of those who washed the outside but were defiled within.[90]

Bullinger is right, but his point can be put more forcefully if we are permitted a few liberties. The reference to the propriety of setting aside the law would ring in the reader's ears like this: "How beautifully you do an ugly thing!" or perhaps, "You do illegality great justice!"

Mark 7.24–30 – The Syrophoenician woman

The core of the story is found in vv. 26–8:

[26] Now the woman was a Greek,
                             a Syrophoenician by birth
       And she begged him to cast the demon
                  out of her daughter.
[27] And he said to her,
              "Let the children first be fed;
       For it is not right to take the children's bread
                             and cast it to the dogs."
[28] But she answered him,
              "Yes, Lord;

yet   even the dogs
under the table
eat the children's crumbs."

The irony in this story is often misunderstood, and for that reason, v. 27 is taken as an undisguised indication that Jesus is racist, or in some way hesitant about including Gentiles in his mission. At best, he is ambivalent, and is here "speaking to Himself as well as the woman."[91] Lane's analysis is particularly undiscerning: the woman would not have understood the reference to Gentiles as "dogs." "The table is set and the family is gathered. It is inappropriate to interrupt the meal and allow the household dogs to carry off the children's bread." Thus the saying betrays personal reasons why Jesus is dismissing her request for help. He and his disciples were "at table," i.e. at rest, and it was for this reason only that they had come to the district (p. 262).

If this were the meaning of the saying, the first part of v. 27 would not make any sense: "Let the children first be fed." And clearly this is to discount the building significance of the section as a whole, each story of which in one way or another reaffirms the extension of salvation to the Gentiles. Mark would hardly have placed this story here if he understood its meaning as a banal assertion of Jesus' need of rest, or even as an assertion that her faith must be purified of superstition, as Lane goes on to say.[92] This comment represents a challenge as well to the notion that the saying is to be taken at face value. Mark could hardly have included it here if that were the case. Jesus' use of the diminutive, "house dogs" – κυνάρια – is often noticed, but that only softens and does not eliminate the severity of the saying. On the surface of it, this is a rejection of the woman's appeal because she is a Gentile.

The point of this discussion is that the saying is ironic. To read only what lies "on the surface of it" is to misread it. It is instead to be read as a bit of tongue-in-cheek. This is irony of a special kind. Clavier called it "ironie d'épreuve."[93] In English, it is peirastic irony. Peirastic irony – from πειράζειν – is a form of verbal challenge intended to test the other's response. It may in fact declare the opposite of the speaker's actual intention. An excellent example is to be found in Genesis 19. 2, in which the angels of the Lord test the seriousness of Lot's offer of hospitality by declaring the opposite of their true intentions: "No, we will spend the night in the street."

There are clues that that is exactly how Mark understands this saying. The first – and to my mind this would be sufficient in itself – is the location of the story here in this series of affirmations of the Gentile mission. The second is the wit evident in the construction of the saying itself. This involves several word-plays. The contrast between the "children" – surely a Jewish term – and the "dogs" – a Jewish epithet for Gentiles[94] – the introduction of the scene of a family at table, the use of the term "bread" (which for Mark's readers has by now become overcoded with eucharistic overtones), all combine to suggest just such a challenge, a riddle to be solved, a witticism requiring a wittier response.

The woman's answer is brilliant. It extends the metaphor by adding the element of crumbs, and by placing the dogs under the table. In the process, it overturns the implication of the first part of v. 27. Crumbs fall to the dogs, and do so intentionally. "If the dogs eat the crumbs under the table, they are fed *at the same time* as the children." In this remark Lane is absolutely correct (p. 263).

Mark 8. 1–10 – Four thousand are fed

It does not require stating that this story closely parallels the feeding of the 5,000 in 6. 30–44, and that there are significant differences between them. In particular, the disciples' question in 8. 4 poses a special difficulty: "How can one feed these men with bread here in the desert?" Jesus has, only two chapters before, fed more people with fewer provisions. Paul Achtemeier's view that the narratives preserve a reduplicated cycle of miracles may well be compelling from the point of view of source analysis,[95] but the literary critic will not find that very helpful. His concern must be with the explication of the narrative as it stands. And even the source critic must be cautious about dismissing the second feeding as a mere – mistaken – repetition of the first, as though the one were accurate, the other an imperfect copy. Robert Fowler is right: "If there are tensions and conflicts between the two narratives, as indeed there are, then the evangelist must bear full responsibility for them; they are there because he has put them there."[96]

Fowler's own treatment provides an appropriate point of departure. He goes on to describe the disciples' rather embarrassing question in 8. 4 as an example of Markan irony. This discussion, which represents a chapter of Fowler's doctoral dissertation, is a careful, step-by-step analysis of the process by which the reader is led to reject the literal meaning of the question in search of another, deeper, meaning. The difficulty of the literal meaning is created by the context in which the story is found, coming as it does so soon after the feeding of the 5,000 in Chapter 6:

> In the case of 8:4, the incongruity arises in the implication of the disciples' question that no one, at least no one *they* know, can feed such a crowd in the desert. The reader must reject this implication in the disciples' question because the reader remembers a prior occasion upon which Jesus fed a slightly larger crowd with slightly fewer provisions. (p. 94)

What is the point? Through the various steps of his analysis, Fowler is led to this conclusion:

> The true significance of the disciples' question is now evident. They condemn themselves with their own words by unwittingly admitting that they possess no awareness of what Jesus has done and can do. They are his disciples, but their lack of understanding hinders their sharing in any significant, lasting way his ministry. Even worse, they do not perceive that they are not equal partners in Jesus' ministry. Try as he might, Jesus seems unable to pierce their shell of incomprehension. All of this is skillfully communicated to the reader by the author's use of irony.   (pp. 95f)

But is this entirely adequate? Perhaps it is simply that Mark has used the disciples' question to *show* the reader exactly what the question implies, that the disciples had forgotten what had been plainly done before their eyes? In the form in which Fowler poses the problem, we are not dealing with obtuseness, but with forgetfulness. The disciples had forgotten what had happened in Chapter 6. True, that forgetfulness was the result of misunderstanding about what Jesus had done. But it implies more than that they simply failed to recognize the potencies of his ministry or their part within it. On the other hand, if we recognize that the two feedings *mean* something which the disciples cannot possibly have seen – either here or there – then the question in 8.4 is exactly the irony Fowler has said it is. But more. It is an irony which actually has a double content.

We can discover what those further implications are by recalling that the two stories together are heavily overcoded with details suggesting the extension of the eschatological meal to the Gentiles. The building tensions of the story-line have led in the same direction. The miracle of the second feeding takes place in Gentile territory,

and comes immediately after Jesus' *tête-à-tête* with the Syrophoenician woman over the question of the crumbs which fall from the
children's loaves. Of course the disciples cannot understand all that.
All the essential clues have been embedded in the story-line itself.
It is for this reason that they cannot understand the ironic nuances
of their question in 8.4. They cannot know that what has happened
in Jewish territory must now happen in Gentile territory as well.
In its context, the secondary meaning of their question is something
like this: "Is there enough of 'the bread' to go around?" Their term
"to satisfy" – χορτάσαι – may be instructive here. It suggests a
tertiary nuance in their response when Jesus asks how many "loaves"
there are: there are seven. Commentators often point out the Gentile
connotations of the number seven, and surely those stand as the
secondary meaning of the number here. But there is a tertiary meaning having to do with the implication that seven – the customary
Jewish number for denoting "fullness" – supplies the answer to
the question the disciples do not know they have asked: there surely
is "enough" of "the bread" to satisfy even the Gentiles. So the
exchange between Jesus and the disciples is a subtle irony, playing
the competencies of the reader off against the blindness of the
disciples. Fowler is right that those competencies have to do with the
fact that this narrative *follows* the feeding of the 5,000, but he has
not probed carefully enough the linguistic frames of reference which
have been created for the reader in the intervening material.

Mark 8.11–20 – The Pharisees seek a sign

There is a certain biting wit here which is only evident to the reader,
and only so when the pericope is held up alongside the demand that
Jesus perform a "sign" (v. 11). "Take heed," Jesus tells his disciples.
"Beware of the leaven of the Pharisees and of Herod" (v. 15). But
what exactly is the "leaven" of the Pharisees and of Herod? On the
surface of it, this is another witticism, a sharp barb. In the ancient
world, leaven is an universal metaphor for evil and corruptive influences.[97] The concern of the Pharisees for liturgical precision, and
the OT proscriptions against leaven in ritually prepared food (Ex.
12.18; 13.6f; Num. 28.16f), together give this warning its particularly
sharp bite. Yet this is no empty warning. Fowler points out that the
Pharisees and the Herodians have been malevolent factors since
3.6,[98] but it is not that which is in view here. Nor is it that Jesus is
warning the disciples against some particular moral evil on the part

of the Pharisees. It is an interesting tactic that he simply "gets in the
boat with the disciples" and leaves them standing there that way.
It is interesting, partly because it is itself a statement to them, a
symbolic gesture. It has something of the character of a sign, but
it is a sign of refusal.

Jesus' denunciation in v. 12 is particularly potent: "Why does
this generation seek a sign? Truly I say to you, no sign will be given
to this generation." The English of the RSV is quite inadequate,
perhaps because the Greek here is so difficult to render: "If this
generation *should* receive a sign ..." The point, however, is clear.
"Leaven" is habitual moral blindness, blindness which refuses to
see the workings of God unless they are plainly displayed. Jesus
refuses their demand, not because there are no signs to be given, but
because there have already been so many and they have refused to
see them. The denunciation in v. 12 is an apocopated curse formula,
cut off short, but not before it discloses tremendous underlying
stresses.

Those stresses finally burst forth in the saying to the disciples in
v. 14: "Beware of the leaven, the blindness, of the Pharisees." How
ironic it is that the disciples – possessors of the mystery of the
kingdom – should fail even to understand the warning against blindness! Jesus' astonishment is expressed in the explosive indignation
of his response in vv. 17–21:

[17]   Jesus said to them,
         "Why do you discuss the fact that
         you have no bread?
                  Do you not yet   perceive
                                     or understand?
                  Are your hearts hardened?
[18]   Having   eyes   do you not see?
         And having   ears   do you not hear?
         And   do you not remember?"

         ...

[21]   "Do you not yet understand?"

There have been "signs" given to this generation, but they are hidden,
mysterious. One must possess "understanding" to perceive them.
The failure of that understanding Jesus calls the "leaven" of the
Pharisees. It is that which is warned against. The failure of the
disciples even to understand the warning considerably sharpens the
irony here, and that moves the tensions and dissonances of the story

to another plane. We have come to the moment at which the blindness of the disciples is to be exposed on massive terms. As the narrative develops we shall discover that we have been prepared for the deepest irony in the book: Peter, as the representative of the disciples, will declare that Jesus is the Christ, and yet entirely misunderstand what that declaration means. There is one further stage in that preparation. In the story of the "twice-touched" blind man in 8.22–6, Mark will hint that the disciples, too, will have their momentary glimpse of the truth, but it will be sight, not insight, a flash, but not sustained illumination.

In summary: Mark 8.27–30 – Peter's confession

Thus far we have explored a widely ranging variety of verbal ironies in Mark, including witticisms, "peirastic" challenges, and expressions of outright sarcasm. These have been found not only in the dialogue, but such turns of phrase have also been found embedded in the narration *as such*. Alongside these verbal twists and complications, Mark has placed a standard body of "reliable commentary" – the disclosures in the prologue, narrator's asides, inside views, explanatory clauses, exclusionary strategies. All of this orchestrates the responses of an audience which brings to the narrative particular kinds of competencies and particular vested interests. It is in the nuanced interplay of those competencies and that reliable commentary that the ironies in Mark gain their clarity and power.

Since the very beginning the reader has known what the characters in the story have not. With this pericope, the disciples broach that knowledge, and for the moment their insight in a limited way merges with that of the story's reader. "You are the Christ," Peter tells Jesus in 8.29. But the reader has known that from the very first verse. He has also almost certainly known that the story will end in Jesus' passion. That knowledge has been part of the enabling frame of reference which has permitted him to see beneath the story's surface to the deeper significances lying embedded there. Jesus, the Christ, must be given over to the hands of men and be killed.

It is strange and significant that the necessity for Jesus' death has never yet become a matter of Mark's sustained focus. Peter does not yet see it, and neither does the reader. Jesus *will* die. That the reader knows. But does he understand that this death is *necessary*, that it is itself messianic? Perhaps it is that the reader, like the disciples, is being set up for a dramatic reversal which is fully potent only in the figure of the immolated victim on the cross. As he reads further he will discover that impaled on the cross along with Jesus are all the fondest aspirations he might attach to the figure of a Messiah who is also Son of God and Vanquisher of Demons (and perhaps Romans, too!). When that Messiah has met his end, Mark's readers will be left with a messiah who makes his début in ordinary dress. Here the ironic dimensions of the narrative will reach their deepest reverberations: "The rule of God overturns all worldly expectations; the most important are the least; those losing their lives are saving them; and the king rules from a cross." [99] That is to say, it is in his person itself, in all his ignominy and suffering, that Jesus' messianic power and dignity are given their most potent expression. But that insight is true only "for those who have ears to hear," for those "who have been given the secret of the Kingdom of God." For everyone else – unyielding reader included – everything about Jesus is in riddles.

Discipleship training   Mark 8.22 – 10.52

It is generally agreed among commentators that 8.27–30 represents a major turning-point in Mark's narrative. With Peter's confession the narrative takes on an entirely different complexion. Hereafter the focus is on suffering, on the necessity of the passion, on the significance of the passion for Jesus' disciples, and upon the details of the passion itself. It is an interesting phenomenon that the next major section on teaching – and on teaching about the demands of discipleship – should be bracketed on either side by stories about blind men, and that Jesus' disciples should continue in their blindness. For here the disclosures of Jesus' identity will become explicit, and the eschatological allusions which opened the first half of the book will have their parallels in the story of the transfiguration story which comes at the opening of the second half. This time, however, they come in such a way that the *disciples* can see them. The identity of John the Baptist as harbinger of the Messiah will be repeated, too, this time also for the disciples. The voice will speak again from the cloud, and the thundering affirmation of Jesus' "Sonship" will be addressed – for the first time – to the disciples. Very much of what has preceded has prepared for this. It is significant that what the characters from their various vantage-points have taken in only piecemeal the reader has overheard or been told in its entirety. In this major section it comes to the surface of the narrative, comes to be driven home with increasing clarity and force, not only for the story's characters, but also for the reader. The reader overhears the clear disclosures and reacts to the deepening blindness of the disciples.

It is for this reason significant that at the precise moment of Peter's confession the blindness of the disciples becomes explicit. They now know that Jesus is the Christ. They do *not* know what that title will require of him, or what it will require of them. If this is the pivotal transition in the narrative, and this the pivotal confession, it is also the narrative's supreme irony. Peter's confession is accurate only in its vocabulary. The political implications with which it is loaded run in entirely the wrong directions, and the reader is forced to a crisis of loyalties which mirrors that of the disciples. Against the backdrop of the passion prediction, Peter's confession is extremely difficult. It signals to the reader the blind irony of his confession. As Peter intends it, the confession − "You are the Christ" − is a shadow of the truth. He is dazzled by visions of splendor, apparently, is blinded by a flash of false light. Against the backdrop of Peter's confusion, the realization that Jesus "must suffer and die" is true light, but it is searing, excruciating in its intensity.

So there is rhetorical tension here. That tension is deepened by a number of ironic movements. One would expect that the momentary identity of knowledge would lead to a common point of view, and that that would eliminate the ironies in the section. In fact, there are fewer of them, but the ones which are here are somewhat more pointed. The disciples continue to blurt out *double entendres*, but now the *double entendres* are ironies which they *should* have known. The judgment of the reader becomes sharper. The continued blindness of the disciples which emerges as the dominant motif of the section has its implied counterpart: the reader's knowledge about Jesus becomes crystal clear.

Mark 8.31; 9.31; 10.33−4 − The passion predictions

For the sake of economy, we shall treat the predictions of the passion together, but, as we do, we should note the rhetorical effect of having Jesus tell his disciples three separate times that he must go to Jerusalem to die. The verbal parallels between the three predictions are very close, and they appear to be reiterated in the vocabulary by which their fulfilment is described. Why, then, the repetition? Does that not introduce redundancy into the narrative? Like other ancient writers, Mark is fond of reiteration as a strategy for emphasizing this or that narrative element. Why? It is one way of orchestrating the reader's reactions.

How that stress works requires a momentary reflection on the dynamic functions of reading aloud, as opposed to reading silently. When one reads aloud, especially when one reads aloud to another person or to a congregation, there is no opportunity to pause for explanations of the various narrative elements. Explanations of that sort − to which we are ourselves quite accustomed − are in fact intrusive. They halt the flow of the narrative and introduce foreign elements. When one reads aloud, however, he can interpret through modulations in the volume or the texture of his voice, and through the introduction of pauses. It is the pauses which interest us here. When the reader is silent, the element of expectancy may become especially pregnant, and the listener may be drawn in more closely. The silence is a challenge − "Listen closely!" But such silences are extremely fragile. They must not be too long, and they must not be disrupted by external interruptions. Thus, whatever else he does, the narrator must keep going, must maintain the flow of his narrative lest the interest of the audience wander and die. Reiteration is a way of overcoming this basic liability of oral recitation. By means of reiteration, a story-teller can introduce and then reinforce elements which otherwise might escape the listener's notice. Reiteration also creates a certain cadence in narrative, and with the cadence a sense of building excitement, and even of the inevitability of the story's outcome.

So it is here. The three predictions of the passion build in precision, and each reinforces the potencies of those which have preceded. With that reiteration, Mark creates in the reader's consciousness exactly what he has said of the predictions themselves: Jesus "said this plainly" (8.32). The plainer are the predictions, the more difficult and obtuse appear the disciples. The reader becomes more and more horrified, not that Jesus must go to Jerusalem and die, but that his disciples were blind to that fact. That is, the reiteration of the passion prediction establishes a kind of narrative foil for the repeated bumblings of the disciples. In their blindness they continue to blurt out ironies which in their own ways reinforce the reactions of the reader. We shall deal with the ironies which follow the first and last of the predictions.

Mark 8.31–9.1 – Peter's rebuke/If any man would come after me ...

In this passage, the narrator does not actually report Peter's words. But the fact that Peter would *rebuke* Jesus is significant. Lane is right: the disciples were totally unprepared to receive what was for them a radical idea: "A rejected Messiah was incompatible with Jewish convictions and hopes" (p. 304). This language is extremely strong. Elsewhere, the term for rebuke, ἐπιτιμᾶν is the technical language of exorcism. Here it would probably mean "to scold," except that Jesus introduces the imagery of Satan in his own "rebuke" of Peter in v. 33. Thus we have an irony: Peter has scolded Jesus, has rejected Jesus' peculiar brand of messianism, but in that way has aligned himself over against "the very plan of God." Ethelbert Stauffer has pointed out a literary parallel to exactly this notion in Gen. Rabbah 56, on 22.7, in which Satan "rebukes" Abraham in an attempt to dissuade him from following through on his plan to sacrifice Isaac.[100] It may be that there is an historically closer parallel in 1 QS 3.13 – 4.26, in which the writer of the Manual of Discipline tells us that a man's evil promptings come from Satan, from the "Angel of Darkness."[101] In our passage, too, Peter's well-meaning but desperate attempt to turn Jesus from this course of action aligns him, not with God, and not merely with men, but with Satan himself. Thus, he, too, must be rebuked in turn (v. 33).

Peter's rebuke of Jesus provides occasion for the further teaching on self-denial which follows in 8.34 – 9.1. These verses are necessitated by Peter's failure to comprehend the meaning of Jesus' prediction of his own self-denial. It is common to hear in these words the clearest teaching in the Gospel about the necessity of suffering as a consequence and condition of discipleship, and they surely are that. But they also clarify and interpret Jesus' prediction of his own death. From that stand-point, they have a self-reflective quality. They address the speaker as well as the hearer. What attentive listener can fail to hear the pathos in these words, coming so soon after Jesus has declared his intention to go to Jerusalem and die?

[34]   If any man would come after me
    let him   deny himself
           and take up his cross
           and follow me

[35] for   whoever would save his life
             will lose it;
          and whoever loses his life
                       for my sake
                       and the gospel's
             will save it.
[36] For what does it profit a man,
             to   gain   the whole world
             and forfeit   his life?
[37] For what can a man give
             in return for his life?

   Technically, the double significance of this declaration is ironic in
that it means something for Jesus which is hidden from the listeners.
The disciples *should* know, but do not. The crowds simply cannot
know. The fact that they are called together for the first time in
v. 34 indicates by an exclusionary strategy that they have heard
nothing of the passion prediction. Usually in Greek tragic literature,
irony on the lips of the protagonist as he marches toward his doom
evokes a deepening sense of horror in the listener. We can see that
movement with special clarity in the reiterated verbal ironies in
Sophocles' *Oedipus the King*, or in Euripides' *Alcestis*. Here, however, the horror is mitigated by an almost tangible sense of the pathos
of the words, the crying out of Jesus' depths. In the prediction of
the passion he has indicated that his approaching death is "necessary."
Here, he ponders death by martyrdom as a matter of active decision.
It is a decision that he himself has had to make, a new temptation
with which Mark begins the second half of the book. That pondering
is masked by the direct address to the disciples and the crowds, and
by the generalizing "if any man" in v. 34. And yet, in terms of its
rhetorical import, the subtle probing of this catena of sayings has
the effect of a soliloquy. To my mind, the pathos here rivals that of
Hamlet's famous "To be or not to be?" or Shylock's eloquent
defence, "Am I not a man? Cut me, will I not bleed?"

Mark 10.32—45 — The third passion prediction/ Precedence among the disciples

The irony in this story is quite close to the surface of the narrative,
a kind of "comedy of errors" on the part of James and John. Two
considerations prevent the story from being debased to the level of

the merely comical, however. First, there is the seriousness of the topic. When James and John ask to sit on Jesus' right hand and on his left "in his glory" (v. 37), they do not know that they are asking for martyrdom. Jesus makes that clear in his response in v. 38 – "You do not know what you are asking" – and in his prediction that they will, in fact, receive the object of their unknowing request. If it is a sobering prediction, it is also one which prevents us from seeing only humor here. Secondly, Jesus' response and the ensuing discussion of servant-hood (in vv. 42) become the basis for a clear paradigm for all disciples, and that paradigm is related directly to the rather ponderous ballast line with which the pericope closes: the reason the disciples must serve one another is that "the Son of Man also came not to be served, but to serve, and to give his life as a ransom for many."

Yet this exchange actually plays upon a series of *double entendres*, all of which are misunderstood by James and John, and correctly understood by the reader. To borrow Robert Fowler's term, Jesus is here winking off-stage at the reader. We may begin with their request:

[37] "Grant us to sit
       one at your right hand
       and one at your left
       in your glory."

Verse 38 indicates to the reader that their question is ironic. What they ought to understand, but cannot, is that for Jesus (and the narrator of the story) Jesus' "glory" is his crucifixion. Their question therefore has a secondary significance they cannot have intended: "You do not know what you are asking," Jesus tells them in v. 38. The image in their minds is almost certainly political, and if so, it foreshadows the much deeper ironies of the soldiers' mockery in Chapter 15. That is, just as the soldiers will mistakenly satirize Jesus for his political aspirations, so James and John here mistakenly express in political terms their own aspirations of "glory." That they are unknowingly referring to the crosses which will stand on either side of Jesus' own is telegraphed to the reader in v. 40: "To sit at my right hand or at my left is not mine to grant, but it is for those for whom it has been prepared." We shall later find exactly this language in the descriptions of the brigands in 15. 29:

[10.37] "Grant us to sit
         one at your right hand
         and one at your left
         in your glory."

[15.29] And with him they crucified two robbers,
    one on his right hand
    and one on his left.

It is obvious that they do not, that they cannot, recognize the allusion. What the reader would have recognized may ultimately be difficult to determine. Nowhere else in the narrative has Mark referred to the crucifixion as Jesus' "glory." Would the reader have brought intertextual competencies to bear? We cannot know for certain. If the reader knows — as is almost certain — that at his death Jesus is to be paraded out as a brutal illustration of Roman tyranny, the irony of their request is driven a level deeper: they have unwittingly asked to take the places of the "brigands" on the crosses on either side of him. The play upon their political aspirations here becomes almost explicit. Jesus, of course, is aware of the irony, and he counters with an ironic question in v. 38:

"You do not know what you are asking.
Are you able to drink the cup
    that I drink,
or to be baptized with the baptism
    with which I am baptized?"

By now, the reader is clear that the question about the cup is a reference to Jesus' coming death, and that clarity will be reinforced when we later find him in prayer in the garden of Gethsemane. "Abba, father," he will pray, "Remove this cup from me; yet not what I will, but what thou wilt" (14.36; see also 14.23). That is still ahead for the reader, but the ominous associations of the term "cup" would be clear from the various intertextual frames of reference he will bring with him to the reading (cf. e.g., Ps. 11.6: Hab. 2.6). James and John, however, miss the point entirely. Instead, they readily, even hastily, agree that they are "able to drink the cup."

What must they have had in view? There are apparently two options. The first is suggested from time to time in the literature: the cup and the baptism need only have meant a reference to the general turmoils and dangers[102] of the coming revolution, perhaps of the eschatological woes. The second is more attractive: the cup at least is a reference to the station of "cup-bearer" and thus of wine-taster at the King's table. We have references to wine-tasters in the ancient world (cf. Xenophon, *Xeiropaidia*, LCL, vol. 1, pp. 34f); the practice was apparently common enough that it would have been clear to the disciples – and to the reader – without further prompting.

The first movement of this pericope creates the occasion for the second, in which Jesus makes explicit the significance of his death as a paradigm of leadership among the disciples (vv. 41–5). There is nothing ironic about the second movement. It is straightforward and clear, like the three passion predictions. Yet in this place it clarifies and drives forward the ironic implications of the first movement: in clamoring after power, the disciples abandon the very program by which this particular messianism will succeed. One is, after all – and truly – called to a discipleship of sacrifice. Jesus has tried to warn them of this before, in 8.34–9.1, and in 9.33–7. In their clamoring after the seats "on the right hand and on the left" – ironic references to the crucifixion – they are, again unwittingly, asking for exactly that which is pivotal to the role of disciple. The ominous threat in v. 39 – "The cup that I drink you will drink, and with the baptism with which I am baptized you will be baptized" – is not a threat, after all. At bottom it is a promise which seats James and John close to the truest "glory" of all.

Mark 10.46–52 – The healing of blind Bartimaeus

With this story we are brought to the very outskirts of Jerusalem, and therefore to the end of the journey which has filled the better part of the past three chapters. The language has grown ponderous, and has been punctuated by the three great predictions of the passion. The blindness of the disciples has been marked out for special emphasis. With every step they have grown more deeply confused, and their growing resistance to the unfolding eventualities of the plot has provided a literary contrast to Jesus' own clarity and his deepening resolve. Jesus knows – and they suspect – that this is his death march, stepped off to ominous cadences. For three chapters now the narrative has had all the hollow vigor of a dirge.

The story of the healing of blind Bartimaeus changes all that. Here there are multitudes once again, or, as Mark says in v. 46 "a worthy crowd." We are not told the disposition of the crowd, but we have the impression from their attempt to silence Bartimaeus that they will not tolerate anything that impedes Jesus on his journey. The impression of enthusiasm is a clear one, and will be deepened in the report of the triumphal entry in the next pericope. Here the focus is on the dialogue, and almost all other descriptive elements are subordinated to that. Yet even the dialogue deepens the sense of hubbub. There is a kind of antiphonal chant, the crowd taking the part of the chorus, Bartimaeus responding with the recitative.

> "Jesus, Son of David,
> have mercy on me!"
>
> > "Be silent!"
>
> "Son of David,
> have mercy on me!"
>
> > "Call him."
> > "Take heart,
> > he is calling you."
> > "What do you want me
> > to do for you?"
>
> "Master,
> let me receive my sight."
>
> > "Go your way,
> > your faith has
> > made you well."

Note the effect of the counterpoint here — the demand, the resistance, the demand again, the stopping, the questioning, the repeated demand. These together build into the story a sense of urgency and expectancy which is a critical element of its rhetorical power.

It is in the declaration that Jesus is "Son of David" that the ironic dimension of the story is found. We have noted already in Chapter 1 Howard Kee's brief treatment of that irony. Kee's treatment is brief enough that it can be quoted in its entirety:

> Even the detailed attempt to clarify the difference between the rout of power by which the nations exercise authority and the route of service and acceptance of suffering that Jesus and his followers must follow does not penetrate to the disciples. How the roles of Son of Man and Son of God (King) fit together eludes them. Ironically, there is one man who can discern who Jesus is: the blind Bar-Timaeus, who calls out to Jesus for help as he is passing through Jericho (10:46–52). Addressing Jesus as Son of David, Bar-Timaeus not only affirms Jesus' role as king, but by associating Messiah and Son of David with restoration of sight, implicitly recalls that in the eschatological kingdom the eyes of the blind will be opened (Isa. 35:5; 42:7; 42:16; 43:8), that this

promise is given to the city of David (Isa. 29:1, 18), and specifically that the power to open blind eyes is assigned to the Anointed (in Septuagint, *christos*) of Yahweh (Isa. 61:1). In sharp contrast to the imperceptive disciples, the blind beggar is able to see clearly who Jesus is.[103]

There is scholarly speculation about the genre of this story. Sometimes it is pointed out that its form is closer to that of a call narrative than to that of a healing *per se*.[104] If that is so, the story represents a fitting conclusion to Mark's major section on discipleship and on the blindness of the twelve. At the same time, the frames of reference built up by the preceding march to Jerusalem suggest a deeper symbolism beneath the surface of an irony about a blind man who discerns who Jesus is. The Messiah brings not only sight but insight, insight which expresses its clarity in terms of willingness to "take up one's cross and follow" Jesus, even in the teeth of what on the surface appears to be ultimate catastrophe.

Judgment on Jerusalem   Mark 11.1 – 13.37

With the triumphal entry Jesus' story reaches the place of its own catastrophe. In the previous section, the overburdening possibilities of catastrophe were a central unifying factor. Along with that central concern we saw a second: the blindness of the disciples. Here in the final chapters there will again be two emphases, not one. In the passion proper (Chapters 14–15) the authorities will denounce Jesus, and we shall see him abused and finally executed. That movement against Jesus is anticipated by a section of events which move in exactly the opposite direction (Chapters 11–13). If, as Quesnell has correctly indicated, Mark is "clustering" stories by theme, it is clear that the theme of this section is judgment against Jerusalem, and thus against the official Judaism which resides there. We have encountered this notion already in the early affirmations of the wilderness in which John's call to repentance was first given expression: Jerusalem, the symbolic center toward which the plot moves, will ultimately prove to be exactly that place which rejects the eschatological figure who is the subject of John's heraldry.

Here, what was implicit in the narrative affirmation of the wilderness becomes explicit in the concatenation of stories which all deal in one way or another with the final reassertion of Jesus' authority, and with the judgment he wields against what is clearly a corrupt and corrupting influence in the city itself. But there is more: with the judgment leveled against the institutions of official Judaism, Jesus will take to himself the prerogatives of authority which they represent. Donald Juel has argued, for example, that the testimony of the witnesses at the trial is "false testimony," yet ironically true: Jesus will destroy this temple and build another, "not made with hands."[105] In the same vein, T. A. Burkill has argued that the blasphemy of which Jesus is accused at the trial is itself – I add "ironically" – an act of "shamelessly willful *blasphemia.*"[106]

This is a section of dramatic reversals: the conquering Messiah will storm Jerusalem on a colt, his army a mob of pilgrims armed with palm-fronds, their battle-cry an ancient hallal which is overcoded with implications they cannot understand. The cleansing of the temple will draw its economy to a dramatic close. The official "representatives of God" will behave diabolically. "The stone which the builders rejected" will become the "head of the corner." The trial will run in two directions, and Jesus will be vindicated at the moment of his condemnation. The burlesque of a coronation which the soldiers will perform will be, in fact, exactly the right counter-point for Jesus' declaration that the Messiah–King must go to Jerusalem to die.

The point of this recitation is that the overwhelming reversal of meaning which transforms the narrative's central elements is ironic in its fundamental operations. They mean something for the reader which is impossible for the characters even to perceive, much less understand. We ought to have expected some such development, given the rhetorical strategies which have been operative in the narrative thus far. Since the very first the reader has known more than the characters, and has understood the ongoing events of the narrative from a significantly different vantage-point. The result has been the deepening of the rift between the two points of view until they have come to hold almost diametrically opposed interpretations. In the language of Chapter 4, the reader's background has been carefully prepared by the competencies which the first half of the book have generated in his consciousness. If for no other reason than that, the narrative has taken on an inherently ironic understructure.

But Mark has not been content with resting the ironic reversals of the final chapters on the reader's prior preparation. Instead, he has consciously drawn into the picture additional clues which increase the distance between the reader and the characters. These additional clues are of three kinds. First, perhaps most obviously, these final chapters are heavily embedded with allusions to scripture and to extra-canonical traditions. Proper reading must therefore be informed by extensive intertextual competencies. With reference to those allusions, the elements of the story-line will appear heavily overcoded, and that overcoding will deepen the story's ironic significances. My teacher, Howard Kee, has examined over 160 occurrences of direct quotation, allusion, and tertiary influences in Mark 11–16.[107] Kee's observation that Mark is synthesizing texts in the course of his allusions is important (pp. 176–9). It suggests the deliberate transformation of existing literary traditions under the influence of the structures and substructures of the events Mark records. But this element of trans-formation is not unilateral. By overcoding his stories of the passion with allusive language, Mark summons to the reader's consciousness existing frames of reference, frames which shape his interpretations of the events as they unfold. We have seen this technique before; here we shall see it used more often and with greater clarity.

A second source of overcoding will also have influenced the reader: his own experience of suffering and catastrophe will find particularly deep resonances here, especially in the Olivet Discourse in Chapter 13. That discourse appears on Jesus' lips in the form of a prophecy, but it is a prophecy with a cipher (13.14) which may now be lost. Even so, we can with fair certainty guess without the cipher that the dis-course would have had special dimensions of significance for Mark's community. Kee has pointed out already that the presence of a cipher generates and deepens the reader's sense of belonging to an elect group, a group marked out in part by its possession of esoteric wisdom:

> Only those to whom the "mystery" has been given – i.e. by God – are able to perceive what is taking place (4.11). When the final violent acts of the evil powers (13.14) take place just prior to the end (13.13), it is only the divinely enlightened "reader" who will be able to understand.[108]   (13.14)

This sense of participation in an elect group may be critical factor in the group's very survival, especially in contexts of severe external challenge. As Kee has shown, the content of Mark's work has rein-forced in several ways the sense that the "wisdom" or "mystery" of God is reserved for an elect group, the community for which the Gospel was composed (pp. 93–6). This observation complements that one: Mark's rhetorical strategies and the texture of his language *effect* in the reader's mind exactly the inclusive sense of special revelation he describes as the promise made to the disciples. The Gospel's form is congruent with its content.

The presence of overcoded language may be coupled with Mark's careful arrangement of the material to suggest a third factor. This third clue increases the distance between the reader and the story's characters: it will be clear to the reader that Jesus' actions are symbolic. This is particularly true of the events in Chapters 11. The triumphal entry will be so clearly a symbolic act that it will effect what T. A. Burkill once called a "Strain on the Secret."[109] In a similar vein, the intercalated relationship between the cursing of the fig tree (11. 12–14; 20f) and the cleansing of the temple (vv. 15–19) will suggest much more deeply embedded significances than acts of mere anger or brutality.[110] It is important to note that, as *acts*, these two elements are fully observable to the characters inside the story. The crowds will wildly endorse Jesus' actions, but they are not properly prepared to grasp their inner significances, and their enthusiasm itself will betray the fact that they have misunderstood. In Chapter 14, an unnamed woman will symbolically anoint Jesus for burial (vv. 3–9). The extravagance of that anointing will apparently provoke Judas' act of betrayal (vv. 10f), an indication that he at least is blind to the deeper significances Jesus indicates are resident in the act itself.

We raise the matter here because it requires a refinement in the scope of the material we now must cover. We have seen that the narrative has become by this time inherently ironic. We have also seen that Mark will deepen that inherent ironic tendency by heavily overcoding his stories with allusive language. We have seen further that, by careful stage-management, he will suggest that Jesus' activities are symbolic in some way, and that that symbolism will be largely lost on the story's characters. These three factors together pose a special dilemma of explication: the dramatic irony here is now thoroughgoing. Hereafter, any fully adequate treatment would have to be encyclopedic in its scope. Our space and resources are more limited. We shall instead focus on representative details, and will leave for another time the full-scale discussion the ironies in these chapters require.

Mark 11. 1–10 – The triumphal entry

The obvious messianic overtones of this pericope hardly require rehearsal.[111] The reference to the Mount of Olives serves as more than a mere geographical note, it suggests clear eschatological associations (cf. Zech. 14. 4 [also Josephus, *Ant.* xx. 169–72; *War,* 11. 261 – 3]). The colt may bear messianic significances (NB. Zech. 9. 9; possibly also Gen. 49. 11); and the homage represented by the strewn garments recalls the popular acclamation of Jehu in 2 Kings 9. 13. The designation of Jesus as "He who Comes in the Name of the Lord" in v. 9 – on the surface of it drawn from an antiphonally recited pilgrims' hallel in Psalm 118 – had come in Judaism to have messianic overtones.[112] The designation of Jesus as "Son of David" (11. 10) appears to have been carried over from the cry of blind Bartimaeus in 10. 47f.

It is the acclamation of the crowds which must command our closest attention:

[9] "Hosanna!"
"Blessed is the 'Coming One' in the name of the Lord."
[10] "Blessed is the 'Coming Kingdom' of our father David."
"Hosanna in the highest."

I have here purposely rendered the technical designation "He Who Cometh" – ὁ ἐρχόμενος – in a wooden fashion to facilitate comparison with the reference to "The Coming Kingdom" – ἡ ἐρχομένη βασιλεία – with which it is parallel. In Greek these two final verses form rather a tidy chiasm. They appear in that way to have a certain formal structure which reinforces the impression of an acclamation. The first half of the chiasm is drawn primarily from Psalm 118. 26, where it appears to have served as a priestly blessing pronounced in the course of an antiphonal, liturgical recitation. Here, however, it is balanced against an interpretative couplet. "Blessed is He who Comes in the Name of the Lord" is reinterpreted to form a clear proclamation that in "The Coming One" lies the hope of the restored Davidic Kingdom.

But the crowds have no way of knowing the deep significances of what they are proclaiming. William Lane has pointed out their failure of insight: "Despite the enthusiasm of their homage, there is no awareness on the part of the people that the time of fulfilment has actually arrived and that the Kingdom has actually drawn near in the person of Jesus himself."[113]

Lane is only partially correct. The crowds see in Jesus the figure of David, now entering the city in a clearly messianic gesture. What they do not understand is that "The kingdom of our father David which is coming" will arrive in its greatest potency when the pretender to its throne will be anointed with spittle and crowned with thorns and enthroned on a cross to die. It is an irony which borders on the paradoxical. In the sense in which we find it here, the acclamation of the crowds is a kind of counter-point to the mockery of the soldiers. Either one is a parody of the truth. But they are so in different ways, and to different rhetorical effect.

We might secure this irony in another way. The events of the next few pericopae are clear judgments against official Judaism and the ongoing institutional operations of the temple. Would the crowds have hailed Jesus King if they had known the end toward which the story is now leading? Hardly. They are fundamentally blind to the greater drama in which they play the parts of bit-players.

We have said that the irony of the acclamation here is a kind of counter-point to the mockery of the soldiers. Before we leave this discussion we might pause and *contrast* those two events as a way of probing their rhetorical significances. Here we may take guidance from Gilbert Bilezekian's suggestion that the triumphal entry functions much like the dramatic *hyporcheme*:

> The *hyporcheme* was a well-known dramatic convention practiced especially by Sophocles. It consisted of a joyful scene that involves the chorus and sometimes other characters; takes the form of a dance, procession, or lyrics expressing confidence and happiness; and occurs just before the catastrophic climax of the play. The hyporcheme emphasizes, by way of contrast, the crushing impact of the tragic incident. (p. 127)

There is reason for caution. It may be that in his eagerness to correlate Mark with Greek tragedy, Bilezekian has overlooked rhetorical and literary parallels which are nearer to hand. Nevertheless, he has provided us with a comparative vantage-point from which to clarify the role of the triumphal entry in Mark's overarching strategy: the hosannas, the waving palm-branches, the crowds, the procession itself, together provide a moment of dramatic relief, in which are momentarily suspended the tensions building within the reader's consciousness. In this way, the catastrophes which follow – especially the mockery of the soldiers – are deepened in their calculating savagery.

The passion Mark 14. 41 – 15. 47

With the discussion of the triumphal entry as possible *hyporcheme*, we are brought naturally to the ironies of the trial and crucifixion. In our exploration of Mark's rhetorical strategies, we have discovered a deeply seated sense of inclusion in an esoteric secret, something shielded from those outside. That sense is here deepened to the level of a paradoxical theological affirmation. For Mark, it is theologically and ironically fitting that the Messiah should be rejected in just this way by the ranking officials of Judaism, should be subjected to just this sort of mock coronation, should die in just this fashion at the hands of Roman soldiers, with real brigands on either side. As a scenario it is the perfect burlesque of the truth it caricatures. Mark is not the only one to discover in the passion an ironic parody of theological truth. We have noted already the presence of irony in John's report of Caiaphas' unknowing prophecy in 11.50: "It is well for one man to die on behalf of the people." But John has developed that irony into an extraordinarily rich treatment of the passion itself. In that, his strategies parallel Mark's, but they are closer to the surface, and thus more easily discerned. With Mark, the ironies are equally pervasive, but more subtle. The trial, the mockery, and the crucifixion are riddled with irony. The ironies play upon the shifting significances of the events as *events*, and thus they are dramatic and not merely verbal: that is, they are embedded in the framework of the narrative itself. We might have guessed as much from the heavy preparation the reader has experienced, but Mark has not left us without further clues. In the discussions which follow we shall take as our starting points the verbal ironies, the sarcasms, and unwitting challenges which are found on the lips of the narrative's characters.

Mark 14. 53–72 – Peter's denial/The trial of Jesus

We shall treat these two pericopae together, since they are intercalated in Mark. The chapter begins with Jesus' prophecy to Peter: "Before the cock crows twice you will deny me three times" (14.30). Peter's reply has overtones he cannot fathom: "If I must die with you I will not deny you" (v.31). In this way we are set up for the scene of the denial which follows at the end of the chapter.

The intercalation suggests some relationship between these two scenes. In fact, they balance one another: Jesus stands trial before the highest religious tribunal in the land; Peter stands "trial," too, before a mob of bystanders, interrogated by a harmless servant girl. It is no accident that both scenes are heavily overcoded with the language of jurisprudence. The maid recognizes Peter, and blurts out an accusation which innocently recalls the stipulations of discipleship: "You were with the Nazarene, Jesus" (v. 67). Peter "swears" his innocence, in the process pronouncing a curse which is ironically more potent than he could ever have imagined: "I swear I do not know this man of whom you speak" (v. 71). Peter's curse is a fabrication – a self-serving tie told in a moment of distress – and yet never were truer words spoken. Peter in fact does *not* know this Jesus. The crowing of the cock, which determines the temporal and psychological climax of the story, brings home the fact that, in denying Jesus, he is in fact denying his own identity and his call as a disciple. The effect of the cock-crow is dramatic in the extreme, and it forces a reversal of meaning for the events it punctuates. Peter's natural fear intensifies, and release from the emotional tension is eventually sought in the blasphemy of a curse that would nullify the continuing effect of a past that has now become for him an object of shame (14:71). However, the Markan motif of a predestined relative *apistia* at once reasserts itself. Prompted by the second cock-crow, Peter recalls Jesus' solemn prediction, and he breaks down and weeps. This tearful denouement signifies that he is finally ashamed of his having been ashamed of an erstwhile allegiance to the prisoner now being charged with the very crime he has himself just committed. In the end, Peter is guilty not only of a failure of loyalty to his friend, but also of responsibility to his Lord. It is this forced reversal which suggests a secondary nuance to the verse with which the complex begins: "Peter followed at a distance" (v. 54).

The trial of Jesus

In one sense, Peter's agitated behavior is a foil for the behavior of Jesus. Both are on trial. The object of the interrogation is roughly the same: who, after all, is Jesus, and what is the basis of his claim to exercise authority? Peter becomes more agitated as Jesus becomes more silent. There is a sense in which Peter's final disavowal (in v. 71) counterbalances Jesus' ultimate claim to authority as he answers – for the only time – the question of the high priest (in v. 62):

[62]   "You will see the Son of Man
            seated at the right hand of Power
            and coming with the clouds of heaven."

[71]   "I do not know this man of whom you speak!"

It is a loose parallel, but it reinforces the literary foil Mark has been developing between the two men.

There is another sense, however, in which the proper foil for Peter is not Jesus but the authorities. They, like he, become guilty of uttering the ultimate blasphemy. We return to Burkill: "As the evangelist understands the matter, the court's decision to condemn Jesus to death on a charge of blasphemy is itself an instance of shamelessly wilful *blasphemia*; and this in turn means that, no less than the demons, the Jewish authorities are doomed to destruction" (p. 59). There are ironic nuances in all of this which the authorities cannot possibly perceive. They cannot know that there is a "reader" who will discern beneath the surfaces of their condemnation of Jesus an even more potent self-imprecation. And perhaps that is the point – they are stone-blind to this cosmic drama in which they are playing such significant roles. In their blindness they fail to see that the roles they play have been written out beforehand.

There are two particular lines in this script which these "actors," these "hypocrites," do not understand. The first is the testimony brought against Jesus in v. 58:

"We heard him say,
'I will destroy this temple that is made with hands.
    and in three days
I will build   another,   not made with hands.' "

In his 1973 doctoral dissertation, *Messiah and Temple*, Donald Juel has dealt extensively with the irony of this statement.[114] Juel's argument is careful, and does not require to be restated in detail. His basic assertion is that exactly that challenge is brought up at the crucifixion itself (15. 29). There it is clearly sarcastic, and yet for Mark's reader just as clearly true. If the charge is ironically true at the crucifixion, it is also ironically true at the trial. There are other clues. In his reading of the preceding chapters, Mark's reader has been prepared already with frequent polemics against the temple. And he can hardly avoid the dramatic effect of the temple curtain tearing apart at the precise moment of Jesus' death in 15. 38[115] Juel is not alone in supposing that the Christian community is itself the "temple not made with hands."[116]

The second irony here carries the first a level deeper. We had seen in our discussion of the healing of the paralytic in 2. 1–12 that Jesus' identity as prophet is significant for Mark. As such it is subtly underscored in a number of places, some of which anticipate the rhetorical movements of the trial itself. Here, in v. 65, that concern is reiterated in an ironically pregnant moment. The authorities demand that Jesus *prophesy*, at precisely the moment his prophecy of Peter's denial is being fulfilled in the courtyard below (vv. 66–72)! The reader has been set up by the text's unfolding rhetorical strategies. This is a trial with two verdicts. Jesus is vindicated by the reader at precisely the moment that the authorities condemn him and hand him over to Pilate for formal trial and execution.

Mark 15.1–15 – The trial before Pilate

We need pause here only for summary remarks. Mark's account of the trial before Pilate is loosely paralleled by John, and the ironic tendencies here are fully visible there. In Mark's account of the trial there are two primary points of stress. The first is the reiterated title "King of the Jews" around which the charge and plea are made to turn (vv. 2, 9, 12). In Mark, as in John, the mockery of the soldiers will be an ironic acclamation of Jesus as "King of the Jews," and that fact should suggest the same here. In the reader's eyes the irony of a Messiah who achieves his end by suffering at the hands of a Roman procurator is nowhere given more potent expression: the charge is right after all: this is, in fact the "King of the Jews."

The second point of stress is the release of Barabbas, a convicted insurrectionist. To recognize the significance of Barabbas in Mark's rhetorical strategies, we must pause to note that the charge brought before Pilate – that Jesus pretended to be "King of the Jews" – is different from the verdict handed down in the sanhedrin the night before – that Jesus was guilty of blasphemy. That is, the sanhedrin is guilty of duplicity by manipulating the charge with the punishment in view. This is calumny of the worst kind. That it is ironic is suggested by William Lane: "It must be considered highly ironical that having branded Jesus as a blasphemer because he failed to correspond to the nationalistic ideal, the council now wanted him condemned by the pagan tribunal on the ... allegation that he made claims of a distinctly political nature" (pp. 550f).

The very shift is enough to expose the accusation as malicious, but Mark is not content to leave it at that. Enter Barabbas. Barabbas provides a test, not of the judicial system, but of the integrity of the charge. From Pilate's vantage-point, the choice between Jesus and Barabbas is a master-stroke. It would provide occasion for the release of an innocent man by setting the crowds over against their own authorities. In the end it proves to be a tactical blunder, because the crowds – at the instigation of the chief priests – demand the release of Barabbas instead. When presented with an acknowledged insurrectionist, they choose his release. In this way Mark makes it clear that the charges against Jesus are trumped-up, and the duplicity of the chief priests is exposed for what it is. At the same time, Mark makes it clear that in Pilate's eyes the execution of Jesus was a miscarriage of justice. Jesus is no rebel, yet it is precisely as a rebel that he is to be executed. If anything, it is the chief priests who are guilty of encouraging insurrection.

Mark 15. 16–32 – The mockery of Jesus

There are three different scenes in which Jesus is subjected to humiliation: in 14. 65 he is mocked by the Jewish authorities; in 15. 16–20 he is mocked by the Roman soldiers; and in 15. 21–32 he is derided by the passers-by at the scene of the crucifixion. We shall deal only with the last two. Robert Tannehill has already pointed out, however, that all three scenes are ironic in their overarching strategies:

> The rejection and scorning of Jesus, prominent in the passion announcements in chapters 8–10, are dramatized in the passion story by scenes of mocking. These scenes are systematically placed, one following each of the main events after the arrest ... The last two of the scenes are vivid and emphatic. All three are ironic and suggest to the reader important affirmations about Jesus.[117]

Mark 15. 16–20 – The mockery by the soldiers

The irony is developed in an almost allegorical fashion in this pericope. The mockery Jesus suffers at the hands of the soldiers represents an extraordinarily complex interplay of surface and deep significances. It would serve our purposes little to explore them in detail. They are readily seen. Who can miss the sarcastic pathos of the cloak, or the crown of thorns, or the spittle? On the surface of it, this is gallows humour, pure and simple, a farce played out in a kind of refined brutality. But it is more. Like the trial, it represents a perfect masque of the truth it parodies.

Mark 15.21–32 – The mockery at the crucifixion

Here, too, the mockery is ironic. We have seen that the challenge to Jesus in vv. 29f may be ironic: "You who would destroy the temple and build it in three days, save yourself and come down from the cross." Again we may refer to Tannehill:

> The command "save yourself" is meant ironically, for the speaker intends to highlight Jesus' powerlessness. The thought is continued by the statement in 15:31: "Others he saved, himself he cannot save." Although intended as a mockery, this statement summarizes so well Jesus' story as told in Mark that it must be regarded as one of the points at which key elements of the total development come to expression ... (p. 80)

We might state that somewhat differently. As he overheard Jesus' paradoxical *teaching* to the disciples, the reader was being prepared to recognize the deeper Christological nuances of the passion. In his encounter with the miracles and the other symbolic gestures, he has learned that with Jesus, more is going on than meets the eye. The feedings were ciphers for the eucharist. The stilling of the storm, and, more clearly, the exorcism were symbolic bindings of Satan. The journey to Tyre and Sidon were signals of the extension of the gospel to the Gentiles. The cleansing of the temple drew its formal operation to a symbolic but quite final close.

It is that preparation which demands that the reader reinterpret the events of the crucifixion on another plane. In an article to which we drew attention in Chapter 1, Tannehill has suggested that the Christological nuances of the passion story ultimately confront the reader with a crisis of judgment, a crisis which demands exactly that reaction Jesus himself had so clearly anticipated in his teaching about suffering.

By way of summary: the epilogue   Mark 16.1–8

Against the excruciating symbolism of the crucifixion scene, the epilogue appears terribly abbreviated. The story ends as abruptly as it began.[118] We have discussed already in Chapter 1 the ironies created by that abrupt ending – the sense that all is not finished, and with that the ongoing work of evaluation required of the reader. We shall not rehearse those effects in detail here. Instead, we shall simply ask how it is that Mark's ending has such a terribly wrenching effect on the reader. How has Mark brought us to this moment?

In the first place, the plot has moved at a sustained clip, at each stage reaffirming Jesus' mastery over the situations with which he is confronted. We have followed his movements back and forth across the Sea, in and out of Galilee, and in and out of the confused loyalties of his disciples. We have followed his inexorable march to his death in Jerusalem, a march which has led him — in its own way triumphantly — across the open nerve-endings of "official" Judaism. In Mark, Jesus has been the very soul of power. We have felt that dynamism at every turn. Mark has been careful, however, to curtail any notion that Jesus' power is the result of personal charisma, or collusion with satanic forces. It is nothing other than the embodiment of the "Kingdom of God" bursting into the world. That the story should end with Jesus dangling on the machine of his death is a literally stunning turn of events, one for which even the passion predictions and the foreshadowing cannot entirely prepare. Against that catastrophe, the epilogue provides hardly an adequate closure for the book.

And that is precisely the point. The ironies in Mark have left the reader with a deep sense that more is going on than meets the eye, that this story — including its catastrophe — is meaningful in a dimension not readily available on the surface. The reader is forced back into the book again. In the end, the ironies of the story-line will raise a host of significances which will continue to haunt the reader long after the story has been drawn to a close. What can be the meaning of this crucified Messiah, this empty tomb? What can be meant by the prophecy of a meeting in Galilee, found on the lips of a strange young man? What is the appropriate response? But perhaps these are best understood, not as unresolved questions, but as challenges to the reader. Donald Juel has found those challenges embodied in the reactions of the women, and it is with his question that we close this chapter: "What sort of good news closes with 'And they said nothing to anyone, for they were afraid'?"

6

BY WAY OF SUMMARY

It may be a little odd to follow a treatment of the Gospel with an uninvited postscript. Odd, but not unprecedented. Very much more could be said if we were to extend our discussion to include narrative elements other than, and different from, irony. I suspect that in the light of those fuller discussions, our understanding of irony itself would take on a somewhat different aspect. Nevertheless, we can say some things.

First, it is important that the various effects of the narrative are tightly interwoven. The narrative is taken in as though it were an integrated whole. From this point of view, although the various thematic elements of Mark are distinct, and cannot be reduced to one another, they are also interrelated, and must be understood together. There are two reasons why this is so. First, polyvalence in narrative suggests that story elements may serve varieties of functions in the story-teller's overarching strategies. We discussed polyvalence in Chapters 2 and 3. There we pointed out that elements may be included which are clearly historical, but which serve the function of orienting the reader within the world of the story itself, or of directing the reader's attention to significances which the story-teller supposes are resident within the story's deeper structures. It is often the same with elements of genre, such as the silencing of the demons in the course of acts of exorcism. Such elements may well be required by the generic structures of the story, and at the same time serve apologetic functions of orienting functions which are critical to the story-teller's larger strategy. Second, the polyvalence of narrative meaning suggests that story elements which are generically different may serve similar or related rhetorical strategies. We encountered this notion briefly in our comments about the organization of story elements under the government of the story's core cliché. The clustering of stories by theme or theological motif may represent Mark's own implicit affirmation of this interest. When the messianic banquet is symbolically extended to the Gentiles in 8.1–9, that movement is clarified and reinforced by a widely ranging concatenation of story elements. We find another, quite similar feeding in 6.30–44, a controversy about ritual defilement in 7.1–13, a "scholastic dialogue" with the disciples in 7.14–23, and an account of a witty, "peirastic" exchange with a Syrophoenician woman in 7.24–30. So the movement of the story-line as a whole moves toward the feeding of the 4,000 by building upon and reinforcing story elements which are both widely distributed and diverse in character.

These two realities of narrative language suggest our second major comment: Mark's use of irony to leverage the reader in one arena may intensify the effect of the others. Story elements work synergistically to predispose the reader's reactions to what follows. As we have seen, he does this through exclusionary strategies, through the timed disclosure of information (especially the superscription!), through asides to the reader, through winks and overcodes, through carefully orchestrated parallelism, and through allusions to outside literary and liturgical traditions. Through it all he signals to the reader that, in the story of Jesus, "more is going on than meets the eye." All of those signals are woven into the fabric of the narrative itself, a fabric which the characters inside the narrative cannot see.

It is also important that Mark's reader encounters these story elements in this particular sequence. The "rhetorical play" between the text and its subtext continuously slips over and generates new competencies. Those competencies can then be assumed in the stories which follow. This is critical. With each episode, Mark paints upon the reader's consciousness the mute background against which the rhetorical play of all subsequent episodes can be worked out. That background is also exclusionary, since the critical difference between the insight possessed by the story's characters and that of the reader may be said to reside in the textures of the story itself.

So the core of the ironies lies in the tension between exclusionary strategies and veiled revelations. The exclusions prevent the story's characters from hearing or understanding the full implications of the story in which they are a part. The revelations make certain that the reader is continually and subtly confronted with just that deeper level of significance. In the play between these two, the reader is not only allowed to view the silhouette of Jesus' full messianic identity, but he is asked to take a position, to declare himself. We might put this differently. To ignore the tension between these exclusionary strategies and revelations would be to cripple Mark's ironies, and to cripple the ironies would be to flatten out the narrative into a straightforward report, rather than a nuanced and provocative telling. The very fact that this Gospel evokes such deep reactions on the part of its reader is testimony to the subtlety and skill with which its ironies have been crafted.

With the third comment, these two become concrete. The reader's reaction to the text is not only visceral. The ironies also function on the level of ideological point of view: they summon the reader to share the world-view from which they are posed. To recognize that they are there, but to resist that summons, is to place oneself in the position of the ironic victim, and to come under the implied condemnation of the story. We have discussed differences of point of view on a theoretical level in Chapter 2. Here we can be concrete. Mark's ironies express a crisis of loyalties between Christianity and traditional Judaism, at every point along the way calling into question those institutions and attitudes which oppose the emergence of this new and different expression of piety. A survey of the specific ironies would reveal challenges leveled against the institution of the temple, against an exclusivist posture toward the Gentiles, against any piety which rejects as unworthy the "people of the land" – including tax-collectors and sinners, and against any brand of messianism which disregards or denies the necessity of suffering.

How are we to reconstruct the circumstances which gave rise to such concerns? Whatever else we say about the matter of historicity, it is clear that these are challenges which would have been critical for the survival of Mark's community. The fact that they are posed subtly, through the development of narrative dissonance, should not prevent us from recognizing their deep potencies: it is not that Mark sought to combine dissonant story elements into a more or less coherent narrative, and that he failed in that attempt. Rather, it is that he deliberately generated dissonance in an attempt to force the reader to take a position, and thus to come to faith.

But faith in what? Or in whom? The ironies in Mark's narrative suggest to the reader that the differences between Jesus and the story's other characters ultimately rest on a deeper plane than mere differences of opinion about piety. The difference is one of esoteric insight. The very fact that the ironies represent implicit judgment would be enough to secure that fact, but Mark is not willing to leave it at that. Instead he carefully points out to those around Jesus – and to the reader as well – that those who understand, those on the inside, "have been given the mystery of the Kingdom," while for those who do not, "everything is in riddles" (4.10–12).

The fourth general comment applies to theological and sociological implications: if our understanding of Mark 4.10–12 is correct, Mark's ironies point beyond themselves to the wider mystery represented in the narrative itself. This is theologically significant, but it is also significant sociologically. Insight into the presence and character of a mystery may be a critical factor in the process of group-boundary definition. It is specifically so when the narrative's chief character identifies those who do not possess the mystery as "outsiders"! It is partly in this way that the group clarifies its relationships and differences from the other communities with which it competes. Even this can be refined. It is not simply that Mark's community excluded those who lacked insight into the mystery of Christ. Rather, the sense of communality itself is founded on the basic agreement that "this – and not that – is what life is like." We have noticed already in Chapter 1 the growing number of scholars for whom the narrative itself is parabolic, or for whom Jesus is the "parable of God." We should not be surprised, then, if the ironies in Mark's sacred story of Jesus are appropriated as ciphers of the structures of reality itself. That is, the "esoteric wisdom" of the eschatological community ultimately involves insight, not into Jesus' life, but into the life of the believer, for whom the issues addressed in the Gospel are not only regnant in their own right, but representative of the issues of life generally. If for Mark the events of Jesus' life are ciphers of a deeper reality, they are also sign-posts which direct the reader to look more deeply into his own reality. If he can approach his own struggles with perceptions schooled by Mark's faith that, in the plan of God, "more is going on than meets the eye," he may discover resonances and significances there which give the lie to the rule of Satan. Only in this way can he find the courage to affirm God in the face of a broken and suffering world, and to take up his cross and follow a broken and suffering Christ.

NOTES

Introduction: the problem of irony in Mark

1 James E. Miller, *Word, Self, and Reality* (NY: Dodd, Mead & Co., 1972), pp. 46f.
2 On which see: Lucille Smith, ed., *York Plays* (1885; rpt. NY: Russell, 1963); and Earle Birney, "English Irony Before Chaucer," *University of Toronto Quarterly*, 6 (1936/7), 542.
3 Jakob Jónsson, *Humour and Irony in the New Testament* (Reykjavík: Bókaútgáfa Menningarsjóds, 1965).
4 Albert Descamps, *Les Justes et la Justice dans les évangelies et les christianisme primitif* (Louvain: Publications Universitaires de Louvain; Gembloux: J. Duculot, 1950), pp. 98–110, esp. pp. 103f.
5 Luke has somewhat softened the impact of the contrast by adding a qualifying phrase, "I came not to call the righteous, *but sinners to repentance*" (5.32).
6 William Lane, *The Gospel According to Mark* (NICNT; Grand Rapids: Eerdmans, 1974), p. 541; cf. also Robert Tannehill, "The Gospel of Mark as Narrative Christology," *Semeia*, 16 (1979), 79.
7 Wayne Booth, *A Rhetoric of Irony* (University of Chicago Press, 1974), pp. 28f.
8 Madeleine Boucher, *The Mysterious Parable: A Literary Study* (Washington, D.C.: Catholic Biblical Association of America, 1977), p. 18.
9 Werner Kelber, *The Oral and Written Gospel* (Philadelphia: Fortress, 1983), pp. 117–29. Kelber lists in support of this thesis the following scholars: Wilder (1964), Weeden (1971), Borsch (1975), Crossan (1975), Tannehill (1977), Donahue (1978), and Malbon (1980). Perhaps the most influential discussion of double levels of significance in Mark is Erich Auerbach's brilliant literary study, *Mimesis* (Princeton, NJ: Princeton University Press, 1953), pp. 35–43.
10 Kelber, *The Oral and Written Gospel*, p. 123; quoting Boucher, *The Mysterious Parable*, p. 83.
11 Gilbert Bilezekian, *The Liberated Gospel: A Comparison of Mark and Greek Tragedy* (Grand Rapids, MI: Baker, 1977), pp. 122–4.
12 Joseph T. Shipley, *Dictionary of World Literature, Criticism, Forms, Technique* (NY: Philosophical Library, 1943), p. 331.
13 Donald Juel, *Messiah and Temple: The Trial of Jesus in the Gospel of Mark* (SBLDS no. 31; Missoula: Scholars Press, 1977).

182

14 Nils Dahl, "The Purpose of Mark's Gospel," in *Jesus in the Memory of the Early Church* (Minneapolis: Augsburg: 1976), p. 56. Perhaps no problem has so preoccupied Markan scholarship as this one. First given concrete expression in Wilhelm Wrede's study, *Das Messiasgeheimnis in den Evangelien* (Göttingen: Vandenhoeck & Ruprecht, 1901), it has generated an enormous body of literature. For a survey, see James Blevins, *The Messianic Secret in Markan Research, 1901–1976* (Washington, D.C.: University Press of America, 1981), and, more briefly, David Aune, "The Problem of the Messianic Secret," *NovT* 11 (1969), 1–31.

15 Donald Juel, *An Introduction to New Testament Literature* (Nashville: Abingdon, 1978), pp. 176–201, esp. pp. 182–96.

16 Robert Fowler, *Loaves and Fishes: The Function of the Feeding Stories in the Gospel of Mark* (SBLDS no. 54; Chico, CA: Scholars Press, 1981).

17 For more on reliable commentary as a literary consideration, see Booth, *A Rhetoric of Irony*, pp. 169–209.

18 Fowler, "Authors and Readers: Reader Response Criticism and the Gospel of Mark," Chapter IV of *Loaves and Fishes*, pp. 149–79.

19 Robert Tannehill, "Tension in Synoptic Sayings and Stories," *Interp*, 34 (1980), 138–59.

20 Howard Clark Kee, *Understanding the New Testament* (4th edn.; Englewood Cliffs, NJ: Prentice-Hall, 1983), p. 114.

21 For a discussion of the literary functions of this *inclusio*, see Paul Achtemeier, " 'And He Followed Him'; Miracles and Discipleship in Mark 10:46–52," *Semeia*, 11 (1978), 115–45.

22 Robert Tannehill, *The Sword of His Mouth* (Philadelphia: Fortress, 1975), p. 55.

23 Laurence Perrine, *Story and Structure* (NY: Harcourt, Brace & World, 1959), p. 66.

24 An enormous amount of ink has been spilled over the question of Mark's ending, almost of all of it dealing with the difficulty of the *text*. For a specifically *literary* approach, see Andrew T. Lincoln, "The Promise and the Failure – Mark 16:7, 8," *JBL*, 108 (1989), 283–300, and the articles cited in notes 26 and 27 below. Lincoln's article crossed my desk too late to be considered in the body of my discussion.

25 Thomas Boomershine, *Mark the Storyteller: A Rhetorical–Critical Investigation of Mark's Passion and Resurrection Narrative* (unpublished Ph.D. dissertation, Union Theological Seminary, New York, 1974), p. 7.

26 Donald Juel, *Introduction to New Testament Literature*, pp. 169ff.

27 Norman Petersen, "When is an End Not an End?" *Interp*, 34 (1980), 151–66.

28 See above, note 7.

29 D. C. Muecke, *The Compass of Irony* (London: Methuen, 1970); *Irony, The Critical Idiom* (London: Methuen, 1970).

30 Edwin Good, *Irony in the Old Testament* (London: SPCK, 1965).

31 See Robert Alter, *The Art of Biblical Narrative* (NY: Basic Books, 1981), p. 15.

32 For irony in the Old Testament, see: Edwin Good, *Irony in the Old Testament*; W. L. Halladay, "Style, Irony and Authenticity in Jeremiah," *JBL*, 81 (1962), 44–54; James G. Williams, " 'You have Not Spoken

Truth of Me': Mystery and Irony in Job," *ZAW*, 83 (1971), 231–55; "Irony and Lament: Clues to Prophetic Consciousness," *Semeia*, 8 (1977), 51–75; Menakhem Perry and Meier Sternberg, "The King Through Ironic Eyes," (Hebrew) *Ha-Sifrut*, 81 (1968), 263–92; Robert Alter, *The Art of Biblical Narrative* (NY: Basic Books, 1981), pp. 18–20.

For irony in Jesus, see: Henri Clavier, "L'Ironie dans l'Enseignement de Jésus," *NovT*, 1 (1956), 3–20; "Les sens multiples dans le Nouveau Testament," *NovT*, 2 (1958), 185–90; Elton Trueblood, *The Humour of Christ* (NY: Harper and Row, 1964), Chapter III: "Christ's Use of Irony," pp. 53–67; Jakob Jónsson, *Humour and Irony in the New Testament*; W. Harnisch, "Die Ironie als Stilmittel in Gleichnissen Jesu," *EvT*, 32 (1972), 421–36; Jerry Gill, "Jesus, Irony and the 'New Quest'," *Interp*, 41 (1980), 139–51.

For irony in Luke, see: James Dawsey, *The Lucan Voice: Confusion and Irony in the Gospel of Luke* (Macon, GA: Mercer University Press, 1986).

For irony in John, see: Henri Clavier, "L'ironie dans le quatrième evangile," *StEv*, 1 (1959), 261–76; George W. MacRae, "Theology and Irony in the Fourth Gospel," in *The Word in the World: Essays in Honour of Frederick L. Moriarty*, ed. Richard J. Clifford and George MacRae (Cambridge, MA: Weston College Press, 1973), pp. 83–96; David Wead, "Johannine Irony as a Key to the Author–Audience Relationship in John's Gospel," in *Biblical Literature: 1974 Proceedings of the Section of Biblical Literature of the American Academy of Religion*, ed. Fred O. Francis (Tallahassee: American Academy of Religion and Florida State University, 1974), pp. 33–44; and, most recently, Paul Duke, *Irony in the Fourth Gospel* (Atlanta: John Knox Press, 1983). Discussions of irony in John's report of the trial are plentiful. See the commentaries by Richardson (1959), p. 194; Brown (1970), pp. 873–89, 895; Morris (1971), pp. 792f; and Lindars (1972), p. 554.

For irony in Paul, see: Aida Besançon Spencer, "The Wise Fool and the Foolish Wise: A Study of Irony in Paul," *NovT*, 23 (1981), 349–60.

2 The social functions of ironic narrative

1 William Lane, "The Gospel of Mark in Current Study," *SJTh*, 21 (1978), 20–1.
2 Howard Clark Kee, *Christian Origins in Sociological Perspective: Methods and Resources* (Philadelphia: Westminster Press, 1980), p. 127. More extensive discussions are to be found in the collection of essays edited by Joseph Strelka, *Literary Criticism and Sociology* (Yearbook of Comparative Criticism, vol. 5; University Park, PA: Pennsylvania State University Press, 1973).
3 René Wellek and Austin Warren, *Theory of Literature* (NY: Harcourt Brace Jovanovich, 1956), p. 95.
4 Peter Berger and Thomas Luckmann, *The Social Construction of Reality* (Garden City, NY: Doubleday, 1966). Berger rapidly followed this collaborated effort with several monographs of his own, including one which is particularly germane to our exploration of the NT evidence:

The Sacred Canopy: Elements of a Sociological Theory of Religion (Garden City, NY: Doubleday, 1969).

5 On which see Kenneth Hamilton, *Words and the Word* (Grand Rapids: Eerdmans, 1971), as well as the excellent discussion in Robert Funk, *Language, Hermeneutic and Word of God: The Problem of Language in the New Testament and Contemporary Theology* (NY: Harper and Row, 1966).

6 The idea that the mind structures reality is not restricted to the linguistic sciences. For a broadly ranging survey of various positions, see Charles Hampden-Turner, *Maps of the Mind: Charts and Concepts of the Mind and its Labyrinths* (NY: Collier, 1981).

7 There is a good introduction to the New Hermeneutic in Paul Achtemeier's work by that title (Philadelphia: Westminster, 1969). A fine representative collection of essays, including essays by Fuchs and Ebeling, is to be found in James M. Robinson and John Cobb Jr., eds., *The New Hermeneutic* (NY: Harper and Row, 1964).

8 See Cassirer's magnum opus, *The Philosophy of Symbolic Forms* (New Haven: Yale University Press, 1953–7), and his programmatic exploration, *An Essay on Man* (New Haven: Yale Univesity Press, 1944), esp. chapters I and II, pp. 1–26.

9 Kenneth Burke, *Language as Symbolic Action* (Berkeley: University of California Press, 1966), esp. pp. 3–9.

10 Hans Georg Gadamer, *Wahrheit und Methode* (Tübingen: J. C. B. Mohr, 1960), p. 419.

11 H. Richard Niebuhr, *The Responsible Self* (NY: Harper and Row, 1963).

12 Richard Bandler and John Grinder, *The Structure of Magic, II: A Book about Language and Therapy* (Palo Alto, CA: Science and Behavior Books, 1975). A related approach is to be found in David Gordon, *Therapeutic Metaphors: Helping Others Through the Looking Glass* (Cupertino, CA: META Publications, 1978).

13 Noam Chomsky, *Language and Mind* (NY: Harcourt Brace Jovanovich, 1968). There is a good discussion of the significance of Chomsky for theological study in Irene Lawrence, *Linguistics and Theology* (Methuchen, NJ: Scarecrow Press, 1980).

14 Joyce Hertzler, *A Sociology of Language* (NY: Random House, 1965). See also M. A. K. Halliday, *Language as Social Semiotic: The Social Interpretation of Language and Meaning* (Baltimore: University Park Press, 1978); Berger and Luckmann, *The Social Construction of Reality*, pp. 47–128; Berger, *The Sacred Canopy*, pp. 12f, 17–21; and the papers delivered to the "Conference on the Interrelations of Language and Other Aspects of Culture," held in Chicago, March 23–7, 1953 (these have been collected and edited by Harry Hoijer in *Language and Culture* [University of Chicago Press, 1954]).

15 Edward Sapir, "Language," in *Encyclopedia of the Social Sciences* (NY: Macmillan, 1933). This essay is also found in *Culture, Language and Personality: Selected Writings of Edward Sapir*, ed. D. G. Mandelbaum (Berkeley, CA: University of California Press, 1957), pp. 7–32. For convenience, page references are to the Mandelbaum edition.

16 George Herbert Mead, *Mind, Self and Society from the Standpoint of a Social Behaviorist* (University of Chicago Press, 1934).

17 Benjamin Whorf, *Collected Papers on Metalinguistics* (Washington, DC: Department of Foreign Services Institute, 1952), p. 4.

18 Sapir, *Culture, Language and Personality*, p. 162.

19 Sapir, "Language," p. 16.

20 The terms are Robert Merton's. See his *Social Theory and Social Structure* (Chicago: The Free Press of Glencoe, 1957).

21 In his discussion of "Science and Linguistics" (*Technological Review* 42 [1940], 229–31, 247f), Whorf argued for the creation of a language which would be geared to the specialized needs of science, one which would not be restricted to the specific patterns or structures of English.

22 Luis Alonzo-Schökel, "Hermeneutics in the Light of Language and Literature," *CBQ*, 25 (1963), 374.

23 Hertzler, *Sociology of Language*, p. 366.

24 Whorf, *Language, Thought and Reality*, pp. 213f.

25 Robert Tannehill, *The Sword of His Mouth* (Philadelphia: Fortress, 1975).

26 Philip Wheelwright, *The Burning Fountain* (Bloomington, University of Indiana Press, 1968). See also his earlier study, *Metaphor and Reality* (Bloomington: University of Indiana Press, 1962). In addition, one should note the entire special issue of *Semeia*, 9 (1977) devoted to polyvalent narration, esp. the articles by Susan Wittig ("A Theory of Multiple Meanings," pp. 75–104) and the volume's editor, John Dominic Crossan, ("A Metamodel for Polyvalent Narration," pp. 105–47).

27 Sallie (McFague) TeSelle has turned the defence of metaphor and allusion to theological advantage. See esp. her studies, *Speaking in Parables: A Study of Metaphor and Theology* (London: SCM, 1975), and *Metaphorical Theology: Models of God and Religious Language* (Philadelphia: Fortress, 1982). A briefer introduction to TeSelle's thought is to be found in her article, "Imaginary Gardens with Real Toads: Realism in Fiction and Theology," *Semeia*, 13 (1978), 241–62. For a careful exploration of *Metaphor and Religious Language*, see Janet Martin Soskice's volume by that title (Oxford: Clarendon, 1985).

28 Wilder's contributions are impossible to enumerate here. For a bibliography and *vita*, see *Semeia*, 13 (1978), 263–87. For an academic biography, see John Dominic Crossan's tribute: *The Fragile Craft: The Work of Amos Niven Wilder* (Chico, CA: Scholars Press, 1981); and the appreciation by Will Beardslee, in *Semeia*, 12 (1978), 1–11.

29 For a distillation of Beardslee's extensive research, see his summary study, *Literary Criticism of the New Testament* (Philadelphia: Fortress, 1970).

30 Ray Hart, *Unfinished Man and the Imagination* (NY: Herder and Herder, 1968).

31 Alfred Schutz, *Collected Papers I: The Problem of Social Reality*, ed. Maurice Natanson (Phaenomenologica 11; The Hague: Martinus Nijhoff, 1971), pp. 340–56.

32 The term was apparently coined by Erich Auerbach in *Mimesis* (Princeton University Press, 1953). It refers to the state of being "along-side," in contrast to being "with." On this view, reality is desultory.

33 Bruno Bettelheim, *The Uses of Enchantment: The Meaning and Importance of Fairy Tales* (NY: Alfred Knopf, 1976).

34 The pioneering work on aetiologies in the OT is that of Herman Gunkel, *The Legends of Genesis* (Chicago: The Open Court Publishing Co., 1907). For more recent studies, see Burke Long, *The Problem of Etiological Narrative in the Old Testament* (Berlin: Topelmann, 1968), and Brevard Childs, "The Etiological Tale Re-Examined," *VT*, 24 (1974), 387–97. For discussions of aetiologies in the NT, see Martin Dibelius (*From Tradition to Gospel* [NY: Charles Scribner's Sons, 1934], pp. 104–32), who distinguishes "aetiologies proper to the cultus" from "personal legends," while noting that the latter may well serve the purposes of the former; and Rudolf Bultmann (*The History of the Synoptic Tradition*, trans. John Marsh [NY: Harper and Row, 1963], pp. 244–307), who, however, avoids the term itself.

35 Mircea Eliade, *The Sacred and the Profane: The Nature of Religion*, trans. W. R. Trask (NY: Harper and Row, 1961).

36 Mircea Eliade, *Cosmos and History: The Myth of the Eternal Return*, trans. W. R. Trask (NY: Harper and Row, 1954), p. 3.

37 See Mircea Eliade, *Rites and Symbols of Initiation* (NY: Harper and Row, 1975).

38 See Robert McAfee Brown, "My Story and 'The Story'," *Theology Today*, 32 (1975), 166–73.

39 Ted Estess, "The Inenarrable Contraption: Reflections on the Metaphor of Story," *JAAR*, 42 (1974), 415–34, esp. pp. 430–4.

3 The literary functions of narrative

1 Alfred Schutz, *Collected Papers I: The Problem of Social Reality*, ed. Maurice Natanson (Phaenomenologica 11; The Hague; Martinus Nijhoff, 1971), pp. 340–56.

2 J. R. R. Tolkien, "On Fairy Stories," in *The Tolkien Reader* (NY: Ballantine Books, 1966), pp. 36f.

3 Seymour Chatman, *Story and Discourse: Narrative Structure in Fiction and Film* (Ithaca, NY: Cornell University Press, 1978), pp. 27–31.

4 Gérard Genette, *Narrative Discourse: An Essay on Method*, trans. Jane E. Lewin (Ithaca, NY: Cornell University Press, 1980), pp. 33–86. See also Meier Sternberg, "Gaps, Ambiguity and the Reading Process," Chapter 6 of *The Poetics of Biblical Narrative: Ideological Literature and the Drama of Reading* (Bloomington: Indiana University Press, 1987), pp. 186–229.

5 Livia Polanyi, "What Stories Can Tell Us About Their Teller's World," *Poetics Today*, 2,2 (1981), 97–112.

6 Louis O. Mink, "History and Fiction as Modes of Comprehension," *New Literary History*, 1 (1970), 541–58.

7 In his study of *Ntsomi* folk tales, Harold Sheub (for whom I am indebted to Robert Culley, *Studies in the Structure of Hebrew Narrative* [Philadelphia: Fortress, 1976], pp. 13–20) has identified at the heart of each tale a "core cliché," which governs the arrangement of its details. We might call this the story's *point*. Our reason for telling a story

significantly affects the selection and arrangement of its parts. In oral literature, the same story, told in differing circumstances and with differing purposes, may be arranged and rearranged with a great deal of freedom. It is the story's "core cliché" which keeps that freedom in check.

8 Boris Uspensky, *A Poetics of Composition: The Structure of the Artistic Text and Typology of a Compositional Form*, trans. V. Zavarin and S. Wittig (Berkeley: University of California Press, 1973). Uspensky's work is widely discussed within NT literary scholarship. See, for example, Norman Petersen, " 'Point of View' in Mark's Narrative," *Semeia*, 12 (1978), 97–121.

9 Robert Weimann, *Structure and Society in Literary Theory* (Charlottesville: University of Virginia Press, 1973).

10 Louis Mink has it right: "The features which enable a story to flow and us to follow, then, are the clues to the nature of historical understanding. An historical narrative does not demonstrate the necessity of events but makes them intelligible by unfolding the story which connects their significance. History does not as such differ from fiction, therefore, insofar as it essentially depends on and develops our skill and subtlety in following stories" ("History and Fiction as Modes of Comprehension," p. 545).

11 Robert Scholes and Robert Kellogg, *The Nature of Narrative* (NY: Oxford University Press, 1966), p. 240.

12 On the surface of it, the distinction between showing and telling rests upon the observable presence of a narrator. In his study of *The Rhetoric of Fiction* (University of Chicago Press, 1961), Wayne Booth has traced within literary theory the growing sentiment that an observable narrator is necessarily intrusive, and that the artistry of a work is marred by his presence (pp. 3–20). It is aesthetically better to let the elements "speak for themselves." In this way the movement within literary criticism itself has tended toward the affirmation of "showing" only, and has understood "telling" pejoratively. If the distinction between showing and telling, therefore, has limited usefulness for contemporary theory, that fact should not prevent us from employing it in our clarification of the movements of ancient literature. In point of fact, our intention runs in a different direction. The assumption that the biblical narrator is only "present" when he is "telling" appears to be widely spread among readers of the scripture. "The biblical writers seldom intrude upon their story." This is then employed in defence of their *objectivity*. But this may be blind to the activity of selection and arrangement by which the narrator continues to expose his point of view even when he has "stepped out of sight behind his characters." Booth's concluding comment is exactly right: "... We must never forget that though the author can to some extent choose his disguises, he can never choose to disappear" (p. 20).

13 Elder Olsen, *Tragedy and Theory of Drama* (Detroit: Wayne State University Press, 1961), p. 79.

14 Albert Lord, *The Singer of Tales* (Harvard Studies in Comparative Literature; Cambridge, MA: Harvard University Press, 1960).

15 Augustine Stock, *Call to Discipleship: A Literary Study of Mark's Gospel* (Wilmington, DE: Michael Glazier, 1982).

16 Gilbert Bilezekian, *The Liberated Gospel: A Comparison of the Gospel of Mark and Greek Tragedy* (Grand Rapids, MI: Baker, 1977).

17 Curtis Beach, *The Gospel of Mark: Its Making and Meaning* (NY: Harper and Row, 1959).

18 Ernest W. Burch, "Tragic Action and the Second Gospel: A Study of the Narrative of Mark," *JRel*, 11 (1931), 346–58.

19 Gérard Genette, *Narrative Discourse: An Essay on Method*, trans. Jane E. Lewin (Ithaca, NY: Cornell University Press, 1980), pp. 33–86; Genette is here building upon the Russian formalist distinction between "fabula" – the primary *content* of the story, its events, its characters, and the intersecting relations between them – and "sjužet" – the emplotment of the "fabula" in narrative form. The distinction between "story time" and "narrative time" is widely observed, but with an equally widely ranging vocabulary. We may here list some of those theoreticians who have offered possible terms: A. A. Mendilow (*Time and the Novel* [NY: Humanities Press, 1952], pp. 65–71): Chronological time/Fictional time; Seymour Chatman (*Story and Discourse* [Ithaca, NY: Cornell University Press, 1978], pp. 62f): Story time/Discourse time; Norman Petersen ("Story Time and Plotted Time in Mark's Narrative," in *Literary Criticism for New Testament Critics* [Philadelphia: Fortress Press, 1978]): Story time/Plotted time.

20 For a wider discussion of this problem as it relates to Markan studies, see Norman Petersen, "Story Time and Plotted Time in Mark's Narrative."

21 Philip Harsh, *Handbook of Classical Drama* (Stanford, CA: Stanford University Press, 1944), p. 27.

22 An excellent brief introduction to Markan framing techniques is to be found in Joanna Dewey, *Markan Public Debate: Literary Technique, Concentric Structure, and Theology in Mark 2:1–3:6* (SBLDS 48; Chico, CA: Scholars Press, 1980), pp. 20–3. See also Robert Fowler, *Loaves and Fishes: The Function of the Feeding Stories in the Gospel of Mark* (SBLDS 54; Chico, CA: Scholars Press, 1981), pp. 164f; David Rhoads and Donald Michie, *Mark as Story: An Introduction to the Narrative of a Gospel* (Philadelphia: Fortress, 1982), p. 51. For a list of Markan interpolations, see Howard Clark Kee, *Community of the New Age: Studies in Mark's Gospel* (Philadelphia: Westminster, 1977), pp. 54–6.

23 Eric Kahler, *The Inward Turn of Narrative* (Princeton University Press, 1973).

24 Wesley Kort, *Narrative Elements and Religious Meaning* (Philadelphia: Fortress, 1975).

25 Hauerwas' work is extensive, and is correlated in significant ways with advances in theories of moral and faith development. See esp. *A Community of Character: Toward a Constructive Christian Social Ethic* (Univesity of Notre Dame Press, 1981), and "The Self as Story: Religion and Morality from the Agent's Perspective," *Journal of Religion and Ethics*, 1 (1973), 73–85.

26 Titus Livius, *Ab Urbe Condita*, trans. B. O. Foster (LCL; London: William Heinemann, 1919), pp. 5–7.

27 Seymour Chatman, *Story and Discourse*, p. 126; this discussion runs through to p. 138.

28 Howard Clark Kee, *Community of the New Age*, p. 58.
29 Edward M. Forster, *Aspects of the Novel* (NY: Harcourt, Brace and World, 1927), pp. 65–82.
30 Shimon Bar-Efrat, "Literary Modes and Methods in View of 2 Samuel 10–20 and 1 Kings 1–2" [summary of dissertation in Hebrew], *Immanuel*, 8 (1978), pp. 24f.
31 Theodore Weeden, *Mark: Traditions in Conflict* (Philadelphia: Fortress, 1971), p. 18.
32 One need mention in this regard only the wonderful stories of Washington Irving, or the opening chapter of Joseph Conrad's *Heart of Darkness*.
33 C. S. Lewis, "On Stories," in *Essays Presented to Charles Williams*, ed. C. S. Lewis (Oxford University Press, 1947), p. 91.
34 The term is Samuel Sandmel's; see his "Parallelomania," *JBL*, 81 (1962), 1–13.
35 See, however, Howard Clark Kee's essay, "The Function of the Scriptural Quotations and Allusions in Mark 11–16," in *Jesus and Paulus. Festschrift für Werner Georg Kümmel*, eds. E. Earle Ellis and Erich Graßer (Göttingen: Vandenhoeck und Ruprecht, 1975), pp. 165–88, see esp. pp. 173–5.
36 On which, see Harsh, *A Handbook of Classical Drama*, pp. 28–32, esp. p. 30.
37 To my mind, the finest discussion of the verbal sensitivities required in effective reading is Umberto Eco's superb study, *The Role of the Reader: Explorations in the Semiotics of Texts* (Bloomington: Indiana University Press, 1979). We shall have cause to refer to Eco in Chapter 4.

4 Text and Subtext: toward a rhetoric of irony

1 Peter Berger, *The Sacred Canopy: Elements of a Sociological Theory of Religion* (Garden City, NY: Doubleday, 1969), pp. 3f.
2 Umberto Eco, *The Role of the Reader: Explorations in the Semiotics of Texts* (Bloomington: Indiana University Press, 1979).
3 Literary theorists are not the only ones who have pointed this out. Within psychological research there is now emerging a hybrid discipline – "cognitive science" – which investigates the activity of thinking. For accounts, see: Morton Hunt, *The Universe Within: A New Science Explores the Human Mind* (NY: Simon and Schuster, 1982); and more briefly and to somewhat narrower aim, Daniel Goleman, *Vital Lies, Simple Truth: the Psychology of Self Deception* (NY: Simon and Schuster, 1985), esp. Chapter Two, "The Machinery of the Mind," pp. 55–90. Both Hunt and Goleman point out that active thought can take place only by continual reference to a system of information already existing in long term memory.
4 For a history of the term, see especially J. A. K. Thomson, *Irony: An Historical Introduction* (Cambridge: Harvard University Press, 1927). A fair survey may be found in D. C. Muecke, *The Compass of Irony* (London: Methuen, 1969), pp. 7–9, 12–13, 46–52. For a somewhat more narrowly focused survey, see Norman Knox, *The Word Irony and its Context, 1500–1799* (Durham, NC: Duke University Press, 1961),

esp. Chapter 1, "The Meaning of Irony: Introduction and Summary," pp. 3–23.

5 Joseph T. Shipley, *Dictionary of World Literature: Criticism, Forms, Technique* (NY: Philosophical Library, 1943), p. 331. This is what Muecke calls "General Irony" in Chapter 3 of *The Compass of Irony*, pp. 119–58. It is this understanding of irony which Soren Kierkegaard develops in his *The Concept of Irony, With Constant Reference to Socrates*, trans. Lee M. Capel (London: Collins, 1966).

6 David Amante, "The Theory of Ironic Speech Acts," *Poetics Today*, 2 (1981), 80.

7 Seymour Chatman, *Story and Discourse* (Ithaca: Cornell University Press, 1978), p. 29.

8 On which, see Noam Chomsky, *Language and Mind* (NY: Harcourt Brace Jovanovich, 1968); the entire first issue of *Semeia* (1974; ed. Robert Funk); Richard Bandler and John Grinder, *The Structures of Magic, I: A Book about Language and Therapy* (Palo Alto, CA: Science and Behavior Books, 1976); Daniel Patte, *What is Structural Exegesis?* (Philadelphia: Fortress Press, 1976); and Alfred M. Johnson, Jr., ed., *Structuralism and Biblical Hermeneutics* (Pittsburgh Theological Monograph 22; Pittsburgh: Pickwick, 1979).

9 Edwin Good, *Irony in the Old Testament*, pp. 33f. There is a remarkable elaboration of linguistic subtleties in this story in Robert Alter, *The Art of Biblical Narrative* (NY: Basic Books, 1981), 37–41.

10 For an evaluation of the present situation, see Howard Clark Kee, *Jesus in History: An Approach to the Study of the Gospels* (NY: Harcourt, Brace & World, 1970), and his *Community of the New Age: Studies in Mark's Gospel* (Philadelphia: Westminster, 1977), esp. Chapter 2, "The Literary Antecedents of Mark," pp. 14–49.

11 Alter makes this illuminating comment: "It is only in exceptional moments of cultural history that these conventions are explicitly codified, ... but an elaborate set of tacit agreements between artist and audience about the ordering of the art work is at all times the enabling context in which the complex communication of art occurs" (p. 47).

12 In a recent study of *Traditional Sayings in the Old Testament* (BLS 5; Sheffield: Almond Press, 1982), Carole Fontaine has investigated the role of proverbs in OT culture, using as her guide the discipline of paroemiology – "That 'branch' of folklore studies which collects and collates proverbs, analyzes local and international variants and makes some attempt at tracing the cross-cultural diffusion of proverbs" (p. 29). Studies of narrative have progressed in a parallel fashion, basing much of their comparisons on Vladimir Propp's *Morphology of the Folk-Tale* (Austin: University of Texas Press, 1968). For an excellent introduction to orality from one whose specialty lies outside the arena of biblical studies, see Jan Vansina, *Oral Tradition as History* (Madison: University of Wisconsin Press, 1985).

13 Moses Hadas, in the introduction to *Euripides*, trans. Moses Hadas and John McLean (NY: Bantam, 1960), p. vii.

14 On this question, see esp. Howard Clark Kee, "The Function of the Scriptural Allusions in Mark 11–16," in *Jesus und Paulus*, eds. E. Earle

Ellis and Erich Grasser (Göttingen: Vandenhoeck & Ruprecht, 1975), pp. 165–88.

15 Gilbert Bilezekian, *The Liberated Gospel* (Grand Rapids: Baker, 1977), p. 127.

16 Boris Uspensky, *A Poetics of Composition: The Structure of the Artistic Text and the Typology of a Compositional Form*, trans. Valentina Zavarin and Susan Wittig (Berkeley: University of California Press, 1973), esp. Chapter 1, "Point of View on the Ideological Plane," pp. 8–15.

17 The problem is complicated by the fact that the notion of an "unreliable" narrator is a relatively recent literary development. In classical literature, presumably all narration was reliable (except where obviously tongue-in-cheek, as in Lucian's wonderful tale, *A True Story*). On reliable and unreliable narration, see esp. Wayne Booth, *The Rhetoric of Fiction* (University of Chicago Press, 1961), pp. 169–211.

18 Harsh includes this proviso: "But there is no certain criterion for determining when the chorus is speaking in character and when it is expressing the views of the poet" (pp. 19f).

19 Wayne Booth, *A Rhetoric of Irony* (University of Chicago Press, 1974), pp. 222f.

20 Robert Alter, *The Art of Biblical Narrative*, p. 76.

21 Menakhem Perry and Meier Sternberg, "The King Through Ironic Eyes," *Ha-Sifrut*, 1 (1968), 263–92; see further, *Ha-Sifrut*, 2 (1970), 608–63. For this information I am indebted to Alter, *The Art of Biblical Narrative*, pp. 17f. Sternberg has continued to evolve his literary exegesis (see: *The Poetics of Biblical Narrative: Ideological Literature and the Drama of Reading* [Bloomington: Indiana University Press, 1987], pp. 190–222).

22 Max Eastman, *The Enjoyment of Laughter* (NY: Simon and Schuster, 1936), p. 203.

23 Sternberg, *The Poetics of Biblical Narrative*, p. 198.

24 Erich Auerbach, *Mimesis: The Representation of Reality in Western Literature* (Princeton University Press, 1953), Chapter 1, "Odysseus' Scar," pp. 1–19.

5 The evidence of irony in the Gospel of Mark

1 For years the standard reference has been that edited by Bruce Metzger, *Index to Periodical Literature on Christ and the Gospels* (Leiden: Brill, 1966); this is current through 1961. In a similar vein, but more recent, is the work of Hugh Humphrey, *A Bibliography for the Gospel of Mark, 1954–1980* (NY: Edwin Mellon Press, 1981). From time to time reviews of the literature appear in print; noteworthy among these are essays by James Brooks ("Annotated Bibliography on Mark," *SJTh*, 21 [1978], 75–82); and Howard Clark Kee ("Mark's Gospel in Recent Research," *Interp*, 32 [1978], 353–68). A book-length bibliographic study by Sean Kealey provides extensive guidance (*Mark's Gospel: A History of its Interpretation from the Beginning until 1979* [NY: Paulist Press, 1982]).

2 Concern for economy and order also presents us with several matters of housekeeping. Unless otherwise noted, the text we will be using will

be the 26th edition of the *Novum Testamentum Graece*, ed. Erwin Nestle and Kurt Aland, *et al.* (Stuttgart: Deutsche Bibelstiftung, 1979). I have been tremendously helped by Franz Neirynck's diagram of the text, "Mark in Greek," *EphTheoLov*, 47 (1971), 394–463. Wherever possible, I have followed the English of the RSV, 2nd edn (1971).

3 For a critical discussion of the importance of sequence, see Menakhem Perry, "Literary Dynamics: How the Order of a Text Creates its Meanings," *Poetics Today*, 1 (1979), 35.

4 Paul Achtemeier, *Mark* (Philadelphia: Fortress Press, 1975), p. 23.

5 In classical Greek, usually "a reward for good tidings," but this is rare in our period. William Lane (*The Gospel According to Mark* [NICNT; Grand Rapids: Eerdmans, 1974]; hereafter = "Lane") understands "gospel" as "an historical event which introduces a new situation into the world" (pp. 43f). Especially worthy of note is the Priene inscription (105, lines 40f), celebrating the birthday of Augustus in 9 BCE. See the discussion and photograph in Adolf Deissmann, *Light from the Ancient East* (Grand Rapids: Baker Book House, 1978), p. 366.

6 It seems clear that the omission occurred by accidental haplography. Given the abbreviations of *nomina sacra*, the text here would have been extremely cumbersome (on which see Bruce Metzger, *A Textual Commentary on the Greek New Testament* [NY: United Bible Societies, 1971], p. 73). Ralph Martin's suggestion that the words were omitted to avoid piling up genitives in "this awkward and verbless sentence" is less likely (*Mark: Evangelist and Theologian* [Grand Rapids: Zondervan, 1972], p. 27). A concise discussion may be found in Lane, p. 41, n. 7. For a comprehensive study, see A. Globe, "The Caesarean Omission of the Phrase 'Son of God' in Mark 1:1," *HTR*, 75 (1982), 209–18.

7 R. A. Guelich ("The Beginning of the Gospel" – Mark 1:1–15, *BibRes*, 27 [1982], 5–15) argues that verses 1–3 stand together as a unit, and that they head, not the whole Gospel, but only the prologue. G. Arnold, ("Mk 1:1 und Eröffnungswendungen in griechischen und lateinischen Schriften," *ZNW*, 68 [1977], 123–7) adduces literary parallels from Greek and Latin authors in support of the same contention.

8 Robert Fowler, *Loaves and Fishes: The Function of the Feeding Stories in the Gospel of Mark*, SBLDS 54 (Chico, CA: Scholars Press, 1981), p. 158. See also Donald Juel, *Messiah and Temple: The Trial of Jesus in the Gospel of Mark*, SBLDS 31 (Missoula: Scholars Press, 1977), pp. 47f. We may note that this observation was made as early as 1957 in an article by Fowler's mentor, Nils Dahl, which appeared in the *Svensk exegetische årsbok* (English translation), in Dahl's "The Purpose of Mark's Gospel," in *Jesus in the Memory of the Early Church* (Minneapolis: Augsburg Publishing House, 1976), pp. 52–65, esp. p. 56.

9 See Mark 1.45; 2.2; 3.7f; 4.1; 5.31; 6.14f, 34, 53–6; 8.1–9.

10 Willi Marxsen, *Mark the Evangelist* (NY: Abingdon, 1969), pp. 38–40. Marxsen argues that the "successiveness" is ultimately the expression of logical priority – the Baptist's story is the "pre-history" of the Gospel (p. 40).

11 James Moulton and George Milligen (*The Vocabulary of the Greek Testament* [Grand Rapids: Eerdmans, 1949], p. 483) give three examples of unqualified παραδίδωμι to show arrest, and Matthew's parallel account (4. 12; cf. 11. 2–4, which requires it) indicates that he – whatever else, a contemporary reader – understood the expression as a reference to John's arrest, rather than to his execution.

12 Note the repeated use of παραδίδωμι in the passion predictions (9. 31; 10. 33) and in the extended account of the betrayal by Judas (14. 10, 11, 18, 21, 41, 42; cf. 3. 19).

13 On the eschatological significance of Elijah, see SBK, I, p. 598. In particular, see: *Sifre Deut.* 41: "If you keep the law, expect Elijah;" and *Pirque R. Eliezar* 43 [25a]: "Israel will fulfill the great repentance when Elijah blessed of memory comes."

14 The identities of language between Mark's description of John the Baptist and the description of Elijah in 2 Kings 1.8 (LXX) are often noted. We may diagram briefly:

Mark 1. 6	2 Kings 1. 8
καὶ ζώνην δερματίνην	καὶ ζώνην δερματίνην
περὶ	περι ζωσμένος
τὴν ὀσφὺν αὐτοῦ.	τὴν ὀσφὺν αὐτοῦ.

15 Of the eleven words contained in Mark's description of John, five are hapax or rare in Mark's Gospel. Only the definite article, the pronouns, and the prepositions are found elsewhere.

16 Thomas Howard, *Christ the Tiger* (Philadelphia: Lippencott, 1967), p. 10.

17 Walter Bundy, "Dogma and Drama in the Gospel of Mark," in *New Testament Studies*, ed. Edwin Prince Booth (NY: Abingdon, 1942), pp. 74f. T. A. Burkill has made a similar observation in *Mysterious Revelation* (Ithaca, NY: Cornell University Press, 1963), p. 16.

18 See esp. A. Feuillet, "Le Baptême de Jésus d'après l'Évangile selon Saint Marc (1,9–11)," *CBQ*, 21 (1959), 468–90; "Le Baptême de Jésus," *RevBib*, 71 (1964), 321–52. Feuillet discusses a variety of literary parallels, among them, the rending of the heavens (Isa. 64. 1 [MT 63.19]); the voice from heaven (Ps. 2); the dove (Isa. 42. 1). P. Garnet, ("The Baptism of Jesus and the Son of Man Idea," *JSNT*, 9 [1980], 49–65) adduces parallels with Noah, and thus – indirectly – with Enoch, as well as 4 Ezra 13; Ezek. 8. 3. Paul Bretscher ("Ex. 4. 22–23 and the Voice from Heaven," *JBL*, 87 [1968], 301–11) discovers an overlooked parallel with Exodus 4. 22f. In the voice itself – a *bath qol*? – Howard Kee finds a parallel in the OT tradition of theophanies and divine auditions: Moses at Sinai (Ex. 3. 4ff), Elijah at Horeb (1 Kings 19. 12ff), Daniel on the Tigris (Dan 10. 2ff); see his *Jesus in History: An Approach to the Study of the Gospels* (NY: Harcourt, Brace and World, 1970), p. 102.

19 See especially P. Pokorný, "The Temptation Stories and their Intention," *NTS*, 20 (1974), 115–27.

20 Frederick Borsch, *The Son of Man in Myth and History* (Philadelphia: Westminster, 1967).

21 Exorcism may also be an implicit component of the story of the leper in vv. 40–5. See the discussion at that place.

22 Wilhelm Wuellner, *The Meaning of "Fishers of Men"* (Philadelphia: Westminster, 1967). This position was introduced in a limited way as early as 1959 in an article by C. W. F. Smith, "Fishers of Men. Footnotes on a Gospel Metaphor," *HTR*, 52 (1959), 187–203. For a more recent discussion, see J. D. M. Derrett, *"Esan gar halieis* (Mk. 1 16). Jesus's Fishermen and the Parable of the Net," *NovT*, 22 (1980), 108–37.

23 John Meagher, *Clumsy Construction in the Gospel of Mark: A Critique of Form- and Redaktionsgeschichte* (Toronto Studies in Theology 3; NY: Edwin Mellon Press, 1979). See also Donald Juel, *An Introduction to New Testament Literature* (Nashville: Abingdon, 1978), p. 180.

24 This is true however one punctuates this verse. For a discussion see Bruce Metzger, *A Textual Commentary*, p. 75.

25 See the discussion between Leander Keck ("Mark 3:7–12 and Mark's Christology," *JBL*, 84 [1965], 341–58) and T. A. Burkill ("Mark 3:7–12 and the Alleged Dualism in the Evangelist's Miracle Material," *JBL*, 87 [1968], 409–17). Keck has argued against the notion that the text derives mainly from Mark's hand, yet even so allows that the demonic confession is Markan.

26 For this observation I am indebted to F. W. Danker, "The Demonic Secret in Mark: A Re-examination of the Cry of Dereliction (15:34)," *ZNW*, 61 (1970), 65: "On the one hand, Jesus is declared to be a lawless man, possessed by a demon. On the other hand, the human opposition making the judgment is itself the agent of demonic forces."

27 Robert Fowler, *Loaves and Fishes*, pp. 167f.

28 Stanley Fish, *Self-Consuming Artifacts: The Experience of Seventeenth-Century Literature* (Berkeley: University of California Press, 1972), p. 60.

29 Rudolf Bultmann, *The History of the Synoptic Tradition*, trans. John Marsh (NY: Harper and Row: 1963), esp. pp. 12–26. See also, recently, U. Müller, "Zur Rezeption Gesetzeskritischer Jesus Überlieferung im frühen Christentum," *NTS*, 27 (1981), 158–85.

30 See the summary discussions in Taylor, *The Gospel According to Mark*, pp. 191f; in R. T. Mead, "The Healing of the Paralytic – A Unit?" *JBL*, 80 (1961), 348–54; and in H.-J. Klauck, "Die Frage der Sündenvergebung in der Perikope von der Heilung des Gelähmten (Mk. 2,1–12 parr.)," *BibZeit*, 25 (1981), 223–48.

31 The notion of a direct causal relationship between sickness and sin may be found in a variety of places in the biblical tradition. Cf. Luke 13.2; John 9.2. See Gustav Stählin, "᾿Ασθενής κτλ.," *TDNT*, 1 (1964), 490–3.

32 Thomas Brudesheim, "Jesus and the Disciples in Conflict with Judaism," *ZNW*, 62 (1971), 193f.

33 See Morna Hooker, *The Son of Man in Mark* (Montreal: McGill University Press, 1967), pp. 87f; T. A. Burkill, *Mysterious Revelation* (Ithaca, NY: Cornell University Press, 1963), p. 131; Joanna Dewey, *Markan Public Debate: Literary Technique, Ring Composition and Theology in Mark 2:1–3:6* (Chico, CA: Scholars Press, 1980), p. 220, n. 19. A review and critique of Hooker is to be found in Barnabas Lindars, *JTS*, 19 (1968), 266–8.

34 Jakob Jónsson, *Humour and Irony in the New Testament* (Reykjavík: Bókútgáfa Menningarsjóds, 1965), p. 178.
35 Morna Hooker, *The Son of Man in Mark*, p. 88.
36 Joanna Dewey, *Markan Public Debate*, p. 220, n. 19.
37 Robert Fowler, *Loaves and Fishes*, pp. 167f, following Robert Tannehill, "The Disciples in Mark: The Function of a Narrative Role," *JRel*, 57 (1977), p. 391.
38 I. Howard Marshall, *Commentary on Luke* (Grand Rapids: Eerdmans, 1978), p. 214.
39 Howard Clark Kee, *Community of the New Age* (Philadelphia: Westminster, 1977), pp. 117–19.
40 This is the first instance of the term in Mark. What it means – here and elsewhere – has been the subject of continuing and intense debate. See esp. the monographs by Frederick Borsch, *The Son of Man in Myth and History*, p. 321; and Morna Hooker, *The Son of Man in Mark*, pp. 81–93. Taylor, *The Gospel According to St. Mark*, pp. 197–200, presents five options.
41 Gilbert Bilezekian, *The Liberated Gospel: A Comparison of the Gospel of Mark and Greek Tragedy* (Grand Rapids: Baker, 1977), p. 123. See also Fowler, *Loaves and Fishes*, p. 162.
42 See esp. Carl Schneider, "κάθημαι κτλ.," *TDNT*, 3 (1965), 440.
43 Gottlob Schrenk, "διαλέγομαι κτλ.," *TDNT*, 2 (1964), 96f.
44 The view that this verse is ironic is now quite widely held in NT scholarship. We may simply list scholars who have endorsed this view in one form or another: Taylor ("apparently"), Jónsson, ("it is biting irony"), Jerry Gill, Lane, Descamps, Grönbech, Klostermann (with hesitation), Clavier, Hoskyns.
45 See esp. Johannes Behm, "νῆστις," *TDNT*, 4 (1967), 924–35.
46 Behm (p. 929) points out that fasting was one of the marks of the Jew. Cf. Tacitus, *Hist.* v. 4.
47 This position has been developed already by Alistair Kee, "The Question about Fasting," *NovT*, 11 (1969), 161–73; and by J. Zeisler, "The Removal of the Bridegroom: A Note on Mark ii. 18–22 and Parallels," *NTS*, 19 (1973), 190–4.
48 Albrecht Oepke, "ἀπόλλυμι κτλ.," *TDNT*, 1 (1964), 395.
49 Cf. 1.24, 2.22; 3.6; 4.38 (possibly); 8.35 (certainly) *bis*; 9.22, 41; 11.18; 12.9 (certainly). NB. the occurrences of the term in 8.35.
50 All of the place names except for Galilee follow the verb ἠκολούθησεν. This gives the list a hint of artificiality, thus also of intentionality.
51 Ulrich Mauser, *Christ in the Wilderness* (London: SCM, 1963), p. 125.
52 The affinities of this section run in two directions. On the one hand, the pericope establishes a summary of Jesus' growing popularity, and as such it stands in contrast to the judgment leveled by the authorities in 3.6. It may parallel the summary and transition in 1.14f (as well as the one in 6.53–6). On the other hand, it looks ahead to the material which follows: the crowds (vv. 7f anticipate 4.1; 5.28–31; and 6.56); the boat (v. 9 anticipates 4.1); the demoniacs (vv. 11f anticipate 3.20–7; 5.1–20). Whether the section is Markan (as Leander Keck has argued "Mark 3:7–12 and Mark's Christology," *JBL*, 84 [1965], 341–58) or

not (as argues T. A. Burkill, "Mark 3:7–12 and the Alleged Dualism in the Evangelist's Miracle Material," *JBL*, 87 [1968], 409–17), and whether or not a summary, it still can function as a critical element in Mark's developing Christology.

53 James the son of Alpheus may be the "James the Less" in 15. 40, but this is uncertain, and for purposes of character development it is insignificant, because James the Less does not appear until much later in the narrative.

54 Karl Rengstorff's comment is especially appropriate: "In the calling of the twelve, Jesus visibly orders both His own and their work in accordance with the divine plan of salvation and in relation to its goal, the preparing of the community of God ... In them Jesus made visible to everyone His claim upon Israel, and He did so in such a way that it was evident that He did not merely claim a select group but the whole people in all its divisions" ("δώδεκα κτλ.," *TDNT*, 2 [1964], 326).

55 Jan Lambrecht, "The Relatives of Jesus in Mark," *NovT*, 16 (1974), 241–58.

56 So we read οἱ παρ᾽ αὐτοῦ. But this is not a matter of universal agreement. On the range of meanings, see Taylor, *The Gospel According to St. Mark*, p. 236: the expression may mean "envoys, ambassadors," "disciples" (so, recently, David Wenham, "The Meaning of Mark iii. 21," *NTS*, 21 [1975], 295–300), "friends" (so, ASV; RSV; AV; C. F. D. Moule, *An Idiom Book of New Testament Greek* [Cambridge University Press, 1963], p. 52), "parents, relatives" (so: NEB; Bultmann, *History*, p. 29: "It seems impossible to doubt that vv. 20f and 31–44 belong together"; Kee, *Jesus in History*, p. 133). It is probably significant that the transition from v. 21 to v. 30 would read smoothly if the intervening material were excised.

57 The Christian significance of these parables is widely discussed in the literature. For a bibliography, see Warren S. Kissinger, *The Parables of Jesus: A History of Interpretation and Bibliography* (Metuchen, NJ: Scarecrow Press, 1979). This note can supply only a sample of the relevant material: Nils Dahl, "The Parables of Growth," *StTh*, 15 (1951), 132–65; G. H. Boobyer, "The Redaction of Mark iv. 1–34," *NTS*, 8 (1961), 59–70; Eta Linneman, *Jesus of the Parables* (NY: Harper and Row, 1966), pp. 117f; J. W. Pryor, "Markan Parable Theology: An Inquiry into Mark's Principles of Redaction," *ExpT*, 83 (1972), 242–5; E. E. Lemcio, "External Evidence of the Structure and Function of Mark iv. 1–20, vii. 14–23 and viii. 14–21," *JTS*, 29 (1978), 323–8; G. Sellin, "Textlinguistische und semiotische Erwägungen zu Mk. 4. 1–34," *NTS*, 29 (1983), 508–30. By and large, the very fact that parable scholarship has felt a consistent need to work backward to the underlying traditions here is evidence of the conviction that these parables have been reworked by Mark or his community.

58 Whether these verses are authentic tradition or *vaticinia ex eventu* is a critical question. See Bultmann, *History*, p. 187.

59 E.g. Joachim Jeremias, *The Parables of Jesus*, trans. S. H. Hooke (NY: Scribner, 1963), pp. 16f.

60 On this matter, see Howard Clark Kee, *Community of the New Age*, pp. 93–6.

61 In this I abandon the RSV (which renders simply "parables") in favor
    of the more widely held view that the parables are "dark sayings" or
    "riddles." On this question, see J. Drury, "The Sower, the Vineyard
    and the Place of Allegory in the Interpretation of Mark's Parables,"
    JTS, 24 (1973), 375f. Cf. esp. Deut. 28.37 (LXX); Ps. 77.2 (LXX);
    Prov. 1.6 (LXX); Ecclus. 13.26.
62 For a history of the interpretation of these verses, see Geraint Jones,
    The Art and Truth of the Parables (London: SPCK, 1964), pp. 225–30.
63 There are a number of interrelated questions: (1) Is this a genuine
    dominical saying, or has it been fabricated by Mark or his community?
    No: W. O. E. Oesterley (*The Gospel Parables in the Light of their Jewish
    Background*, p. 54) suggests that the hardening theory as it is found here
    parallels – and probably derives from – Paul (NB. Rom. 10.18, in
    which Paul quotes to the same effect Isa. 53.1 and 6.9f!); in 1 Cor.
    5.12; 2 Cor. 4.5 and 1 Thess. 4.12, οἱ ἔξω is used as a designation for
    those who are outside the church; the term μυστήριον is lacking in the
    gospels except for here and in the synoptic parallels (Matt. 13.11; Luke
    8.10). Yes: E. F. Seigman ("Teaching in Parables [Mark 4,10–12; Lk.
    8,9–10; Mt. 13,10–15]," *CBQ*, 23 [1961], 171) notes that the quotation
    from Isa. 6.9f is closest to the Palestinian Targum, and that the antithetic
    parallels are a characteristic of Jesus' undisputed sayings. To this we may
    add the observation that the term μυστήριον is not unknown from Jewish
    apocalypticism (on which see the article by Priscilla Patten mentioned
    in note 67 below; cf. also 1 QS 11.3–4, in which the elect are supposed
    to perceive the secret of the Kingdom).
        (2) What is meant by μήποτε in the final line? Jeremias, (*Parables
    of Jesus*, p. 15) thinks that μήποτε represents Aramaic *dalmah*, but that
    this is ambiguous. It may mean "in order that," "lest perhaps," or
    "unless." Jeremias himself favors the last view, and in that way resolves
    the difficulty, although perhaps too easily. T. W. Manson ("The Purpose
    of the Parables: Re-examination of St. Mark iv. 10–12," *ExpT*, 68
    [1959], p. 134) translates "in case."
        (3) Is Jesus' use of parables intended to clarify his message, or to
    obscure it? To confuse: T. A. Burkill ("The Cryptology of Parables in
    St. Mark's Gospel," *NovT*, 1 [1956], 246–62, esp. p. 246). This is the
    usual meaning of *mashal*. Note also the private explanations 4.11f and
    4.33. The fact that the disciples do not understand is also evidence in
    this regard: they were supposed to have apprehended because the secret
    "had been given" them. To clarify: the basic significance of Jesus'
    parables appears at times to have been painfully clear (as: 12.1–12);
    the parables are constantly reinforced by the exhortation to "listen"
    (although this may be a call to listen for deeper meaning!); John W.
    Bowker asks ("Mystery and Parable: Mark 4:1–20," *JTS*, 25 [1974],
    p. 302): "Would Jesus trick his listener?". It is sometimes suggested that
    rabbinic parables universally clarify, rather than obscure (but not so:
    cf. 2 Sam. 12.1–6[!], and the frequent parallelism between the term
    παραβολή and other terms for "riddle" or "dark saying" in the LXX).
64 Carey Moore, "Mark 4.12: More Like the Irony of Micaiah than Isaiah,"
    in *A Light Unto My Path*, ed. Howard Bream *et al.* (Gettysburg

Theological Series 4; Philadelphia: Temple University Press, 1974), pp. 335–44.

65 Jerry Gill, "Jesus, Irony and the 'New Quest'," *Interp*, 41 (1980), 139–51.

66 Bruce Hollenbach, " 'Lest They Should Turn Again and Be Forgiven': Irony," *Bible Translator*, 34 (1983), 312–21.

67 Priscilla Patten, "The Form and Function of Parable in Select Apocalyptic Literature and their Significance for Parables in the Gospel of Mark," *NTS*, 29 (1983), 246–58.

68 Bultmann (*History*, pp. 54f) describes this technique as "scholastic dialogue," and he points out that it was commonly used in the perpetuation of rabbinic tradition.

69 If μόδιος means "peck-measure" (so: Walter Bauer, *A Greek–English Lexicon of the New Testament and Other Early Christian Literature*, trans. William Arndt and F. Wilbur Gingrich (University of Chicago Press, 1957), p. 527), the reference may be to hiding a lamp, or, as Jeremias suggests "smothering it with a vessel" (see his *The Parables of Jesus*, p. 120; cf. Josephus, *Ant.* v. 223, in which μόδιος is a vessel used to hide a lamp). Jakob Jónsson (*Humour and Irony in the New Testament*, p. 96) thinks this a joke: who would be so foolish as to light a lamp, then hide it? The rabbis would, that's who. According to Jónsson, rabbinical requirements prohibited one from extinguishing a light lit on the eve of the Sabbath, it must burn all night, and therefore required covering (M. *Sabb.* XVI. 7).

70 See R. Stuhlmann, "Beobachtungen und Überlegungen zu Markus iv. 26–29," *NTS*, 19 (1973), 153–62.

71 This is perhaps most clearly evident when Mark's language in v. 38 is compared to that of the synoptic parallels. Moffatt renders this verse freely, but, I think, sensitively: "Teacher, are we to drown, for all you care?"

72 P. Achtemeier, "Person and Deed. Jesus and the Storm Tossed Sea," *Interp*, 16 (1962), 169–76.

73 "I said to him, 'Is there something else about you, Asmodeus?' He said to me, 'The power of God which binds me with unbreakable bonds by his seal knows that what I have related to you is true. I beg you, King Solomon, do not condemn me to water' " (Test. Sol. 5. 11). Solomon then exercised mastery by "encircling" (drenching?) the demon with ten jars of water.

74 H. C. Kee, "The Terminology of Mark's Exorcism Stories," *NTS*, 14 (1967/8), 232–46.

75 Vernon Robbins ("Summons and Outline in Mark: The Three-Step Progression," *NovT*, 23 [1981], 97–114) has recently argued that Mark consciously developed rhetorically related clusters in groups of three. See also his study, "Mark 1.14–20: An Interpretation at the Intersection of Jewish and Graeco–Roman Traditions," *NTS*, 28 (1982), 220–36.

76 K. M. Fisher and U. C. von Wahlde ("The Miracles of Mark 4.35–5.43: Their Meaning and Function in the Gospel Framework," *BTB*, 11 [1981], 13–16) have discovered what they take to be a chiastic structure in the broader movements of Mark. In this structure, the miracles balance the parables:

          3.12–19   – Choice of the twelve
          3.20–36   – Rejection of Jesus by some
          4.1–34   – Parable collection
          4.35–5.43   – Miracle collection
          6.1–6   – Rejection of Jesus at Nazareth
          6.7–33   – Sending of the twelve

77 On which, see esp. G. R. H. Horsley, *New Documents Illustrating Early Christianity* (North Ryde, Australia: Macquarie University, 1981), pp. 25–9.

78 See J. Schneider, "ὅρκος," *TDNT*, 5 (1967), 462f.

79 In his *History of the Synoptic Tradition* (p. 209, n. 1) Bultmann notes the following with reference to 1.24: "We have to call attention to the unusual situation that the demon appears in the role of the threatened man, who utters his 'protective' words, while Jesus takes on the role of the demon! (cp. Mk. 5:7)."

80 Werner Kelber, *Mark's Story of Jesus* (Philadelphia: Fortress Press, 1979), p. 32. Cf. also J. F. Graghan, "The Gerasene Demoniac," *CBQ*, 30 (1968), 522–36, and before that, Harald Sahlin, "Die Perikope vom gerasenischen Besessenen und der Plan des Markusevangeliums," *StTh*, 18 (1964), 159–72.

81 There is a great deal of discussion about this saying, most of it born of the saying's deep ambiguities. In point of fact, κοιμᾶν is a common euphemism for death throughout the literature of the period (cf. Albrecht Oepke, "κοιμάω," *TDNT*, 3 [1965], 431–7), yet the denial that she has died appears to controvert that meaning and require a literal sleep here. Thus one sometimes reads the suggestion that she was in a coma or a deep natural sleep (see Taylor, *The Gospel According to St. Mark*, p. 295 [Taylor lists in favor of this view Creed, McNeile, and Plummer]; Lane rejects this possibility on the basis of the Lukan parallel [pp. 196f; cf. Luke 8.55], but this is to import evidence which is alien to Mark). To my mind, the suggestion fails to carry conviction because the normal generic structures of the story require that she be dead. That is, miracle stories are generally so structured that the testimony of the witnesses establishes the exact conditions requiring cure, and the movements of the patient afterward demonstrate the efficacy of the cure. So it is here. The testimony of the witnesses indicates that she had literally died, and the fact that she walks, as well as the requirement that she be given food, represent distinctive proofs that she had been raised from a literal death.

82 For example, Origen, *Contra Celsum* vi. 36, who says, erroneously, that Jesus is nowhere described as an artisan in the gospels; Justin Martyr (*Dialog.* 88) describes him as a maker of ploughs and yokes (an allusion to Matt. 11. 29f?). Origen's remark may, however, reflect the equivocation of the MS traditions. Here, P45 fam 13 33 372 543 565 579 700 on, read ὁ τοῦ τέκτονος υἱός. Taylor thinks this is correct (p. 300), but clearly it is an assimilation to Matt. 13.55, and the reading adopted by the NA 26 would in any case have claim to originality because it is more difficult.

83 Walter Wink, *John the Baptist in the Gospel Tradition* (Monograph Series 7; Cambridge University Press, 1968), p. 10.

84 See Robert Fowler, *Loaves and Fishes*, pp. 158f.
85 The bibliography on this pericope is enormous. Very much of it revolves around the explication of the details of the story in the light of messianic expectations. For a survey, see Richard Hiers, *Jesus and the Future: Unresolved Questions of Eschatology* (Atlanta: John Knox Press, 1981), 72–86, 143, n. 16.
86 This view has been current since Augustine. The details are internally consistent. They involve matters of vocabulary, symbolic numbers, ethnically different locations, and literary context. These are too many to be coincidental.
87 This appears to be the dominant scholarly position, although challenges have been raised against it. In 1952 G. H. Boobyer ("The Eucharistic Interpretation of the Miracles of the Loaves in St. Mark's Gospel," *JTS*, 3 [1952], 161–71) argued that the language of Acts 27. 35 was a closer parallel. But the parallels between the two feedings and the Last Supper in Mark are close enough to suggest some direct line of association between them. Against Boobyer read B. van Iersel, "Die wunderbare Speisung und das Abendmahl in der synoptischen Tradition," *NovT*, 7 (1964), 167–94. Van Iersel points out that familiarity with the language of the eucharist could even have created unconscious assimilation. With this comment he answers in advance the objection of Robert Fowler (*Loaves and Fishes*, pp. 138f). Fowler takes the view that the eucharist has not yet been introduced into the reader's consciousness, and that any allusions would be shielded from the reader. Clearly this is an attempt to incorporate the reception–critical observation of the linear quality of language into the resolution of an interpretative crux. To my mind it fails to carry conviction because it confuses competencies assumed in the text – e.g. the habitual familiarity with the technical language of the eucharist – with competencies generated by the text. The reader does not need to wait until Chap. 14 to hear eucharistic language; such language rings already in his ears. For a fuller treatment, see esp. A. Shaw, "The Marcan Feeding Narratives," *Church Quarterly Review*, 162 (1961), 268–78; I should here register my hesitation, however: Shaw carries the details of the two feedings over with such precision that they have become virtual allegories. My own position calls for an evaluation closer to the interpretation of the parables: Mark has a single main point. He wishes only to suggest the eucharist here, as a kind of secondary frame of reference. Here is answered Fowler's second objection. The term "eucharistic" is "secondary and vague" (p. 139). Fowler is objecting to the use of the term by modern scholars. Yet his objection is precisely the point. Allusive language is often "superficial and vague." It teases and hints, overlaying the primary language with nuances which are secondary and suggestive, rather than direct and blunt.
88 Quentin Quesnell, *The Mind of Mark: Interpretation and Method through the Exegesis of Mark 6, 52* (Analecta Biblica 38; Rome: Pontifical Biblical Institute, 1969). As Quesnell would have it, the eucharistic implications are the organizing core of the book as a whole (see p. 276!).
89 Richard Batey, "Jesus and the Theatre," *NTS*, 30 (1984), 563–74.

90 E. W. Bullinger, *Figures of Speech Used in the Bible Explained and Illustrated* (1989; reprint: Grand Rapids, MI: Baker, 1968), p. 811. Cf. also Walter Bauer, *A Greek–English Lexicon of the New Testament and Other Early Christian Literature*, trans. William Arndt and F. Wilbur Gingrich (University of Chicago Press, 1957), p. 402.

91 Taylor, *The Gospel According to Mark*, p. 351.

92 Nor is there any indication that this is why Jesus has left Galilee. In 6. 30, in which Jesus explicitly indicates that he is taking his disciples away for rest, he expresses his compassion on the people with an extended teaching session, culminating in his openly distributing bread! Clearly as Mark sees it, the need for rest is a secondary item on Jesus' theological agenda.

93 Henri Clavier, "La méthode ironique dans l'enseignment de Jésus," *Etudes Theologiques et Religieuses*, 5 (1930), 87.

94 Paul also plays upon this term in an ironic saying (Phil. 3. 2: "Look out for the dogs… those who mutilate the flesh"). This, however, is sarcasm.

95 Paul Achtemeier, "Toward the Isolation of Pre-Markan Miracle Catenae," *JBL*, 89 (1970), 265–91.

96 Robert Fowler, *Loaves and Fishes*, p. 91.

97 See Plutarch, *Moralia* II. 659b; TB *Berachoth* 17a.

98 Robert Fowler, *Loaves and Fishes*, pp. 109f.

99 David Rhoads and David Michie, *Mark as Story: An Introduction to the Narrative of a Gospel* (Philadelphia: Fortress Press, 1982), p. 61.

100 Ethelbert Stauffer, "ἐπιτιμάω κτλ.," *TDNT*, 2 (1964), pp. 624, n. 7, 625.

101 In a recent article ("Peter: Stumblingblock and Satan," *NovT*, 15 [1973], 187–90), B. A. E. Osborne has argued that there is a subtle play on words underlying this condemnation of Peter: Peter is said to have aligned himself with the "thoughts of men" (8. 33). But the thoughts of men are themselves under the influence of the evil *yetzer*, and it is for that reason that they are set over against the "thoughts" of God. In TB. *Sukkoth* 52a, one of the seven names of the evil *yetzer* is "stumbling-block", and in Pesikta 165a, the *yetzer* is a rock which causes travelers to stumble at a crossroads. If this sort of thinking is in view in Mark 8. 31–3, there is a subtle play on Peter's name: a moment ago, Peter – the petros – was the corner-stone, here he has become a stumbling-block. A moment ago he spoke under divine inspiration, here he has spoken under the influence of the Evil One. This is a curious and entertaining conjecture, but it is not convincing *for Mark*. It requires intertextual competencies which are altogether too subtle for Mark's reader. Whether Osborne's investigations reveal something of Jesus' own anthropology is another matter, however, and worthy of further consideration.

102 Taylor, *The Gospel According to Mark*, p. 441, is instructive: "In popular Gk. βαπτίζεσθαι was used metaphorically to express the thought of being flooded with calamities."

103 Howard Clark Kee, *Understanding the New Testament* (4th edn.; Garden City NJ: Prentice-Hall, 1984), p. 114.

104 See E. Schuyler Johnson, "Mark 10:46–52: Blind Bartimaeus," *CBQ*, 40 (1978), 191–204; M. G. Steinhauser, "Part of a 'Call Story'?" *ExpT*, 94 (1983), 204–6.

105 Donald Juel, *Messiah and Temple*, esp. pp. 55–8; so, also, Henri Clavier, "Les sens multiples dans le Nouveau Testament," *NovT*, 2 (1958), 190f; Ernst Best, *Following Jesus* (*JSNT* Supplement, series 4; Sheffield, England; University of Sheffield, 1981), pp. 213–25.

106 T. A. Burkill, "Blasphemy: St. Mark's Gospel as Damnation History," in *Christianity, Judaism and Other Greco–Roman Cults*, ed. Jacob Neusner (Leiden: Brill, 1975), p. 59.

107 Howard Clark Kee, "The Function of the Scriptural Quotations in Mark 11–16," in *Jesus und Paulus*, eds. E. Earle Ellis and Erich Grässer (Göttingen: Vandenhoeck und Ruprecht, 1975), pp. 165–88.

108 Howard Clark Kee, *Community of the New Age*, p. 67.

109 T. A. Burkill, "Strain on the Secret: An Examination of Mark 11:1–13:37," *ZNW*, 51 (1960), 31–46.

110 See, for example, the monograph by William Telford, *The Barren Temple and the Withered Tree: A Redaction–Critical Analysis of the Cursing of the Fig-Tree in Mark's Gospel and its Relation to the Cleansing of the Temple* (*JSNT* Supplement, series 1; University of Sheffield, 1980).

111 There is a particularly good survey of the messianic implications here in R. J. McElevy, *The New Temple: The Church in the New Testament* (Oxford University Press, 1969), pp. 59–63. See also J. Blenkinsopp, "The Hidden Messiah and His Entry into Jerusalem," *Scripture*, 13 (1961), 81–8.

112 See especially Sigmund Mowinkel, *He That Cometh*, trans. G. W. Anderson (Nashville: Abingdon, 1956), pp. 155–86.

113 William Lane, *The Gospel of Mark*, p. 398.

114 Donald Juel, *Messiah and Temple*, pp. 55–8.

115 About the torn temple veil, T. A. Burkill has this to say: "In a supernatural fashion the temple itself sets the scoffers at naught by bearing witness to the doom to which it is condemned" (*Mysterious Revelation* [Ithaca, NY: Cornell University Press, 1963], p. 138).

116 See also, for example, Ernst Best, *Following Jesus*, pp. 213–25; Augustine Stock, *Call to Discipleship*, p. 199.

117 Robert Tannehill, "The Gospel of Mark as Narrative Christology," *Semeia*, 16 (1979), p. 79.

118 The problem of Mark's ending as a *textual* difficulty is well-known, and the literature dealing with it is enormous. The textual evidence is not unequivocal, and one occasionally reads attempts to reopen the question in some way. To my mind, until additional MS data are recovered which demand it, the textual question is now best left closed. If anything, literary study (such as that of Norman Petersen, "When is an End not an End? Literary Reflections on the Ending of Mark's Narrative," *Interp*, 34 [1980], 151–66) has reinforced the conclusion that Mark originally ended with v. 8, since it has shown that the short ending makes narrative sense.

SELECT BIBLIOGRAPHY

Literary criticism

Abrams, Meyer H., *The Mirror and the Lamp: Romantic Theory and the Critical Tradition* (New York: Oxford University Press, 1953).

Anscombe, Gertrude Elizabeth, *Intention* (Oxford: Basil Blackwell, 1958).

Auerbach, Erich, *Mimesis: The Representation of Reality in Western Literature* (Princeton University Press, 1953).

Booth, Wayne, *The Rhetoric of Fiction* (University of Chicago Press, 1961).
A Rhetoric of Irony (University of Chicago Press, 1974).

Chatman, Seymour, *Story and Discourse: Narrative Structure in Fiction and Film* (Ithaca, NY: Cornell University Press, 1978).

Eco, Umberto, *The Role of the Reader: Explorations in the Semiotics of Texts* (Bloomington, IN: Indiana University Press, 1979).

Fish, Stanley, *Surprised by Sin: The Reader in Paradise Lost* (Berkeley: University of California Press, 1971).
Self-Consuming Artifacts: The Experience of Seventeenth-Century Literature (Berkeley: University of California Press, 1972).

Forster, E.M., *Aspects of the Novel* (New York: Harcourt, Brace and World, 1927).

Frye, Northrup, *Anatomy of Criticism: Four Essays* (Princeton University Press, 1957).

Gennette, Gérard, *Narrative Discourse: An Essay on Method*, trans. Jane Lewin (Ithaca, NY: Cornell University Press, 1980).

Hardy, Barbara, *Tellers and Listeners: The Narrative Imagination* (University of London, 1975).

Harsh, Philip W., *A Handbook of Classical Drama* (Stanford, CA: Stanford University Press, 1944).

Harvey, W.J., *Character and the Novel* (Ithaca, NY: Cornell University Press, 1966).

Hirsch, Eric D., Jr., *Validity in Interpretation* (New Haven: Yale University Press, 1967).
The Aims of Interpretation (University of Chicago Press, 1976).

Iser, Wolfgang, *The Implied Reader: Patterns of Communication in Prose Fiction from Bunyan to Beckett* (Baltimore: Johns Hopkins University Press, 1974).
The Act of Reading: A Theory of Aesthetic Response (Baltimore: Johns Hopkins University Press, 1978).

Kahler, Eric, *The Inward Turn of Narrative* (Princeton, NJ: Princeton University Press, 1973).

Kermode, Frank, *The Sense of an Ending: Studies in the Theory of Fiction* (New York: Oxford University Press, 1967).
　The Genesis of Secrecy: On the Interpretation of Narrative (Cambridge: Harvard University Press, 1979).
Kort, Wesley, *Narrative Elements and Religious Meaning* (Philadelphia: Fortress Press, 1975).
Lanser, Susan S., *The Narrative Act: Point of View in Prose Fiction* (Princeton University Press, 1981).
Muecke, Douglas C., *The Compass of Irony* (London: Methuen, 1969).
Olsen, Elder, *Tragedy and the Theory of Drama* (Detroit: Wayne State University, 1961).
Perrine, Laurence, *Story and Structure* (New York: Harcourt, Brace and World, 1959).
Scholes, Robert and Kellogg, Robert, *The Nature of Narrative* (New York: Oxford University Press, 1966).
Sedgewick, G. G., *Of Irony, Especially in Drama* (University of Toronto Press, 1948).
Sharpe, Robert B., *Irony in Drama: An Essay on Impersonation, Shock, and Catharsis* (Chapel Hill: University of North Carolina Press, 1959).
Thompson, A. R., *The Dry Mock: A Study of Irony in Drama* (Berkeley: University of California Press, 1948).
Thomson, J. A. K., *Irony: An Historical Introduction* (Cambridge: Harvard University Press, 1927).
Todorov, Tzvetan, *The Poetics of Prose*, trans. Richard Howard (Ithaca, NY: Cornell University Press, 1977).
Toliver, Harold, *Animate Illusions: Explorations of Narrative Structure* (Lincoln: University of Nebraska Press, 1974).
Tompkins, Jane P., ed., *Reader–Response Criticism: From Formalism to Post-Structuralism* (Baltimore: Johns Hopkins University Press, 1980).
Uspensky, Boris, *A Poetics of Composition: The Structure of the Artistic Text and Typology of a Compositional Form*, trans. V. Zavarin and S. Witting (Berkeley: University of California Press, 1973).

Biblical Studies

Achtemeier, Paul, *An Introduction to the New Hermeneutic* (Philadelphia: Westminster, 1969).
　Mark (Proclamation Commentaries; Philadelphia: Fortress, 1975).
Adar, Zvi, *The Biblical Narrative* (Jerusalem: Department of Education and Culture of the World Zionist Organization, 1959).
Beach, Curtis, *The Gospel of Mark: Its Making and Meaning* (New York: Harper and Row, 1959).
Beardslee, William, *Literary Criticism of the New Testament* (Philadelphia: Fortress Press, 1970).
Best, Ernst, *Following Jesus: Discipleship in the Gospel of Mark* (*JSNT* 4; Sheffield, England: University of Sheffield, 1981).
Bilezekian, Gilbert, *The Liberated Gospel: A Comparison of the Gospel of Mark and Greek Tragedy* (Grand Rapids MI: Baker, 1977).

Boomershine, Thomas, "Mark the Storyteller: A Rhetorical–Critical Investigation of Mark's Passion and Resurrection Narrative." (unpublished Ph.D. dissertation; Union Theological Seminary, New York, 1974).

Boucher, Madeleine, *The Mysterious Parable: A Literary Study* (Washington, D.C.; Catholic Biblical Association of America, 1977).

Bultmann, Rudolf, *The History of the Synoptic Tradition*, trans. John Marsh (New York: Harper and Row, 1963).

Dewey, Joanna, *Markan Public Debate: Literary Technique, Concentric Structure and Theology in Mark 2:1–3:6* (Chico, CA: Scholars Press, 1980).

Dibelius, Martin, *From Tradition to Gospel*, trans. Bertram Woolf (New York: Charles Scribner's Sons, 1934).

Dunn, James D. G., *Unity and Diversity in the New Testament: An Inquiry into the Character of Earliest Christianity* (Philadelphia: Westminster, 1977).

Evans, Carl *et al.* eds., *Scripture in Context: Essays On the Comparative Method* (Pittsburgh Theological Monograph Series 4; Pittsburgh: Pickwick, 1980).

Feine, Paul; Behm, Johannes; Kummel, Werner G., *Introduction to the New Testament*, trans. A. J. Mattill, Jr. (14th edn; Nashville: Abingdon, 1966).

Fowler, Robert, *Loaves and Fishes: The Function of the Feeding Stories in the Gospel of Mark* (Society of Biblical Literature Dissertation Series 54; Chico, CA: Scholars Press, 1981).

Frei, Hans, *The Eclipse of Biblical Narrative* (New Haven: Yale University Press, 1974).

Funk, Robert W., *Language, Hermeneutic and Word of God: The Problem of Language in the New Testament and Contemporary Theology* (New York: Harper and Row, 1966).

Good, Edwin, *Irony in the Old Testament* (London: Society for the Promotion of Christian Knowledge, 1965).

Hawkes, Terence, *Structuralism and Semiotics* (Berkeley, CA: University of California Press, 1977).

Henry, Patrick, *New Directions in New Testament Study* (Philadelphia: Westminster, 1979).

Hooker, Morna, *The Son of Man in Mark* (Montreal: McGill University Press, 1967).

Humphrey, Hugh, *A Bibliography for the Gospel of Mark: 1954–1980* (New York: Edwin Mellon Press, 1981).

Jeremias, Joachim, *The Parables of Jesus*, trans. S. H. Hooke (New York: Scribner, 1963).

Johnson, Alfred M., Jr., ed., *Structuralism and Biblical Hermeneutics: A Collection of Essays* (Pittsburgh Theological Series 22; Pittsburgh: Pickwick, 1979).

Jones, Geraint, *The Art and Truth of the Parables* (London: Society for the Promotion of Christian Knowledge, 1964).

Jónsson, Jakob, *Humour and Irony in the New Testament: Illuminated by the Parallels in Talmud and Midrash* (Reykjavík: Bókzútgáfa Menningarsjóds, 1965).

Juel, Donald, *Messiah and Temple: The Trial of Jesus in the Gospel of Mark* (SBL Dissertation Series 31; Missoula: Scholars Press, 1977).

Lane, William, *The Gospel According to Mark* (New International Commentary on the New Testament; Grand Rapids: Eerdmans, 1974).

McKelvey, R.J., *The New Temple: The Church in the New Testament* (Oxford University Press, 1969).

Martin, Ralph, *Mark: Evangelist and Theologian* (Grand Rapids: Zondervan, 1972).

Marxsen, Willi, *Mark the Evangelist*, trans. R.A. Harrisville, *et al.* (Nashville: Abingdon, 1969).

Mauser, Ulrich, *Christ in the Wilderness* (London: SCM., 1963).

Meagher, John, *Clumsy Construction in the Gospel of Mark: A Critique of Form- and Redaktionsgeschichte* (Toronto Studies in Theology 3; New York: Edwin Mellon Press, 1979).

Nestle, Eberhard and Alan, Kurt, eds., *Novum Testamentum Graece* (26th edition; Stuttgart: Deutsche Bibelstiftung, 1979).

Oesterley, W.O.E., *The Gospel Parables in the Light of their Jewish Background* (New York: Macmillan, 1936).

Patte, Daniel, *What is Structural Exegesis?* (Philadelphia: Fortress Press, 1976).

Perrin, Norman, *Rediscovering the Teaching of Jesus* (New York: Harper and Row, 1967).

Petersen, Norman, *Literary Criticism for New Testament Critics* (Philadelphia: Fortress Press, 1978).

Polzin, Robert M., *Biblical Structuralism: Method and Subjectivity in the Study of Ancient Texts* (Philadelphia and Missoula: Scholars Press, 1977).

Quesnell, Quentin, *The Mind of Mark: Interpretation and Method Through the Exegesis of Mark 6,52* (Analecta Biblica 38; Rome: Pontifical Biblical Institute, 1969).

Simon, Ulrich, *Story and Faith in the Biblical Narrative* (London: Society for the Promotion of Christian Knowledge, 1975).

Spencer, Richard, ed., *Orientation by Disorientation. Studies in Literary Criticism and Biblical Literary Criticism Presented in Honor of William Beardslee* (Pittsburgh Theological Monograph 35; Pittsburgh: Pickwick, 1980).

Stock, Augustine, *Call to Discipleship: A Literary Study of Mark's Gospel* (Wilmington, DE: Michael Glazier, 1982).

Tannehill, Robert, *The Sword of His Mouth* (Philadelphia: Fortress Press, 1975).

Taylor, Vincent, *The Gospel According to St. Mark* (Grand Rapids, MI: Baker, 1966).

Trocmé, Etienne, *The Formation of the Gospel According to Mark*, trans. Paula Gaughan (Philadelphia: Westminster, 1975).

Walker, William O., Jr., ed., *The Relationships Among the Gospels: An Interdisciplinary Dialogue* (San Antonio: Trinity University Press, 1978).

Weeden, Theodore, *Mark: Traditions in Conflict* (Philadelphia: Fortress Press, 1971).

Wink, Walter, *John the Baptist in the Gospel Tradition* (Monograph Series 7; Cambridge University Press, 1968).

Sociology of knowledge

Berger, Peter, *The Precarious Vision: A Sociologist Looks at Social Fictions and Religious Faith* (New York: Doubleday, 1961).
The Sacred Canopy: Elements of a Sociological Theory of Religion (Garden City, NY: Doubleday, 1969).
Berger, Peter and Luckmann, Thomas, *The Social Construction of Reality: A Treatise on the Sociology of Knowledge* (Garden City, NY: Doubleday, 1966).
Chall, Leo, "The Sociology of Knowledge," in *Contemporary Sociology*, ed. J. S. Roucek (New York: Philosophical Library, 1958), pp. 286–303.
Eliade, Mircea, *The Sacred and the Profane: The Nature of Religion*, trans. Willard Trask (New York: Harper and Row, 1961).
Fawcett, Thomas, *The Symbolic Language of Religion: An Introductory Essay* (Minneapolis: Augsburg Press, 1971).
Foley, John M., ed., *Oral Traditional Literature: A Festschrift for Albert Bates Lord* (Columbus, OH: Slavica, 1981).
Gager, John, *Kingdom and Community: The Social World of Early Christianity* (New York: Prentice-Hall, 1975).
Halliday, M. A. K., *Language as Social Semiotic: The Social Interpretation of Language and Meaning* (Baltimore: University Park Press, 1978).
Hertzler, Joyce O., *A Sociology of Language* (New York: Random House, 1965).
Hoijer, Harry, ed., *Language in Culture: Conference on the Interrelations of Language and Other Aspects of Culture* (University of Chicago Press, 1954).
Landar, Herbert, *Language and Culture* (New York: Oxford University Press, 1966).
Lord, Albert Bates, *The Singer of Tales* (Harvard Studies in Comparative Literature; Cambridge, MA: Harvard University Press, 1960).
Mead, George Herbert, *Mind, Self and Society from the Standpoint of a Social Behaviorist* (University of Chicago Press, 1934).
Merton, Robert, *Social Theory and Social Structure* (Chicago: The Free Press of Glencoe, 1957).
Mol, Hans J., *Identity and the Sacred: A Sketch for a New Social–Scientific Theory of Religion* (New York: Free Press, 1976).
Propp, Vladimir, *The Morphology of the Folk-Tale*, trans. Laurence Scott (Austin: University of Texas Press, 1968).
Sapir, Edward, *The Selected Writings of Edward Sapir in Language, Culture and Personality*, ed. David Mandelbaum (Berkeley: University of California Press, 1949).
Language: An Introduction to the Study of Speech (New York: Harcourt, Brace, 1960).
Schroeder, W. Widick, *Cognitive Structures and Religious Research: Essays in Sociology and Theology* (East Lansing: Michigan State University Press, 1970).
Schutz, Alfred, *Collected Papers I: The Problem of Social Reality*, ed. Maurice Natanson (Phaenomenologica 11; The Hague; Martinus Nijhoff, 1971).
Schutz, Alfred and Luckmann, Thomas, *The Structures of the Life–World*, trans. R. M. Zaner and H. T. Englehardt, Jr. (Evanston, IL: Northwestern University Press, 1973).

SUBJECT INDEX

actual repertoire, 64
Adam, 98
Aeschylus, 68, 71
aetiologies, 29, 73, 108, 141
allegory, 5
allusion, 53–5, 63, 70–1, 76, 94, 99,
    167, 179
am ha-aretz, 114, 125
anachronisms, 38
Aristotle, 42–3
asides, 60, 78–80

ballast lines, 91, 109, 115, 118
Bar-Jesus, 65
Bartimaeus, 163–5, 169
Bathsheba, 77–87
Beelzebul, 105
bread, 142

Caiaphas, 66
Caligula, 145
call narratives, 101–3
catharsis, 46, 85
characterization, 46–52
    foils, 48
    identification, 46
    moral implications, 51
    names, 48
    roundedness, 50–1
    traits, 47
Cicero, 60
circumstantial selections, *see* contextual
    selections
Clytemnestra, 71
codes, 59
common frames of reference, 59,
    68–9, 70
competencies
    assumed by the text, 58–60, 63–76,
        143
    generated by the text, 58–60, 76–89

contextual selections, 60, 61, 65
controversies, 107–19
convention, 69
core cliché, 38, 133
co-reference, rules of, 59, 65–6
cosmos, sacred, 16–17

Daniel, 65
David, 77–87
Decapolis, 138
demons, demoniacs, 102–7, 121, 132,
    134–8, 178, *see* exorcisms
dictionary meanings, basic, 59
Dionysus, 83
disciples, obtuseness of, 93
Dives, 72
double entendre, 7
doublets, 8
dual time, 44

Eglon, 64
Ehud, 64
Elijah, 95, 144
encyclopedia, 59, *see* repertoire
endings
    indeterminate, 11
    unhappy, 11
epistemology, 36
eschatology (-ical), 93–8, 102, 152, 156
eucharist, 142–3, 146–7, 151–3
Euripides, 72–4, 78, 82–3, 160
Eurykleia, 84
exclusionary strategies, 60, 86–7, 105
exorcism, 178
    at Capernaum, 102–3
    at Gerasa, 135–8
    language in the stilling of the Storm,
        132
    see demons

fasting, 116–17

209

AUTHOR INDEX

INDEX OF CLASSICAL AUTHORS

CITATIONS FROM EXTRA-CANONICAL JEWISH LITERATURE

Ecclesiasticus (Sirach)
38.24–39.11: 141
38.24–8: 141
2 Enoch
22.6: 98
Genesis Rabbah
56: 159
Life of Adam and Eve
4.2: 98
Manual of Discipline
1 QS 3.13–4.26: 148, 159
Martyrdom of Isaiah
2.8: 95
2.9: 95
2.11: 95

Susanna
54–5: 65
54: 65
58–9: 65
58: 65
Testament of Judah
25.3: 125
Testament of Levi
18.10--11: 125
Testament of Solomon
5.11: 132
11.6: 132
Tobit
3.1–6: 86
4.20–1: 86
5.21: 86

CITATIONS FROM CANONICAL LITERATURE

Printed in the United Kingdom
by Lightning Source UK Ltd.
107529UKS00002B/81